TWO
STRANGERS

Norma Iris Pagan Morales

ISBN 978-1-959895-78-7 (paperback)
ISBN 978-1-959895-77-0 (ebook)

Printed in the United States of America

Overview

When her father is murdered by the Mafia in New York City, Carmela Bonanno reluctantly steps into his shoes. She was going to carry on his legacy.

She wanted to start a non-profit group dedicated to furthering the education for the poor. There she meets Charles Palermo, the ex-SEAL, and head of her security team.

She quickly learns that coming to New York might prove to be a deadly decision. Keeping her alive is one of the toughest assignments Charles ever faced. Yet through one disturbing situation after another she continually impresses him with her strength and inner courage.

Even though he fights his feelings for her, it's a losing battle. And when the job is over, he doesn't know how he'll let her go.

Dedication

I dedicate this novel to my sister, Adelin Milagros Pagan Morales. She was the only one that encouraged me to write short stories or novels. You are gone, but not forgotten. I Thank you, sis, because you were the only that was always there for me.

Contents

Chapter 1

The Fire

The noise of the growing mob outside grew louder. A muted roar made by hundreds of angry voices chanting one of the only terrorists he knew, "Death to America".

Charles Palermo checked his weapon one last time and turned in a stoop to face the six other men now trapped with him in the burning interior of an Office building.

Three of his security contractor teammates, and three internationals diplomats who were scared out of their minds and visibly struggling to hold it together.

The sound of more breaking glass shattered the tension in the room. Another fire alarm blared to life from down one of the hallways, signaling that the flames were spreading fast.

Already the smoke was thick enough to make his eyes sting.

"We've got a minute or two, max, before they scale the wall," he said to the man on his right.

Saul, the team leader, and Palermo's best friend, scanned their darkened surroundings, but they both knew there was only one way out. "Call again for an emergency exfil," he told Charles. "Tell them we'll stay in the building as long as possible."

It was their only option, since the place was surrounded by angry protestors. Trying to escape out any of the emergency exits would result in them being shot or beaten to death, and their bodies dragged through the streets by the enraged mob.

"Fire's spreading from the north side," Gaby, the retired Special Forces master sergeant reminded him as Hunter got back on the radio to stress the urgency of their situation. "All exits and staircases on that side are out."

"We'll have to get to the roof and wait there," Saul answered.

"What's the story on that bird?" Charles demanded to the man on the other end of his radio, shoving his finger into his other ear to hear the response over the chaos.

"Working on it, sir." Not good enough. "We've got two protestors officials and the American ambassador with us, and we've only got a few more minutes before that mob gets inside." He and his teammates had already spent the last thirty minutes fighting their way through the rabble to get inside the place and secure the surviving diplomats. Getting out was going to be way harder.

Rounds started slamming into the window above them. Spider webs formed. around the impact sites. Dozens of them. He ducked instinctively when the bullets resistant glass finally cracked. They all hit the deck and covered their heads with their arms as chunks of it rained down.

A split-second later a hail of bullets peppered the far wall behind them, a few feet over their heads.

The roar outside intensified instantly. Two firebombs flew through the shattered window, hit the floor and exploded into a wall of flame. Charles didn't get a chance to hear what the man was saying to him over the radio.

From the sudden rise in volume of that terrible roar, he knew the crowd had finally cleared the wall and were about to storm the building.

Hell. He grabbed his rifle and rolled back into a crouch as the wall of noise pulsed against his eardrums. They were about to be overrun, and all because some dickhead idiot from back home had decided to burn the financial building. This would be a great publicity stunt to show how much he and the rest of America hated those Italian immigrants.

The incident had not only angered the Italians living in New York. It had already cost the lives of more than a hundred innocent people caught in the crossfire including an American humanitarian Italians had captured and killed.

Then they'd used the financial burning incident to justify the man's brutal murder and incite the general populace to attack American interests in the country.

"Go," Saul shouted over the confusion, grabbing the white-faced American ambassador by the upper arm. He hauled the man toward the closest hallway, filled with infernal orange light from the fires while the other two team members took charge of the demonstrators.

In a running crouch Charles followed behind, covering their six. A few yards into the hallway the smoke was already noticeably thicker, making them cough as they raced to find a stairwell that would take them to the roof.

They turned right and stopped short at the sheet of flame licking the walls and ceiling ahead of them, blocking their exit. Turning left, they ran blindly down another hallway just as the enraged mob breached the building.

Charles could hear the shouts and pounding footsteps closing in on them, moving closer with every heartbeat. Shots rang out behind them, way too close.

Whirling, he went to one knee and brought his M4 up, fired at the shadowy shapes that appeared around the corner. He dropped three of them before he jumped to his feet and raced after his teammates' hazy silhouettes as they disappeared into the smoke down the corridor in front of him.

"Over here! Hurry!"

He spun and followed Gaby's shout, staying low to keep out of the worst of the choking, toxic smoke. Thirty yards in, the air began to clear slightly. He could just make out the doorway at the end of the hall and ran straight for it. He wasn't fast enough.

More attackers spilled into the corridor behind them and opened fire. A burst of rounds plowed into the wall next to Charles's head. He whipped around and returned fire, dropping two and wounding another.

To his right and slightly above him he could hear his teammates' thudding footsteps as they rushed the diplomats toward the roof. He chased after them, turning every few seconds to shoot at the men pursuing them.

The dim emergency lighting in the stairwell flickered on and off, casting spooky shadows everywhere. His lungs burned from the smoke; his heart slammed as he raced up the concrete steps. Two floors. Three. And the mob was still coming after them.

At the fourth, and top floor he turned the corner on the stairs and came to a skidding stop when he saw his team gathered next to a steel exit door.

Gaby was staggering back from it, swearing, and sweating, rifle held tight in his hands. Someone had already put a round through the lock mechanism, which was still holding somehow.

When Gaby moved aside Saul backed up a step then slammed his boot repeatedly into the ruined lock. Even with the bullet hole and the ex-SEAL's considerable muscle, the door didn't budge.

Saul looked back at him, his expression tense. "Get down to the third floor and try another stairwell."

There was nowhere else to go. "They're right behind us," Charles warned.

"Go," Saul ordered. "I'll watch our six this time."

Not wasting another second, Hunter turned and ran while the others followed him back down the stairs. He careened around the corner, through a door, and tore down another hallway that led to the opposite side of the building. Distant shouts echoed up from below.

His teammates were a few steps behind him. In the thinning smoke his gaze locked on the steel door at the end of the hall. Only steps away, he heard the crowd coming.

He dropped to one knee in firing position as his teammates escorting the diplomats rushed passed and waited. The moment the first attacker cleared the corner he fired, hitting him in the chest.

The guy fell, arms outstretched, knocking back the man behind him. Hunter shot him in the head and didn't pause to watch him hit the floor.

He sprang to his feet and made a desperate charge for the door. Saul saw him coming and stepped aside in time for Charles to smash the lock with the sole of his boot.

As the punishing impact traveled up his leg, he felt the doorway. One more well-placed kick and the heavy door flew open to crash into the concrete wall. The stairwell to the fourth floor and hopefully the roof was clear.

The stairwell below them was going to be full of enraged attackers any moment now.

As the clean air rushed past him, Charles moved aside and glanced over his shoulder at the rest of his team with a nod. Two of them shoved the shaken diplomats through the doorway and followed up the stairs directly behind them to provide protection while Charles and Saul guarded the doorway.

Saul stayed on one knee beside him, weapon up, his gaze trained down the hallway where the enemy were about to rush them when a door suddenly rang against the wall somewhere below them. More men were coming up the stairs at them from the second floor.

Shit. "Let's go," Hunter shouted over the blare of the alarms, the rising shouts from behind and beneath them. The rest of the team were already up the stairs. Charles started going down. He could hear someone kicking at the door to the roof up there. Please open. "Come on!"

Saul was too busy to respond. He fired a double tap in one direction, then rotated and took aim down the stairwell to the second floor. Charles cursed and turned back. He was halfway to Saul when his friend looked back at him with an angry frown. "Go! You've got the only working radio. Get everyone on the roof and onto that chopper."

"Fuck that." No way in hell Charles was leaving him here to guard off the attackers alone.

Saul ended Charles's descent with an upraised fist that commanded him to stop. His voice was calm, his eyes intense as he stared up at him. "That's an order, Charles. Get your ass up there."

Everything in him rebelled at the command, but he knew Saul was right.

His first duty was to the diplomats they'd voluntarily come to save. He'd get everyone to the roof and direct the bird in, then come back for Scottie if necessary. "Roger that."

Suddenly Saul's head snapped around to face the corridor and he fired twice at more attackers. Charles turned and ran, taking three stairs at a time. Four paces up, he heard Scottie grunt.

Charles turned in time to see him struggling to his knees, blood pouring out from beneath the bottom of his tactical vest.

Without hesitation he went down the stairs toward his friend.

"I said go!" Saul's annoyed gaze bored into his, filled with resolve. Charles read the unspoken message there. Saul was prepared to give his life to save the rest of them.

He'd stay and protect them all, fight off the attackers until his last breath. That's what all SEALs were trained to do, and that training never went away, even after they left the Teams.

The thought of Saul making that ultimate sacrifice turned his blood to ice.

He hesitated. Torn between duty and the need to protect his buddy, years of training and discipline kicked in. Swearing, Charles turned and raced for the fourth floor.

The door to the roof was open, and he caught the faint pulse of rotors when he slammed the door open and stepped into the clear air on the darkened rooftop.

Charles blinked and sucked in a calming breath. It took him a moment to come back to the present and remember he was in his own house.

Pulling out of the painful memory, he raised the TV remote and pressed pause, freezing on screen the image of him as he emerged onto the roof.

His throat was dry, his heart pounding like he was still back there rather than sitting on his leather couch at home. He swore he could smell the bitter flavor of smoke, taste the bitterness of it in his mouth. On the TV he stood in the open doorway dressed in his tactical gear, radio in one hand, rifle in the other. In front of him the other security team members were kneeling with their weapons raised, facing outward with the diplomats huddled between them.

That's the image the rest of the world had seen a group of men gathering on the roof while the rescue helicopter came in.

Now, gazing at the high-definition screen mounted on the wall across the room, Charles searched for answers. He'd watched this same footage countless times over the past ten days since he'd been home, torturing himself with what he could have done differently.

Maybe if he'd stayed in that stairwell, he could have saved Saul. Instead, once that hello had begun its descent, he'd gone back inside to drag his unconscious friend over his shoulders and take him out to the waiting bird.

The camera crews on the streets below had captured shots of him appearing with Saul slumped over his shoulders too. He didn't need to see it on screen or in any of the newspapers or magazines again.

That awful moment was permanently burned into his memory without another visual reminder. Willing his pulse to slow down, Charles hit the power button and turned off the TV.

The recorded image of him vanished, replaced by his reflection in the black of the screen. In the empty silence the roar of the attackers slowly faded from his ears.

He leaned back into the leather couch with a sigh and stared at the darkened screen. Though the images were gone, in his mind he was still back in that dimly lit stairwell watching Saul bleed all over the floor as he struggled to bring his weapon up into firing position.

The news crews had only captured the chaotic scene from the outside of the

Financial building. Ironic that the rest of the world would never see what had happened inside, while Charles couldn't close his eyes without seeing it imprinted on the backs of his eyelids.

In the stillness of his living room, the sound of waves crashing onto the shore came through the screen door that led out to the large deck outside. He and

Saul had built it last fall when his buddy had come to stay with him for a few days here on St. Simon's.

They'd enjoyed many a beer on that deck together while staring out over the rolling Atlantic. It used to be Charles's favorite spot in the house. Since coming home this time, he hadn't set foot on it once.

The shrill ring of his cell phone broke the quiet. He got up and walked to the granite counter that separated the living room and kitchen. When he saw the number on the screen, he almost didn't answer it. Something maybe morbid

Curiosity made him do it anyway. "Bill. What's up?"

"How are you doing', Charles?"

How do you think I'm doing? "Good," he said, because what else was there to say? "What can I do for you?" No sense wasting time on pleasantries. Bobby wouldn't be calling just to bullshit. Charles went back to sit on the couch and picked up the pen he'd been using, twiddling with it to keep his free hand busy.

"You ready for tomorrow?" Ted asked without explanation. The owner and president of Security didn't believe in pussy footing around, which was just as well because Charles didn't either.

In the reflection of the sliding glass door, Charles could see his travel bag hanging near the back door. Inside it was his freshly pressed black suit. "Yeah," he lied, glancing down at the pad of paper on the coffee table and all the scratched out lines that filled the first half of the page.

"So, what do you need?"

"You."

That was the last thing he wanted to hear right now. Charles closed his eyes briefly and fought back a weary sigh, not even bothering to pretend he misunderstood. "Why?"

"I'm short on guys and I need someone over here who knows the area, knows how things work with the locals and officials. You're one of my best, Charles. This is a big one. I want you to be team leader this time." Because Saul was gone.

The familiar hollow sensation started up in his gut at the reminder. He tipped his head back to rest it against the couch and considered what his boss was asking. "Who've you got for me?"

"Gaby"

The Bonanno's name set off a pain inside him, dragged up those horrific few hours when his team had spontaneously rushed to the financial building to try and save the diplomats trapped inside. "Who else?"

"Two newer guys. Marines. One ex-Force Recon and the other a Scout/Sniper. Both came highly recommended."

He considered the logistics of it, prepared to hear Tom out and then turn him down. "What's the job?"

"Personal security detail." His boss paused. "Johnny Bonanno's daughter."

Charles's fingers tightened around the phone so tight they went numb.

"What?" It came out a croak.

"She's coming here to pick up where her old man left off. Gets in two days from now."

Did that whole family have a death wish? Charles ran a hand over his face. Johnny Bonanno had just been killed over there in a very barbaric way because of his connection with the Mafia. And the anti-American sentiment wasn't any better over there now than it had been at the time of the murder. "Stupid timing." Smack at the end.

This would only make the radicals bolder if they wanted to try anything. As if they needed more incentive to carry out attacks on Americans, he thought with a disgusted shake of his head.

"Yeah, well, the new school Johnny's foundation financed opens next week.

His Daughter is coming for the grand opening. You know I wouldn't ask you to take this on if it wasn't important. I lost four of my more experienced guys, including

Saul, in the days following Bonanno's murder.

After what happened to him, Gerry contacted me. He wants us to take care of the daughter's security while she's here."

Charles rubbed at the ache that was beginning to form between his eyes. Gerry was an influential politician and had been a close friend of Bonanno's. He and

Tommy went way back, had served in the first Gulf War when they were in the

SEAL Teams together.

Made sense that he'd reach out to Tommy to protect Bonanno's daughter. "Where's the school?"

Tommy didn't answer right away, and Charles knew the answer wasn't going to be good. "Greene Valley."

Of course, it was. He let out a humorless laugh. "She unaware or something?" Maybe she never watched the news or read the newspaper.

"Not at all. Sounded to me like she's carrying out his final wishes, outlined in his will. Figured you could relate to that."

Charles's eyes slid to the pad laid out on the table in front of him. Yeah, he knew all about carrying out the final wishes of someone you loved.

"This contract's real important to me, Charles, so I'm calling in a favor. I want you to head this detail, no one else."

Calling in a favor for this was a low blow, but the fact was, Charles did owe

Tommy. Owed him the greatest debt a man could owe another, his life.

Loosening his fingers from around the phone, he sighed and relented. "I can fly out of New York tomorrow night after the service. Text me the flight details."

Tommy's exhalation was full of relief. "Thanks, brother. I appreciate this."

Don't thank me yet. "Yeah. See you in a couple days."

"You know it. Give my best to Saul's family."

"Will do."

Disconnecting, he tossed his phone aside and picked up the scribbled-on pad.

Every single line there was crossed out. He'd already spent three hours at this without being any closer to knowing what to write.

Words just didn't seem adequate. His gaze strayed to the framed picture of him and Saul hanging on the wall across the room.

They were out on a fishing boat together off Myrtle Beach, arms across each other's bare shoulders, huge grins on their faces. A heavy ball of grief settled in his gut. No matter how much he hated it, it was his duty to eulogize his best friend tomorrow, then see him put into the ground.

Whatever words he put to paper would never do Saul justice. Nothing could. Except maybe sending him off with the giant party they'd promised each other should one of them die before the other. Maybe, if Charles got lucky in New York over the coming days, he might just get the chance to hunt down the same militants who were ultimately responsible for Saul's death. If he did, he wouldn't hesitate to send them to hell where they belonged.

Chapter 2

Charles is Chosen

Bent over his keyboard in his third-floor office, Michael Juliani inspected the latest schematic in his AUTOCAD program. He was concentrating so hard that he jolted a little in his chair when his computer signaled an instant message with a loud ding.

He frowned. He never got instant messages at work. Only at home when he was communicating with one person. His heart rate kicked up a notch. When he read the username along with the message, written in Italian, his insides tightened.

Is she here?

It was him. Michael almost couldn't believe it. They'd never attempted to contact him here at work before, but IM was his contact's preferred method of communication. The man was paranoid about phones being tapped and e-mails being traced, so he was always sending messages via different usernames and accounts to avoid detection and tracking.

Michael straightened and considered his reply. Whatever the contact's network wanted, it must be important for them to take the risk of contracting him here.

Still, the possibility of being caught in communication with them made his heart thump and his palms turn clammy. Casting a surreptitious look around him to ensure his coworkers at the engineering firm weren't close enough to see what was on his screen, he hunched over his keyboard and typed out a brief answer.

I don't know.

A few seconds later, the person reply came back. Find out and contact me immediately. The man signed off. Michael blinked. That was it? No further information about why they wanted him to do the checking though he suspected they were planning an operation of some sort or what they planned to do with the information when he reported back to them. Probably just as well.

The less he was aware of about their plans, the easier it would be to claim his innocence if he got caught later. He wanted to help the cause, not become a victim of it.

Quickly clearing his screen, Michael got busy doing whatever he could think of to erase the evidence of the conversation from the computer's hard drive. He wasn't stupid. Couldn't be too careful these days and he didn't want anything pointing to him in case his Italian's contact tried to implicate his involvement later.

While he worked, his mind rolled with the things he had to check on to find the woman in question.

Carmela Bonanno is going to be next. The Italian Mafia had already managed to kidnap and kill her father, so it made sense that they'd want to eliminate her as well when she arrived.

She was either very stupid for doing so, or very brave. Michael had been shocked to learn she was coming to New York in the article he'd read a few days ago. Apparently, she had designs to take up where her father had left off in his misguided efforts to build schools for the poor.

If Michael could find Ms. Bonanno's location when she arrived in the city, he would gladly give it to his TTP contact and help prevent her foundation's efforts.

Soft footfalls behind him sent a wave of alarm through him. He scrambled to clear the screen back to his desktop by the time, his supervisor and boss, reached him.

She stopped next to his chair and gave him a suspicious look down her long nose.

"What are you doing?" she asked, more demand than question.

"Nothing." He kept his attention on the monitor as he moved items around on the desktop, though he could see her in the screen's reflection against the black background. "Just cleaning up some files."

She frowned, her mouth pulling into a thin line of disapproval that tarnished her otherwise attractive face. Her long dark hair fell down her back in thick waves.

Carmela looked just like a simple American girl; however, she was more than that…

"I asked you to finish up that schematic by noon," she reminded him sharply, making him feel like a boy being scolded. And right out in the open where everyone could see.

He could feel the stares aimed in their direction from around the large open room where the desks were organized into tidy rows.

Jaw tight, he turned in his seat to look up at her, brimming with resentment.

"I'll have it for you by the end of the day."

Carmela sighed and folded her arms across her chest, unintentionally dragging his gaze to her breasts that strained against the fabric of her pale pink shirt. He hated his body's automatic sexual reaction to her.

Another reason he wished women had to wear robes rather than western style clothing that made them look so indecent. "I said by noon," she reiterated.

"I'm doing it as fast as I can." It was hard not to choke on the measured response when he secretly longed to put her in her place. It had taken him two years to get hired at this prestigious engineering firm. He wasn't going to blow his chance at advancement because of friction with his boss. He was smarter than that. Far smarter than anyone here gave him credit for, he thought with a surge of arrogance.

Carmela's gaze flicked to his desktop screen, then back to him, her tight expression telling him just how annoyed she was with his performance.

"Perhaps you need to manage your time better then."

Meaning, stop playing around organizing things that didn't matter and get your work done. Michael battled to keep his contempt of her from showing. Carmela that she was not only his boss, but she was also head of the design group at the firm. She was a stickler for deadlines and had no problem calling a worker to ask if she didn't think he or she was working hard enough. If he had any desire to be promoted, he had to impress her.

That also offended his male pride. "Have it to me by the end of the day or I'll find someone else to finish the project for you." With that unexpected pardon and added threat she turned on the point of her high heel and walked away, those spiky heels clicking against the tiled floor.

Bubbling inside, Michael tapped down his frustration and pulled open the design program in question. If she only knew how much he resented her, he fumed. He'd be fired from the firm within a week if anyone found out exactly what he thought of her and all the women like her, overeducated feminists who took up fashionable spots at the top companies in the country and precious seats in the university applied sciences programs so that he and other men were turned away.

He'd barely gotten into his program on the third try because of women like her, despite his perfect GPA and references. It was wrong. It had to stop.

Educating women was bad. Michael was against all that....

Not that he'd always been so radical in his thinking, of course. His mother was a college educated woman after all, and taught English to elementary school children. The difference was his mother knew her place and didn't act superior to men. She was a good woman. A lot of women in his generation were not.

The stricter interpretation of Islam he'd been exposed to at university had opened his eyes, and seeing so many male classmates turned away from their chosen program in favor of a female student had made him realize that adopting any new law was needed.

She blinked and looked up from her laptop at Ray Dunlop, the fifty-eight-year-old co-founder of Fair Start Foundation, standing in the hotel room doorway. "What? Who?" "Your team leader."

Huh? Was her jetlag so bad that she'd screwed up the date somehow? A quick check of her calendar assured her she hadn't. "He's a day early."

"Yeah, how about that." Ray's sun-weathered features gave nothing away about what he thought of the head of her newly arrived security detail. She knew nothing about the man in question except that he'd been handpicked by Tom, the owner of Titanium Security.

Normally she would have at least read a file on the men in her detail before arriving here in Pakistan but considering recent events, Tom had been left scrambling to find replacement contractors for the job.

"Downstairs?" she asked, a little nervous about meeting the man who would be responsible for her safety for the duration of her visit.

Ray nodded. "In the lobby."

Okay then, apparently for some reason Ray wanted her to see this guy for herself before forming an opinion. She hit save on her list of talking points for the upcoming meeting with the education minister and closed the laptop, giving

Ray her full attention. "So, did you meet him?"

"No, just saw him talking to one of the guys on my detail. Thought I'd come up and let you know, so you can meet him and help put your mind at ease."

Given what had happened to her father here a few weeks ago? Not likely. But meeting the man might make her feel a little better about things or not.

"I'll come down right now." She grabbed her black lightweight sweater and threw it over her shoulders on her way to the door. Ray followed her into the hallway and to the elevator without a word. As the digital numbers on the panel in front of them ticked off the decreasing floor numbers, she cast Ray a sideway glance. He stood near the mirrored side wall without looking at her, face serene, hands clasped in front of him.

His silence was really starting to annoy her. He knew how wound up she was. Why couldn't he say something to reassure her? She was jittery enough now without having any more unpleasant surprises to deal with. The last few weeks had been full of them.

She tried again. "So, what's he like?" A little smile this time. "You'll see."

Carmela blinked in surprise. "You're not going to tell me anything about him?" If he was keeping something from her to spare her, she'd prefer to know ahead of time so she could prepare herself.

"Nope."

Classic Ray. Either he had nothing to report, or there was a reason he was looking forward to watching her reaction to meeting her bodyguard. That didn't ease the anxiety grinding in her belly, but she'd find out soon enough who Organization had assigned to protect her. "Is he American or British?"

"American."

"Former military, or law enforcement?"

"Military."

Ray had managed to find out all that without meeting him. "What branch did he served ?"

A telling pause. Then, "SEALs."

An answering pain of dread echoed around her suddenly hollow stomach.

She struggled to keep the spike in anxiety from showing on her face, and hoped she managed it well enough.

"Really? Well, that's impressive." If it was true.

God, she prayed this guy was legit. "How long ago?"

He shrugged as though it wasn't important. "My guy didn't say."

"Lot of help you are," she muttered as she exited the elevator and reached the lobby door. True to form, Ray grinned and reached past her to press down on the metal bar, swinging the door open for her.

The heels of her nude-toned pumps clicked on the highly polished marble tile as she crossed to the foyer of the lavish hotel. Tom had booked them here. It was supposedly one of the safest hotels in the city because of its solid security presence due to all the diplomats and foreign contractors who stayed here.

Despite knowing that, Carmela had barely slept at all since they'd checked in two nights ago. She probably wouldn't get a full night's sleep again until she made it home safely, far away from this part of the world where armed militants would kill her simply because of what she represented.

The modern sparkling glass and tile lobby was busy, filled with wealthy tourists and businessmen dressed in suits. A far cry from the places where she'd be staying in a few days once they entered New York.

Considering the circumstances, she'd have felt a hell of a lot better if Tom would guard her personally, but that wasn't going to happen and she had to accept it.

In their last conversation before she'd flown here, he'd told her he was working on finding a solid team for her and promised to find someone he trusted. That would have to be good enough.

The bar came into view, a polished mahogany expanse tucked away into a cozy corner of the lounge. She spotted a group of six well-built men seated on leather sofas set against the far wall.

Two she recognized as belonging to Ray's. detail, so she assumed the others must be here for her. The oldest, maybe around forty with reddish-blond hair shaved close to his head, had to be the team leader.

Carmela drew a calming breath to battle her nerves. "That's them?" she asked.

Ray, but the men had spotted her and were already rising from their chairs. To her surprise the redhead didn't approach her.

A slightly shorter man with dark hair broke away from the group and when she got her first good look at him, something inside her stilled. Was this who Tom had sent to lead her in detail?

He was way younger than she'd expected. Around the same age as hers, in his late twenties if she had to guess. Her palms went damp. Was he experienced enough to lead the group of men charged with keeping her safe over here.

When Tom had promised to send her one of his best, someone with a lot of experience, she'd assumed he'd assigned someone much older.

The man kept coming, examining her just as closely. He was around six feet tall or so, with short dark hair and light brown eyes that were a little startling against his tanned complexion.

His features were rugged, too harsh to be called handsome, and from the amount of beard on his face it looked like he hadn't shaved in a few days.

His expression remained neutral as he sized her up, but there was something in his gaze that made her insides tighten in reflex. The flat line of his mouth and the hard twinkle in his eyes made him look cold.

Unapproachable. A light gray polo shirt stretched over his broad chest and shoulders and showed off his well-defined arms. His build spoke of hard work and discipline.

His confident posture, the controlled way he moved told her he'd spent time in the military. But a SEAL?

She'd recently learned the hard truth that not all claims about being a SEAL were legit. He was almost to her now. The dark caramel of his eyes should have made them seem warm, but instead the look in them sent a chill of unease through her.

Now that he was closer, she realized he didn't look at all happy to see her. In fact, it looked like he either never smiled or had forgotten how to. Unless there was yet another problem she was unaware of? Never let them see you sweat.

Over the years her father had told her that more times than she could count.

Easier said than done right now, however. She was totally out of her element here and had to keep reminding herself why she was doing this. No matter the consequences.

Though having no consequences would be awesome. Ray stood a step or two behind her, offering the silent support of his calming presence. Smoothing her hands against the sides of her dress to wipe away the dampness that had gathered on her palms.

Carmela straightened her spine and put on a polite smile as she prepared to meet this hard-edged man who would hold her life in his hands during the next week.

Chapter 3

Meeting Carmela

Given what he'd seen and read about her in her file, Carmela Bonanno wasn't at all what he'd expected, and Charles wasn't the kind of man who liked to be surprised. Not in this line of work.

Next time he talked to Tom, he was going to give him hell for this. Charles held Carmela's gaze as he approached and pushed aside his misgivings about the job.

First off, she was a hell of a lot prettier than he'd realized. The few pictures he'd seen of her hadn't been of good quality, and her face had been all puffy and wet from crying at her father's funeral. She might not be beautiful, but there was something about her that drew his interest.

She moved with a smooth, purposeful gait that spoke of a high level of self-esteem and he had to give her points for maintaining eye contact without flinching because right now he wasn't trying to mask his feelings about this detail.

Taking her out to the tribal region while there was a credible threat against her life? Even if he hadn't read her file earlier, with a single glance Charles could already tell she didn't belong here. It was obvious she was greener than green.

That would only make his job harder. With her long dark brown hair pulled up in a pile of curls, wearing a pale pink sleeveless dress that skimmed her rounded curves and ended just below her knees and those fragile high heels that emphasized a very sexy pair of legs, she looked about as tough as Barbie.

Her face was too open, her startling light green eyes unique enough to draw attention, and they gave away her every thought. Right now, they regarded him with a cautious light, probably because he looked less than pleased.

How the hell was she going to make it in the jungle? Everyone that met her was going to remember her eyes, and that wasn't a good thing. He drew up a few feet from her. Pulling his professional demeanor around him, he opened his mouth to introduce himself and started to offer a hand when she beat him to it.

"I'm Carmela," she announced, holding out a hand, a friendly smile in place.

He shook it politely, a bit surprised by the firm grip she used. Her eye contact never hesitated. She wasn't lacking in confidence, that was for sure. He didn't yet know if that was good or bad though.

In his experience, coming from the kind of money she did manage to give people an overinflated opinion of themselves. He hoped she wasn't like that. "Ma'am. I'm Charles Palermo."

"Nice to meet you." She released his hand and folded her arms across the firm-looking breasts he was trying not to notice beneath the conservative yet nonetheless tempting bodice of that dress. "So, Tom sent you?"

He thought he detected a hint of suspicion in her tone, but having never met her before, he couldn't be sure. "That's right."

"And I understand you were a SEAL?"

"Yes, ma'am."

She nodded once. Those pale green eyes, made even more vivid by her tasteful makeup and thick black lashes, swept over him in thorough assessment.

Not in an appreciative way. His admission didn't get him the reaction he usually got from women when they found out he'd been a SEAL. Not even close.

Instead, when she met his gaze again her expression gave him the foreign feeling that she'd measured him against some unknown yard stick and found him lacking.

"If you don't mind me asking, what Team were you with?" This time he was sure he wasn't imagining the skepticism buried in her polite tone.

A bit taken aback; he eyed her guardedly as he responded. "A few different ones over the years."

Apparently, his ambiguous answer didn't earn him any more points. Her gaze

Hardened and became almost cool. "Ah, and where did you go through BUD/S?"

Okay, this was getting flat out weird and the edge to her tone made it clear she wasn't asking all these questions out of mere curiosity.

Being grilled like this was the last thing he'd expected from her. Tom had told him she was kind and easygoing, and nothing in the dossier he'd read about her suggested she might be difficult to work with. Easygoing wasn't exactly how she was coming across now, however.

He glanced over her shoulder at her co-worker Ray for some indication of what the hell was going on, but the man seemed to be fighting back a smile and didn't say anything as he spun around and walked away.

Turning his attention back to Carmela, Charles set his hands on his hips and fought down his impatience. What the hell did it matter to her what Team he'd been with and where he'd done his initial training? He fought to keep the annoyance out of his voice. "Little Creek, Virginia."

Another nod, and that assessing look that made him feel like she had him under a magnifying glass. Did she think he was lying? His spine stiffened. "And what rank were you when you left the Navy?" she continued.

"I made it to Lieutenant." And that probably doesn't impress you either, does it? Jesus, maybe he should have brought his resume and a list of references with him for her to double check.

A frown creased her forehead, as though what he'd told her wasn't adding up in her head. Or maybe she couldn't envision him as being capable of leading a platoon of men. "How old are you? If that's not too personal." He arched an eyebrow. "Thirty-one." He swore he could read the dread in her eyes as she came to the realization that he was only three years older than her.

Believe me, sweetheart, I'm plenty old enough to guard your little tail for the next few weeks.

"Anything else?" His crisp tone made her lose some of her boldness. A faint tinge of pink hit her cheeks, as though she'd only just realized that she'd been interrogating him in the middle of the lobby. "You're just… not what I expected after talking to Tom, that's all." She flashed a tight, uncomfortable smile.

Yeah, that makes two of us. He'd be damned if he apologized for who he was though. "He hired me for this detail on short notice."

That seemed to make her even more uneasy. She eyed him again, trailing her gaze over his torso and back up to his face as if searching for clues to a puzzle she couldn't quite solve it.

He wanted to ask her if he passed inspection, but instinct told him there was more to this than disappointment or even dislike on her part. As he stood there trying to understand the disquiet in her eyes, realization finally hit him.

She didn't believe him.

Didn't believe he'd ever been a SEAL, much less served as an officer in the

Teams. Seriously? He fought the urge to laugh. The last thing he'd thought he'd bedding this morning was having to prove himself to the woman he'd been assigned to protect.

What proof could he offer her right now, other than his words? Did she expect a demonstration of his skills before she decided if he was qualified to be her head of security?

He doubted it would ease her mind to know that he could tell her exactly how many people stood in the lobby at that very moment, where they were positioned, where each exit was and the location and make of the vehicles parked under the porte-cochere outside the revolving front doors. He had a pistol tucked away at the small of his back and a spare magazine of ammo in his pocket.

Those pale eyes flicked up to his once more. "If you don't mind me asking, how long were you with the Teams?"

Why would he mind that one after everything else? "Six years." Frustrated, he folded his arms across his chest. He knew the move was intimidating because it emphasized his size, but he didn't care if he intimidated her at the moment.

He cocked an eyebrow in silent challenge when she continued to stare at him. "You want my BUD/S class number so you can check up on me? Call up NAVSOC headquarters and have them run my records?"

Her gaze snapped up to his, a hint of steel entering her expression at his acidic tone. "And how would I know if you gave me the real one?"

Okay, to hell with this. He whipped his cell phone out of his pocket and thrust it toward her.

"Call Tom and ask him yourself about my credentials." Flushing, she waved his hand away and lowered her eyes. "I'm sure that's not necessary," she murmured, clearly embarrassed at being called out.

No? For her it seemed necessary. "Maybe you'd rather speak to my former commander at Little Creek instead. I've got his number programmed in here too."

That intelligent gaze lifted to his once more, and he felt a shock in his gut as the underlying hint of vulnerability in her eyes finally registered. He'd seen that look enough to know what it meant. Whatever was going on for her, it was based on fear, not rudeness.

She held up her hands in self-defense. "Okay, I realize I must seem rude by questioning you like this, but I promise I'm not doing it to insult you.

I'm sure you're aware of what happened to my father here a few weeks ago."

Better than she'd ever realize. "I'm sorry for your loss. I wasn't on his protective detail. Our company wasn't even involved. So, I can't be held accountable for what happened to him."

"Yes, thank you, and I never meant to imply that you were." She took a breath, let it out slowly and glanced away before continuing. "I don't know if. you're aware of what happened, but the head of my father's security team claimed he was a SEAL and it turned out he wasn't, not even close. The truth is he washed out of BUD/S after three weeks.

The company he worked for lied about him, his background, and pretty much everything else, including the rest of the men on the team. It turned out they were a bunch of friends who wanted to cash in on the westerners hiring security contractors over here. No one found out about it until...after." She swallowed.

Charles frowned, his annoyance evaporating. Tom hadn't said a word about any of that. No wonder she'd felt the need to question him. Guys lied about being SEALs all the time, mostly to pick up women, but he'd never heard of one of them making it through the rigorous background checks necessary to land a job as a contractor. Which meant the owner of the company Michael

Brown had hired was a slimy jerk. "I'm sorry. That should never have happened."

She waved his words away. "Despite how those sounds, my father was a very intelligent man. The security company was recommended to him by someone he met here in Italy. Someone he trusted. They had to have known the company wasn't legit. I think they may have been in on it, hoping to get their hands on some of the initial ransom demanded when my father was kidnapped."

She rubbed a hand over the back of her neck, visibly distressed.

For some reason Charles found he didn't like seeing her upset. "Is anyone investigating that?"

"Yes. So, when you said you'd been a SEAL, it made me suspicious. I'm sure a lot of guys in your line of work claim to be SEALs when they're not, and I'm not exactly comfortable putting my life into a stranger's hands after what happened to my father. Sorry if I offended you. That wasn't my intention, and I apologize."

Okay, so maybe she was likeable after all. He inclined his head in acceptance of the apology because he could totally understand why she'd reacted the way she had. He didn't appreciate Tom failing to mention the incident with the SEAL wannabe when he'd asked Charles for this favor. For now, he needed to reassure her that he was the real deal.

"Tom was one of my chiefs when I was in the Teams," he told her. "We worked together, and he can vouch for me personally. The organization's background checks are extensive, like all the other security companies checks are supposed to be.

They go back ten years, digging through our pasts, service records, living records. Every company I've ever worked for has checked me out with my former officers, guys I've served with, my neighbors, even my high school teachers.

"These companies often work for the government, so they thoroughly vet all of us because we need certain security clearances to do our jobs. Right now, on this detail you've got me, a former Special Forces master sergeant, a former

Marine Scout/Sniper, and an ex-Force Recon member. That's a hell of a lot of experience and firepower at your back, which hopefully we won't wind up using. We're all legit, or Tom would never have hired us in the first place."

"Okay." Her smile wasn't all that convincing.

They needed to move past this roadblock, fast. "What more can I do to put you at ease about this?" Her expression tightened at his brusque tone, a hint of anger sparking in her eyes for the first time. "Look, I said I was sorry, and I am. I truly didn't mean to insult you or your service record. I just wanted to be sure you were telling me the truth."

"Understood, and I gave it to you, along with ways to check up on me if you want." He had no doubt she'd do so the moment she got back up to her room, and more power to her. "Whatever misgivings you have about me, rest assured

I'm more than qualified to keep you alive for the next six days. I've conducted dozens of high-risk missions, most of those as a SEAL platoon team leader, and

I've never lost a principal yet.

I'll take you into that mountain village where the school is. At the end of the week, I'll put you safely on the plane back to Italy. That's all you really need to know about me."

He swore she hid a turn at his rude words. "Okay." At least her nod was crucial this time, as if she was starting to come around to the idea of him leading the detail.

"So, being that we're going to be spending a lot of time together over the next few days, can we maybe erase this conversation and start over?" The right corner of her mouth rolled up, her eyes holding a hopeful look as she offered a hand and raised her eyebrows. "Truce?" Well, if that verbal olive branch didn't instantly take the edge off his bad mood.

"Yeah, peace." He clasped her hand again, noting how cold her soft skin was. Despite the brave face, she was a hell of a lot more nervous about being here than she let on.

Charles filed that info away in his mind. He'd do what he could to make her feel secure for the rest of her stay in New York. Ignoring the slight tingle her touch had ignited in his palm, he released her and stepped back. She was a job, for Chris sake, not a potential lay.

"Your first meeting's tomorrow afternoon, correct?"

"That's right."

At least she seemed pleased that he'd already memorized part of her itinerary. "You got the rest of your schedule ready for me?"

"It's up in my room."

"I'll come up and get it in the morning." That would give her enough time to unwind and call Tom, give him a turn in the hot seat if she wanted to go over

Charles's background before they saw each other again.

As if she'd read his mind, a spark of displeased humor lit her eyes. "I don't need to call him. I believe you."

"You'll feel better if you talk to him." They both would. Anything that made her feel more confident in his abilities would make his job easier, so her talking to Tom was a win-win.

Her lips twitched in a tiny grin, and it made her look mischievous. Like a luscious fairy with that riot of dark curls cascading down the back of her neck.

In her heels, the top of her head barely reached his chin. While that pink dress wasn't revealing in any way, the way it hinted her curves, made it disturbingly sexier by the minute.

"You're right, it will. It's not because I think you're lying, okay?"

It seemed important to her that he believed that. He nodded once. "Fair enough."

"Want me to tell him you said hello?"

"Yeah, do that." Because God knew, Charles had plenty to say to his boss the next time they spoke.

"Okay, see you in the morning then. Nine o'clock?"

He nodded and watched Carmela cross the lobby toward the elevators, head up, spine straight, her high heels tapping against the marble floor. It didn't escape his attention that every other man in the room noticed her too.

Shaking his head, Charles turned and headed back to the others waiting at the lounge's seating area, wondering what he'd gotten himself into.

Chapter 4

Daily Schedule

The knock on her hotel room door came at exactly nine the next morning.

Charles was punctual, that was for sure. She liked that he cared about attention to detail.

Carmela strode over to answer the door, took a deep breath to suppress the butterflies flitting around in her stomach before pulling it open. She and Charles hadn't gotten off on the best footing yesterday, and it was her fault.

He probably thought she was a total nut and hated the thought of being near her for the next week. She was determined to make amends for any damage she'd caused and smooth things over.

She pulled the door open. Charles stood there with his hair still damp from a recent shower and wearing cargo pants and a collared shirt. "Hi."

"Morning." His intent gaze swept over her, taking in the modest knee-length blue dress and black silk scarf she'd covered her hair and shoulders.

Though there was nothing overtly sexual in the examination, she could sense the male approval there and a shocking burst of heat filled her lower abdomen.

Surprised by her visceral reaction, she nagged herself for it. This was not the time or place for that sort of attraction. Not that she planned to let him know she felt a pull toward him.

"Come on in." She had the finalized printed itinerary laid out on the desk for him to look at. He waited for her to sit before turning the remaining chair around and overlapping it, resting his defined forearms along the top of the backrest. A sexy, confident move that seemed as natural to him as breathing.

She didn't see a wedding band on his left hand, but maybe he didn't wear one while he was working. A secret part of her hoped he wasn't spoken for.

Minor muscles flexed along his right forearm, dusted with dark hair, as he shifted the paper and scanned it for a few moments. The man had ridiculously sexy arms.

What would it feel like to be wrapped up in that kind of strength?

She'd bet a hug from him would feel amazing, though he didn't strike her as the hugging type.

"I want to change where you've got us all staying at the Hilton," he said after a minute, still reading.

"Oh." She craned her neck around to peer at the paper. "Something wrong with it?" Ray had booked the hotel for them.

"There are a few other places I know that'll work better. It will help us blend in better while we're in that area."

He didn't look up at her, his expression calm, his tone matter of fact.

Blending in sounded good. "Okay. Anything else? Do we have an interpreter? yet?"

"I've got someone lined up already. We'll pick him up on the way out of the city. Everything else looks good. For now, anyway." He glanced up, and she was again startled by those light brown eyes.

She couldn't help but stare. "Can I keep this?" When she nodded, he folded it up and slipped it into the pocket of his pants. "So, what did Tom have to say when you called him yesterday?"

She didn't even bother trying to deny it. "Just that you were one of the best guys he's ever worked with, and that I should go out of my way not to bother you.

I told him it was already too late, and he said not to worry because I can work my way back into your good graces with a specific brand of beef jerky you love."

His lips twitched, his eyes warming a few shades to a rich caramel. If he ever truly smiled, it would soften a lot of the harsh angles of his face and make him downright gorgeous.

He was handsomely good looking as it was. Maybe it was better that he didn't smile, otherwise she would have a hard time pretending she wasn't wondering if that hard body felt as good as it looked.

"Don't worry about it. We're good. He should've told me about what happened with the contractors your dad hired. He should have briefed you on our background checks and records beforehand anyway, especially under the circumstances."

The circumstances being that her father had been held down while someone else slit his throat with a knife. On camera. She shoved the grief down before it could break free. "Well, I'm going to get you some jerky when this is all over. It's the least I can do."

"I won't say no to that, but it's not necessary." He returned both sculpted arms to the top of the chair back and focused his attention on her with a slight tilt of his head. "Before we get started, there are some things you need to know about the way I operate."

It was only fair that he has his say, especially after the way she'd practically cross-examined him yesterday. "Okay."

He nodded once. "If I give an order, you follow it, immediately and with no questions asked." His stark tone made it clear he wouldn't tolerate anything else.

He probably thought she was going to be difficult, given his introduction to her. Nothing could be further from the truth. "That's fair."

"if I'm not around and one of the other guys gives you an order, you do the same."

No argument here. "Got it."

"Good." A spark of relief lit his eyes, maybe at how easily she'd acquiesced. to those demands.

After his first impression of her she didn't blame him, but she was all too aware of how woefully equipped she was to be going into an area known to be controlled by the Mafia. Staying alive and in one piece was very important to her. Whatever he and the others told her to do to stay safe, she'd to it.

"I'm sure you realize how high tensions are here right now, especially surrounding the TTP's recent campaign against female education," he continued.

"Wherever possible we'll keep a low profile, stay out of the media spotlight and generally, not do anything to draw attention to you or any of us. Your eye color is going to stand out where we're going, so try not to look anyone in the eye if you can help it, especially men."

She nodded, totally on board so far.

"Also, I'm your bodyguard, not your tour guide. I'm here to ensure your safety, not be your buddy. If you need a friend, you'll have to go to Ray or maybe Gage."

Wow. Okay, good to know what the boundaries were. "Who's Gage?"

"My second-in-command. You'll meet him downstairs later when we go to your first appointment." He held her gaze as he continued. "So, if I don't get talkative with you or don't respond when you try to engage me in conversation, it's not because I'm being stupid. I'm doing my job, and the best way I can do that is to keep some distance from you and stay in the background.

Same goes for the rest of the team. The less you or anyone else notices us, the better."

"I understand." Still, she felt a little pain of disappointment at his declaration. They were going to be in close quarters together at least some of the time over the next week.

Based on what she knew of him so far, she wouldn't mind getting to know Charles a lot better during that time.

"I've got all your health records on file. Is there anything that needs to be updated? Are you on any meds I need to know about?"

"No." She hadn't touched the sedatives and sleeping pills the doctor had prescribed her between the funeral and this trip and didn't plan to take any of them now.

From here on out she had to stay sharp, and that meant not having her mind blurred by anything, even prescribed medications. The sharpest edge of grief had faded to the point where she only got teary about her dad once in a while.

Charles leaned back, and she couldn't help but admire all the muscles shifting beneath that black collared shirt, ground rules and clearly stated boundaries notwithstanding.

"Now, not to scare you, but in case there's a threat or things go sideways, you need to know about our emergency contingencies. Everyone on this team is charged with protecting you if the need arises. If something happens to me, Gage will take over, then the others.

Ray's team will even step in if necessary. If something happens to all of us, you need to find a way to get to the American embassy and contact Tom immediately. He'll take care of things from there. All right?"

All right? Not really, but she nodded anyway, swallowing past the sudden restriction in her throat. She squeezed her fingers together in her lap. "What about security at the school? How will you…"

"Both teams have already been going over that. No offense to you, but it's better that you don't know what we've got planned.

I know it's not easy, especially after what happened to your father, but trust me when I say I'm not leaving anything to chance."

Staring into his eyes, seeing the rock-steady confidence there, she believed him. A shocking prospect, considering she'd only met him a day ago. "Thank you." Her voice came out a bit rough.

Charles shook his head. "Nothing to thank me for. I take my job seriously."

The subtle reminder that she was just a job to him didn't escape her notice.

She'd best remember that and not make an idiot of herself by trying to be friendly with him.

Since she was a people person, and she was grateful for him taking her on, that wasn't going to be easy for her.

"Any questions?"

None that she could think of, so she shook her head.

Charles stood, sweeping that intent gaze over her from face to bare feet and back again, its touch making her belly flutter in feminine awareness. "I'd like to stay while you and Ray go over everything and get up to speed on what's happening with Fair Start Foundation and the school."

It surprised her that he seemed genuinely interested in what they did. She smiled. "Sure, that's fine." She began digging out papers to show him and Ray knocked on the door a few minutes later. Together they spent three hours reviewing documents, lists, contracts, and plans of attack for how they might counter any resistance to their program within the local political machine.

Occasionally Charles asked a thoughtful question but otherwise he absorbed everything in silence, filing it all away into what Carmela could tell was a very quick mind.

By the time they finished, she felt certain she was as prepared as she could be, and that Hunter had a much better understanding of how Fair Start worked. It was almost one o'clock, and she was starving as she and Ray hadn't eaten since early morning.

Eating at the hotel was one thing because it catered to tourists, the restaurants in the city were closed until after sunset. Charles glanced at his watch as she tidied up the desk and stood. "If you're ready, I'll take you down to the truck and we'll get going to your meeting."

"Sure."

In the lobby he stayed at her side to the revolving doors at the front. He went through first and waited for her on the sidewalk. Seconds after she stepped up beside him, a black SUV with tinted windows pulled up in front of them. Charles opened the back left door for her as he visually scanned the area, she assumed for threats.

She climbed inside then Charles shut the door and rounded the hood.

She recognized the driver as the redhead from yesterday who she'd mistakenly assumed was in charge.

Another SUV drove in behind them as Hunter climbed into the front passenger seat. He shut the door with a pop. "This is Gage," he told her without glancing back. "Gage, Carmela. The rest of the team is in the truck behind us."

Gage reached back a hand, which she took automatically, and offered a warm smile. He had vivid bright blue eyes which crinkled at the corners when he smiled, and she couldn't help but respond kindly. "Nice to meet you, Carmela."

His words had a southern drawl. "Likewise." Already she could see he was a lot friendlier than Charles. She buckled her seatbelt, noting the tattoos that covered both his arms from wrist to the sleeves of his black T-shirt.

"Off to the first meeting?" Gage asked Hunter.

"Yep. Another team's already in route." He turned partially in his seat to look back at her. "Ray will meet you in the minister's office."

"Sure."

Gage pulled away from the hotel and turned onto the main street.

The business district was a bustling area of high rises and other corporate buildings, crowded and full of traffic. An entirely different world from the downtown region. The SUV's engine purred as Gage merged onto the highway and picked up speed.

The men didn't talk beyond the occasional comment or question about traffic or alternate routes. Carmela stayed quiet in the back, but it felt weird to be driven around without speaking to the other people in the vehicle.

Like she was a VIP being chauffeured across the city or something. Though she wanted to initiate conversation she resisted the urge, remembering Charles's warning. He'd made it clear they weren't going to be friends, and it didn't feel right to talk to Gage while ignoring him.

Instead, she used the time it took to reach the first meeting location to review her notes and talking points she'd laid out.

By the time they reached the Ministry of Education building, nerves were once again jumping in her belly. Charles escorted her upstairs to the appointed office without a word.

"I'll be in the lobby when you're done," was all he said before leaving. Carmela went into the meeting, relieved to have Ray there with her. The minister, an overweight man somewhere in his fifties, dressed in a business suit stood and shook their hands, then offered Carmela his condolences about her father while an appointed photographer took some shots of them. She put on a smile.

This one's for you, Dad. He'd be proud of her for doing this. Knowing that helped a lot and kept her centered. Even though he was gone forever, his approval still meant a lot to her. She could be brave for him, for his memory and legacy.

Together, Carmela and Ray laid out the purpose for their trip, Fair Start's intentions for the new girls' school in the Green Valley, and their belief that girls deserved the right to a quality education, no matter where they lived.

Ray took his turn, carefully addressing concerns that the Italian government had outlined about working with Fair Start, doing his best to relieve them.

Next, Carmela gave her presentation, gaining confidence with each point she raised. Hell, she'd come all the way from Italy in spite of everything, hadn't she? She believed in what she was doing, enough to set aside her fears and leave her old life behind this mission.

They needed the Ministry's blessing and funding for future operations in the country, and she intended to see that they got both.

When the balding minister smiled and agreed to support their cause, a ripple of goose bumps broke out beneath her lightweight black sweater. They'd done it. Ray looked at her with a grin. He reached over and squeeze her hand.

Forty minutes later, Ray flung an arm across her shoulders on the way down to the lobby.

"If your old man could see you now..." He gave her affectionate squeeze. "You knocked them dead, kiddo. Proud of you."

"Thanks." She was thrilled, excited, and electrified. She was glad she'd come here despite her worries.

"Ready for the next one?" Ray was headed to a meeting with the team of lawyers of the Italian government had. They were assembled to discuss funding, while she was meeting the female Dean of Education of a local university.

"You bet. I'll meet you for dinner at the hotel once I get back from my meeting with the US ambassador, and you can tell me how it went with the university folks."

"Sounds good."

As he'd promised, Charles was waiting for her in the lobby along with Ray's head of security. The two men escorted them back to the waiting SUVs and the drivers turned out of the parking lot in opposite directions.

"So, how'd it go?" Gage asked as he stopped at the first traffic light.

"Great. No, better than great." She couldn't stop smiling. God, they'd done it. The rest was essentially just a formality now.

"Glad to hear it." He reached across the console and thumped a fist into

Charles's shoulder. "Aren't we?" "We are," Charles answered dryly, staring straight ahead.

"Don't mind him, he really is happy for you. I can tell because he's not scowling."

She hid a smile, liking Gage already. Too bad Charles couldn't let his guard down a little with her as well, but she understood why he wouldn't.

"You hungry?" Gage continued. "I picked us up some lunch, which was no mean feat considering pretty much every food place is closed until sundown."

She thought she'd smelled something good when she climbed into the vehicle. "Great, because I'm starving. Thanks," she said when he handed a

Styrofoam container back to her. The scent of cinnamon and cloves and something else sweet tickled her nose. She was so hungry she wanted to devour it all.

"Charles said you're not a vegetarian. Thank God, so I figured a salad with chicken was a safe bet until I get to know you better."

"Sounds perfect, thanks." She popped the lid open to find a sliced chicken breast drizzled with spices and honey on a bed of greens and pieces of ripe mango on top. Oh, yum. It tasted even better than it looked, too. "So good," she moaned around a bite of chicken.

"Right? Stick with me, lady. I know all the good food joints around here."

Charles shot him a bland look and started in on his own lunch but didn't say anything.

Carmela stuffed her face all the way across town and was just closing the container when Gage suddenly turned up the radio.

Since the broadcast was in Napolitano, she couldn't understand what the announcer was saying, but Gage quickly shoulder checked and changed lanes, moving them across to the far-right side of the highway.

"Something wrong?" she asked.

"We must re-route, is all. Accident up ahead is clogging everything up.

I'm going to try a couple tricks to get around it." His tone and demeanor were calm, as though he'd anticipated the possibility long before they began the drive.

He probably had. He certainly knew his way around the city.

"We'll get you there on time, don't worry," Charles added, crumpling up the paper napkin he'd just wiped his mouth with and tucking it into the takeout container.

When they'd tried three different routes without success and came to yet another standstill on the last one, Charles unbuckled his seatbelt and swiveled to face her. He looked down at her feet.

"Can you walk a while in those heels?" "Sure." She set her container on the seat beside her and undid her own seatbelt, assailed by nervousness.

Considering the possible threat to her, walking around out there in broad daylight even with a bodyguard didn't thrill her. Especially in shoes that would leave blisters after a few blocks.

"Let us off at the next intersection," Charles directed Gage. Gage pulled over and half straddled the sidewalk as he bypassed traffic amid the annoyed horns blaring at them.

At the traffic light, he stopped. "Where do you want me to pick you up?"

Charles already had his door open. "I'll let you know when we're done." He opened her door and helped her down from the truck, his grip gentle on her arm despite his obvious strength.

More tingles raced over her skin, and she mentally scolded herself for her body's reaction.

"It's only a few blocks from here," he said to her. "You good with that?"

Though his eyes were shielded by his dark sunglasses, she knew he was studying her reaction. The man didn't miss anything, she'd seen that much already.

"Yes." She wasn't going to complain over a few blisters if that's what he was worried about it. Outside the air-conditioned vehicle, the heat was like a slap.

The sun was almost directly overhead, and it radiated off the baking pavement like an oven. It didn't matter that it was a dry heat, she felt as though someone had aimed a blow dryer at her face and turned it on full blast.

She followed closely behind Charles's fast steps across the street through the grumbled lanes of traffic, stretching out her strides to keep up with him. He kept careful tabs on her, checking on her position every few seconds.

On the far side of the four-lane road, they hit the sidewalk and headed east toward the government buildings a few blocks away. Here it was less crowded, the pedestrians moving in opposite directions on the thin strip of pavement without any problem.

She noticed Charles's head moving constantly and knew he was documenting everything going on around them. Hired security or not, he was out here guarding her back. She found that sexy as hell.

By the time they were a block away from their destination, sweat had gathered beneath her arms and breasts and across her face. She couldn't wait to get inside the building and cool off, maybe duck into the ladies room to take off her thin sweater and scarf. They passed groups of businesspeople talking on cell phones and crowds of others who'd abandoned their deserted buses and taxis in favor of walking.

She stayed directly behind Charles who acted like a human icebreaker, his wide shoulders opening a path through the sea of bodies. Someone jostled her from behind. She bounced off a man in a business suit on her right and reached out blindly for Charles to catch her balance, snagging the back of his shirt. Her fingers hit something hard beneath it and she realized he had a weapon hidden in the back of his waistband.

Without a tie in his stride, he reached behind him and took her hand. His grip was strong but gentle, strengthening her courage and calming her at the same time. Whatever happened, she knew he would be there to take care of her if she needed him.

"Almost there," he said over his shoulder, pulling her along. The sudden loud blare of horns made them both snap their heads to their right. A white delivery-style truck was barreling up the first available unclogged street, right toward the tall buildings on the opposite side of the intersection a half block away.

Charles stopped walking so fast that Carmela bumped into his back. Before she could retreat a step, she felt the unnatural stillness in him, a silent tension that made her jerk her head around to stare at the truck.

It was moving too fast and showed no sign of slowing down. Everyone else was staring now too. The street dead ended at the tall rows of buildings lining it, and there was no way the truck could turn the corner given its speed.

Horns were still loud as the vehicle whizzed past other traffic at breakneck speed. She watched in astonishment as it blew through the stop light and hurtled straight toward the building across the dead-end intersection.

Charles whirled and grabbed her shoulders, pushing her toward the ground.

"Get down!" he yelled.

What? Too stunned to protest, Carmela sprawled flat on the pavement. The breath whooshed out of her as Charles's hard weight landed on her back, squashing her against the burning hot sidewalk.

Someone near her screamed. A split second later she heard the loud bang of an impact, then the still air was ripped apart by an explosion. The force of it tore over her like a raging wind, whipped through her body like a shockwave. Her eardrums and lungs felt like they'd exploded from the pressure.

For a split second the sidewalk rolled and bucked beneath them as if they were on a boat. It took a moment for the truth to sink in. A bomb. Her heart hammered against her ribs. Charles was still on top of her, his arms crossed over her head and face to shield her. She didn't dare move.

People were screaming, running past them, even over them. Hunter grunted when someone stepped on him, but he didn't budge from his position atop her. She could hear glass shattering close by, hitting the ground somewhere behind them with a sharp crash.

The smell of smoke and burning wreckage was already thick in the air, as well as an audible roar that pulsed against her throbbing eardrums.

When the mass of panicking people around them began to thin out, Charles's weight finally lifted from her. She sucked in a shaky breath, her compressed lungs aching with the effort and dared to lift her head. Only to witness a scene straight out of hell.

The truck had plowed straight into the front of the building, leaving a gaping hole where flames now poured out, belching huge clouds of toxic smoke. All the windows in the lower floors were blown out, in addition to those in the buildings on either side and across the street. People were running everywhere, shouting, their faces flooded with panic.

In the openings of the shattered windows, she could see people sticking their heads out of the burning building to look around. Some were waving articles of clothing out of the openings with frantic motions. They were trapped, she realized. Trapped in that crippled, burning building. Fear and helplessness gripped her.

A hard hand cupped her jaw, turned her head. She blinked up into Charles's concerned face. He was saying something to her, frowning. "I'm okay," she managed shakily, and got to her hands and knees. He grabbed her beneath the arms and hauled her upright as though she weighed nothing. When she was on her feet, he kept hold of one upper arm. She was thankful because her legs wobbled.

All around them people crowded into groups, staring at the awful spectacle before them. As she watched, the first victims started to pour out of the ruined building, covered with blood and ash.

Two men emerged carrying another and laid him down on the sidewalk away from the falling glass and rubble. It took a moment for Carmela to realize the man was missing his right arm at the shoulder.

She stared in horror at the lump of glistening bloody flesh sticking out of the sleeve, the blood pulsing out of him while someone tore off their shirt and frantically wrapped it around the severed limb. The wounded man's mouth was wide open, his eyes squeezed shut in an expression of unimaginable agony.

Carmela's stomach stumbled and she tore her gaze away. The howl of distant sirens rose over the cries of the wounded and the roar and crackle of flame. She felt a tug on her arm and looked up into Charles's grim face.

"Let's go," he ordered in a voice made even scarier by his fierce expression.

She wanted to turn and run as fast as her rubbery legs would carry her. "The wounded," she began, feeling the first tremors of shock ripple through her muscles. It was almost a hundred degrees outside, yet she felt like she was freezing. "We have to help." They had to do something. People were trapped inside. Charles had training, and they were close enough to the victims to maybe get some of them out.

Rather than answer, he began dragging her in the opposite direction. She stumbled, realized she'd lost a shoe and glanced back. It was nowhere to be seen, swallowed up by the mob still gathered on the sidewalk, holding their hands to their faces in horror and disbelief, some crying and wailing.

The sounds made her skin crawl in primal reaction. Fire trucks and police vehicles were beginning to show up on scene, sirens and lights going. "Wait," she insisted, yanking against his hold. His fingers were like iron bands around her upper arm.

"We've got to get the hell out of here," he shot back, walking faster. Carmela kicked off her other shoe to save herself a broken ankle as she struggled to keep up.

"Suicide bombers like to wait until the first responders show up to the initial blast."

More screams. Charles jerked his head around and she followed his gaze just in time to see a second white delivery truck racing toward the stricken building.

A scream built up in her throat, but never escaped. Charles swore and tackled her again, this time bringing her down to the sidewalk with a bone-jarring thud. She cried out as he landed on top of her, slamming her ribs and hip bones into the unforgiving concrete. His arms came up over her head to shield her, the force of them scraping her cheek and temple against the rough surface.

Before she could draw breath, another explosion tore through the air, even stronger than the first one. Her teeth clacked together when the shockwave rolled through the ground.

More screams. Closer this time. Terrified and blood curdling. Heavy things slammed into the ground nearby. The heat of the blast washed over her, stinging her skin. Hunks of burning metal whipped past them, gouging out chunks of pavement and concrete where they landed. Carmela was too afraid to move. She couldn't breathe, couldn't think.

Seconds later Charles got up and lifted her once again. Her heart was slamming out of control. She grabbed hold of his shoulders for support and cowered against him, darting glances around to see what was happening. She saw people stumbling around with burns and bleeding wounds. The carnage was horrific.

Her whole body started shaking. He grabbed hold of her hand, clamped his long fingers around hers and yanked forward, away from the scene. She fell, scraping both knees and her free palm. He scooped her up again, tossed her over one broad shoulder, and ran.

Carmela clung to the back of his shirt for balance. Every running step sent her midsection slamming down on his shoulder. All she could do was tense her stomach muscles and hold on. She kept her eyes closed and fought the urge to cover both ears with her hands because she needed to keep her grip on Hunter or she'd fall.

Through the weird numbness creeping over her she could still hear those terrible screams rising and shuddered. Hunter was talking to someone over the walkie talkie, shouting instructions she didn't catch.

Her hands dug into his shirt; fingers frozen there like talons. Were more bombers still coming? Did they have other targets in mind across the city? Any courage she'd thought she had was gone. She should never have come here. What the hell had she been thinking?

After an unknown amount of time Charles stopped and slid her off his shoulder to her feet, steadying her with a firm grip on her waist when she swayed. She blinked up at him, trembling all over.

They were now blocks away from the bombing site, on a road with hardly any traffic. He leaned his face close to hers. "You're okay. Gage is right there," he panted, skin streaked with sweat and grime, not a hint of fear anywhere in his expression. She followed his pointing finger down the road to see the two black

SUVs roaring up. "Come on."

When he grabbed her hand and pulled again, she followed, her legs wooden but at least functioning. Together they ran to the waiting vehicles. Gage jumped out and popped open the back door before climbing back behind the wheel.

Charles shoved her headlong into the backseat and climbed in behind her, slamming the door shut behind them.

The instant it closed he was on top of her again, flattening her facedown against the leather seat. She squeezed her eyes shut.

"Hold on," Gage said as he reversed and shot the vehicle backward at an alarming speed, the engine revving high and loud. Above her, Charles took her hands, setting one against the doorframe and the other against the back of the front seat.

"Brace yourself," he commanded.

For what? She wanted to yell but couldn't get the words out and did as he said. A second later Gage cranked the wheel hard to the right. The truck spun in a sickening half circle, sending Carmela sliding along the slippery leather toward the door.

She cried out and pushed back with her straightened right arm, but Charles was there. He caught her, reinforcing her with his weight and strength as he struggled to hold them in place against the wild swing of the vehicle. The squeal of tires registered for a moment, then she heard Gage shift the transmission and they were driving forward once again, racing away from the scene.

A tense minute passed before Charles finally let her up. She slowly unwrapped herself off the seat and pushed into a sitting position with shaky arms. Her scraped cheek and palms stung and she'd be covered in bruises by morning, but at least she was still alive and in one piece. She still couldn't understand what had just happened.

A hard arm reached around her waist to drag the seatbelt across her body and snap it into the buckle. Immediately she wrapped her arms around herself in an attempt to stem the violent shivers wracking. His gaze was intense, the look in his eyes frightening, but that didn't scare her as much as what she heard him mutter under his breath when he looked away from her to stare out the window.

"Welcome to NEW YORK."

Chapter 5

Charles the Caretaker

Carmela somehow managed to put one sore bare foot in front of the other despite the stiffness in her muscles as Charles steered her into her hotel room. The lock clicked into place behind them, sounding overly loud to her heightened senses. Her heart rate still hadn't normalized. She took slow, deep breaths to calm herself. It wasn't working.

"Let's take a look at you," he said, ushering her into the bathroom with a solid hand on the small of her back. The warmth of his touch registered more than his voice did. She winced when he flipped a switch and bright white lights flooded the room.

With a nudge forward, he settled her on the closed toiled lid and grabbed a facecloth from the rack above it. He ran the tap and moistened it before turning back to her.

"Here. Clean up your cheek while I check your feet."

Feeling stiff all over, Carmela turned her head to look at herself in the wide rectangular mirror above the vanity. Her eyes looked huge in her too pale face and the side of her right cheek was scraped up to the temple.

It was raw and oozing from being mashed against the sidewalk. It could easily have been so much worse.

Lowering her gaze, she pressed the cool cloth to her cheek, ignoring the sudden sting. Charles was crouched at her feet, one bronzed hand reaching for her left ankle. She put out an arm to stop him, recoiling from the intimacy.

She was a heartbeat away from bursting into tears. Having him touch her right now, even if only to check for injuries, would be too much. "They're fine."

He raised his eyes to hers, that steady gaze sending a jolt of heated interest through her overloaded system. "They're bleeding. I want to make sure there aren't any bits of shrapnel in them."

She repressed a shudder and pulled her foot back. "I can do it."

He brushed her hand away with an impatient motion and grasped her ankle in a warm grip. "Just sit still and let me look."

Pushing out a sigh, Carmela allowed him to cradle her foot in his hands, unsettled at the way his touch sent streaks of sensation up her legs. How could he be so calm and steady when it felt like she was going to shake apart.

It was easier to keep a leash on her emotions when there wasn't any physical contact between them. The way he touched her, so gently despite his rough exterior, made her ache to lean forward and wrap her arms around that sturdy neck.

She longed to feel his strong arms around her in return, locking out the rest of the world. She wanted that so badly she almost gave into the urge to reach for him.

He killed the impulse by stretching an arm out above her for another facecloth, wetting it also before turning his attention back to her right foot. "It's scraped up some."

After wiping the sensitive bottom of her foot, he took the left one in his large hand, holding it up so he could see the sole in the light. "There's a splinter of something," he murmured, and a moment later pulled something sharp out of her foot. Her toes pointed in reflex, and she sucked in a breath.

A tiny shard of metal sparkled between his fingers as he held it up for her to see. Then he turned her left hand over and put it in her scraped palm before going back to search for others.

She stared at the fragment with detached revulsion, wondering where it had come from. The building? One of the exploding trucks? A first responder's vehicle? Feeling sick again, she dumped it on the counter with a tiny rattling sound.

"One more, but it's deeper. Hang on a sec." He shifted onto one knee and dug in his back pocket, coming up with a jackknife loaded with all sorts of tools.

With a pair of tweezers at the ready he took hold of her foot again and looked up at her.

"This is going to hurt, but I need to get it out before it buries itself in there and causes more problems."

Carmela nodded and tightened her hands in the folds of her dress. The light blue cotton was torn in several places and stained with dirt from where she'd hit the ground. The right shoulder seam was barely holding together. She pressed her lips together and fought not to wriggle when the tips of the tweezers dug into her tender flesh.

"Sorry," he said without glancing up at her, forehead furrowed in concentration. "It's a way in there." "It's fine," she murmured, wishing he'd just hurry up and get it over with already. Having him kneeling at her feet made her feel silly and only intensified the need for the feel of his arms around her. He'd made it clear where the line between them stood, so she wanted him to leave so she could lock the door and be alone for a while to get herself together.

It took a few minutes for Charles to get the remaining fragment out of the side of her instep. This one hurt more than the other and she tensed. He set the piece on the vanity and she relaxed, ignoring the painful stinging. "Your tetanus vaccines up to date?"

"Yes." This was such an insane conversation. Untold numbers of people had just been blown up, and she and Hunter almost with them. If they'd been any closer to the blasts. She swallowed and wrapped her arms around herself, fighting off another attack of shivers that kept rolling through her.

Charles didn't miss her reaction. "If your legs are steady enough after this, I'd recommend a hot shower. It'll help with the shaking," he offered, again without looking at her. She was glad for the small amount of privacy it afforded her. The truth was she was freaking terrified and barely holding her emotions in check.

Only the fear of humiliating herself in front of Charles kept her true reaction at bay. He'd protected her with his own body, and she hated the thought of seeming weak and emotional in front of him. He was calm, decisive, had been even during the bombings. His hands were completely steady as he tended to her feet.

The pulse in his throat was slow and steady. It was as though the explosions hadn't affected him at all. She didn't even want to think about what sort of training, or what he must have seen in the field during his time in the military that would enable him to compartmentalize such a horrific event so easily.

After pulling a third and final fragment out of her skin, Charles pressed the washcloth to her foot until the bleeding stopped, then stood and rinsed the tweezers in the sink. His elbows were raw and bloody, the heels of his hands. scraped raw.

Her impulse was to tend to him in return, but knew he'd rebuff her help with some gruff comment that would make her feel even worse so she stayed silent.

He searched her eyes before speaking again, as if gauging her emotional state. She bit down hard to stop her jaw from trembling. "Make sure you wash out all those cuts and scrapes as best you can when you shower. With soap if you can handle it."

Yeah, she could handle the sting of soap in her cuts and scrapes. What she couldn't handle what had just happened. What could have happened if they'd been any closer, and his calm apathy right now. She lowered the facecloth from her cheek, tossed it onto the granite vanity with a fleshy plop, and asked the question burning a hole in her brain.

"That wasn't... You don't think that had anything to do with Fair Start, do you?"

Charles shook his hands in the bowl of the sink and reached for the hand towel hanging from a ring on the wall next to the light switch.

In the mirror, he met her gaze. "Highly doubt it. There are a lot of foreign dignitaries in town, so maybe the government buildings were a temptation too great to pass up.

Whoever did it had it planned well in advance though. Packing two separates trucks with that amount of explosive and finding their way to an open route in that mess?" He shook his head, the light casting bronze-tinted highlights in his dark hair.

"Either they got lucky with the accident clogging up traffic, or they set it up that way in the first place. My money's on the second guess."

She shivered at the certainty in his voice, in his eyes. She looked away before he could see the fear in her own. "Thanks for getting those splinters out." Her feet stung and throbbed along with the rest of her, but mostly she just felt cold and tired and…numb. Rather than answer, he leaned a hip against the edge of the vanity and folded his arms across his chest, regarding her in silence. After a long pause she looked up at him.

"Are you, okay?" he asked quietly. The genuine concern in his voice nearly undid her. Not even close. "Yeah." What did he expect her to say? It had to be obvious how rattled she was. Maybe she was crazy, but for a second, she thought she saw a gleam of admiration in his eyes.

"Trust me, a hot shower will help get rid of the shakes. Take your time and make sure you keep warm when you get out. I'll send you some antibacterial ointment and band aids and something to eat." She made a face at the thought of eating but he continued.

"Ray will want to see you as soon as he gets back. You'll need to eat, even if you don't feel like it. It'll help boost your blood sugar and counteract the shock." He sounded like he spoke from experience, and he likely did.

Nodding in reply, she held her breath while he crossed to the door where he paused and looked back at her. "You're safe now and everything's fine. Gage and I are just down the hall if you need anything, okay?"

That glimpse of understanding, of that tiny bit of softness from him made her throat tightens.

"Okay." It came out a mere whisper.

When the door closed behind him with a solid click, Carmela gave up the pretense of being brave and slumped forward. She buried her face in her trembling hands and let the shudders and tears run through her.

By the time she'd calmed enough to shower and finish dressing, almost half an hour had passed. A knock came at the door. Expecting it to be Ray, she was surprised to find Gage standing on the other side of the peephole. "Hey," she said, standing back to let him in.

His bright blue gaze swept over her in a quick assessment, taking in her damp hair and yoga pants, the thick knit sweater she'd wrapped around herself to keep warm.

"Brought you some stuff for your feet." He handed her the ointment and bandages Charles had promised. The pain of disappointment that he's sent

Gage instead of bringing them himself caught her off guard. *He's not going to come back and coddle you, for crying out loud. Get over it.*

"Thanks." She sat on the edge of her queen-size bed and started bandaging the cuts on her feet.

Gage stuck his hands in his back pockets, obviously in no hurry to leave. Had

Charles asked him to stay with her. "So, how you are holding up?"

She stopped what she was doing to meet his eyes. Did he want her to lie?

"Honestly? I'm not sure."

An ironic grin curved his mouth. "Not the nicest introduction to Napolitano."

"No." Worse than she'd ever imagined, and she'd imagined plenty of awful things in the past few weeks.

"Well, if it's any consolation, you held it together better than most civilians would have under the circumstances. You impressed the hell out of Charles, and that's not easy to do."

That intrigued her curiosity. She set the tube of ointment aside. "He said that?"

"Pretty much." He lowered his tall, muscular body into a wing chair near the bed, leaned back into it. "We called Ray to tell him you were all right. You want something to eat while you wait for him to get back?"

"I couldn't eat right now, but thanks." Her stomach was way too risky at the moment to even contemplate putting anything in it, despite Charles's earlier advice.

Gage nodded and opened his mouth to say something else when his cell beeped. Pulling it out of a front pocket in his cargo pants, he checked it and looked up at her with a grin.

"My daughter, checking in on me. Must've seen the bombings on the news and got worried about her old man."

God, how scary for her. Carmela knew all too well what it felt like to know your father was in harm's way and see it splashed all over the news. To stop that line of thought, she wrapped the folds of her sweater tighter around her body and changed the subject.

"You have a daughter?"

"Thirteen. Going on twenty-five." He was smiling as he texted his daughter. back.

She waited until he was done before speaking, curious about him and desperate for a distraction. "Do you see her often?" He had to be close to forty.

How much longer did he want to live this kind of life?

Gage shook his head, regret evident in his expression. "Not as often as I'd like. This line of work means I travel a lot. Even when I'm stateside I teach training courses, things like that."

"That must be hard on her."

"Yeah, especially when I miss birthdays and holidays with her. She's a great kid, though that's more her mother's doing than mine, I'm afraid."

"Oh. Are you still…together?" From what she understood, a lot of marriages didn't work out for Special Operations members.

His smile turned rueful. "No, and we're both better off apart." He shrugged as he set his phone down on one muscular thigh. "We were young and thought everything would magically work out in the wash, but the truth was we never should have gotten married in the first place. Now Janelle lives with her full time." He tilted his head. "What about you?"

"Never been married. Came close to getting engaged a few months ago though. I would have gone through with the wedding, too, if my father hadn't stepped up and pointed out how incompatible we were. Couldn't have been easy for him to say it to me, but thankfully it made me open my eyes before it was too late."

Though deep down she had to admit she'd known there was something wrong with the relationship. She just hadn't wanted to face it until her father confronted her.

Gage grinned, his manner completely disarming. "Disaster avoided."

"Exactly." She smiled wistfully and shook her head. "God, I miss him."

"I'll bet. But coming over here and carrying on his legacy, that's something to be proud of."

If he only knew what a chicken she really was, he wouldn't think so. "Thanks.

You know," she added, "you're a lot easier to talk to than Charles" Gage chuckled. "Yeah, I get that a lot. What can I say, I'm a people person.

Special Forces guys must be since most of our job is spent teaching other people. Did you know that?"

"No, I didn't." "See? You and I have something in common. We're both awesome teachers."

She smiled wider, liking his easy-going nature and his efforts to soothe her mind. "I knew I liked you for a reason. If we get a chance, maybe one day you could show me how to do that wicked turn you did back there with the truck."

His eyes crumpled at the corners and a chuckle rumbled up. "That J-turn's pretty slick, huh? Yeah, I could show you how it's done if you don't tell Charles. "What he doesn't know won't hurt us, right?"

"Exactly." Grinning, he stood. "I like you, Carmela. I know you've had a rough start to your trip, but despite all that I don't want you worrying about anything while you're here.

Charles's one of the best, which is why Tom's got him leading this team. You couldn't be in better hands than his, and the rest of us will take care of you too, I promise you that."

He was so sweet. All those tattoos didn't fool her one bit. She wanted to hug him out of sheer gratitude. "Thanks. I really appreciate it."

Gage was still smiling as he made his way to the door. When he opened it, Ray stood there; fist poised to knock. His face was pale and pinched with worry.

When he saw her, he expelled a sigh and seemed to sag in relief. The moment he stepped inside and held out his arms, Carmela rushed straight into them while

Gage quietly closed the door behind him to give them privacy.

Fresh out of the shower after hitting the hotel gym, Charles glanced up from his phone when Gage entered the room. "How is she?" "Just fine. Ray's with her now."

"Good." He was surprised at how well she'd held up so far. Not too many women he knew could experience something like a double suicide bombing with mass casualties without falling to pieces or becoming hysterical.

Carmela had done neither.

Instead, she'd been silent on the way back to the hotel, closed. Only the trembling on her body and the pallor of her skin had told him just how shaken she truly was. It had taken an act of will stop himself from holding her tight until she felt safe again.

"Any word on who claimed responsibility for the attack yet?" Gage asked.

Charles nodded at the TV, currently showing a news broadcast about the bombing.

More than a dozen people had been killed outright in the blasts, and almost a hundred more were wounded. "TTP, but no surprise there."

"Fuckers." Gage set his hands on his hips. "You want to change the schedule at all?"

Gage knew him too well. "Yeah, I want to delay her arrival at the Gracie Mansion by twelve hours. If someone out there's gunning for her after all, I'm going to give them a smaller window of opportunity to work with.

I've already talked to Tom. I'll update everyone else tonight then hold a full briefing in the morning.

In the meantime, let's go over the map of the school one more time."

Together they reviewed the topography of the school's location, the access. roads leading to and away from it, as well as any other trails visible on the satellite map. Plugging up every access point wasn't an option, so he had to make an educated guess about where the enemy might strike from and make contingencies for it.

Working it over with Gage made the task easier. The man was solid, smart, and a great operator. Charles was glad to have him as his second-in-command.

After a couple of hours' discussion and planning they stopped to eat.

"You going to let her know about the schedule change, or should I?" Gage asked, rising to toss his container in the trash.

"I'll do it." It surprised him how much he wanted to personally check in on her again. "Hell of a thing, what she's doing. I like her."

Charles smirked. "You like everyone, and everyone likes you."

"Not true. My ex-wife would be the first to tell you that."

It didn't bother Charles that Gage was on friendly terms with Carmela. He was good enough at his job that Charles didn't mind relaxing the protocol about interaction between him and their principal on this assignment.

Over the past two years working together Gage had earned his trust, and along with it, the right to operate with more latitude than Charles might allow the others on the team.

Still, had to admit there was a tiny part of him that wished he didn't have to maintain his distance from her. Gage spoke up when Charles reached the door. "Go easy on her, Charles."

He paused and looked back at him with an upraised brow. "Are you seriously telling me how to do my job?"

Gage's expression was all innocence as he held his hands up in self-defense.

"I'm just saying, you don't need to be all hard ass with her. She got the message about not being best friends loud and clear, so she's not going to throw herself at you or anything."

That drew a resentful chuckle out of him. "Occupational hazard, women throwing themselves at me." Although the idea of Carmela throwing herself at him was a hell of a lot more appealing than it should have been.

The attraction was there. She was clever about it, but he'd noticed the glimmer of female interest in her eyes the few times he'd caught her checking him out.

The interest was mutual. Under different circumstances he'd be making moves on her in a big way, but not when she was a client, and he oversaw her safety over here.

"Yeah, my heart bleeds for you, man," Gage said dryly. "Call me if you need backup."

"Not a chance in hell." Gage's laugh followed him out into the hallway.

When Carmela opened the door Charles was surprised to find her alone in the room. She was dressed in a pair of black stretchy pants that hugged her thighs and a light gray sweater that belted at her waist.

Her hair was a mass of coffee brown curls that spilled halfway down her back, and she didn't have a trace of makeup on. Still sexy as hell, even with the scrape on her cheek and her smell.

God, the air was infused with that mix of shampoo, lotion, and feminine warmth.

She smelled so good it gave him the insane urge to bury his face in the curve of her neck and breathe in more of her.

Focus, jackass. He glanced around the room, taking in the rumpled bed where she'd pulled the covers back on one side, the room service tray bearing two sets of dishes wedged into the corner. "Where's Ray?"

"He went back to his room to call his family so I could call mine in private because I knew they'd be freaking out."

"Your mom?"

"And brother." She stepped back and gestured for him to come in, then went and sat against the mound of pillows stacked at the headboard.

"Is your brother involved with the foundation too?" From her file Charles knew he was two years younger than her.

"No, it isn't his thing, so he hasn't been involved from the get-go. He owns a restaurant in Phoenix."

Interesting. He crossed to an armchair positioned across from the foot of the bed and sank into it. "You look better."

She met his eyes, a gleam of humor lighting their pale depths. "What, you didn't like my shell-shocked, I-just-narrowly-escaped-being-blown-up look?"

"I like this look better." More than was professional of him, if he was honest.

She had color in her cheeks again and she seemed much steadier, but that's not what he wanted to talk to her about. "I've decided to make another change to the schedule."

She leaned forward and sat cross legged on the bed, giving him her full attention. "Okay..."

"There's no credible threat against you or anyone involved with the foundation, but after today I'd feel better if we changed the itinerary for when you arrive at the school."

Her brow crumpled. "You mean I won't be there for the official opening?"

"You will, but we'll get you there an hour or so prior to the ceremony, rather than stay the night."

She digested that for a moment, and he could tell her mind was working overtime on that piece of information. "So, what time will we leave here, then?"

"Oh-three-hundred Tuesday morning."

Rather than protest the early hour, she consented with a thoughtful nod.

"What about Ray?"

"He'll be arriving an hour before you. I'll be there ahead of him with the rest of his team. Gage and the others will travel with you to the school."

Her frown deepened. "So, you want to be there hours in advance to set up, but there's no credible threat. Is there an indirect one?" He had to admire her quick mind. "No." Not other than the TTP's vow to eliminate her and anyone involved with the foundation, and he wasn't going to remind her of that because he knew she hadn't forgotten.

Nodding slowly, Carmela broke eye contact and shifted on the bed to play with the sheet. She was silent for a few beats before speaking. "My father knew the risks involved before he was kidnapped," she began, surprising him with the turn in conversation.

"He believed in his cause enough to come here despite them. Then he died," she managed, stumbling over the wording, and Charles knew why. Her father hadn't merely died. He'd been murdered, throat slit, then beheaded with a sword on camera for the US authorities to see. He hoped the hell no one had let her watch the footage. He hated that her life had been touched with that sort of violence.

"When he died, he left instructions in his will that his work with the foundation be carried on," she continued. "I'm a founding Board member in addition to being his daughter.

I believe in what we were doing. He believed in it enough to risk his life for it." She raised haunted eyes to his, and Charles's heart squeezed at the raw pain he saw there.

"I know I don't belong here for God's sake, I'm a high school math teacher but he died for what he believed in. I'm not proud to admit it, but I don't want to be here." Her expression was tortured. "But after what happened, the way he died, how could I not step up and try to make this dream come true for him now that he's gone?"

The weight of responsibility on her shoulders, the grief in her eyes they hit Charles is like a kick in the gut. He squeezed his fingers around the padded arms of the chair, fighting the urge to walk over there and wrap her up in his arms. For Christ's sake, he was only human.

To see this confident, polished woman so lost and vulnerable turned him inside out. She was clearly afraid to be here, yet she'd somehow found the strength to overcome it and do what she felt necessary.

"And these girls." She pushed a hand through the tangle of her hair and blew out a breath, then drew her knees up to her chest and looped her arms around them.

"They want an education badly enough to risk their lives by simply coming to school. How the hell can that happen at this time? I'm not brave, never have been. I'm scared to death about going into that valley because of what happened to my father, but if those girls have the courage to defy the

Taliban and show up to school, I must help them.

What sort of person would I be if I stayed home in the States when they show that sort of bravery daily?"

A normal one, he thought. Few people had the moral conviction to take on something like this. Fewer still had the guts to see it through. He admired her for it. Far more than she'd ever realize. "I understand."

Her eyes cut to him. "You...do?"

He nodded, thinking of Scottie. Charles would have done anything for him.

"But you're wrong."

She blinked in surprise. "About what?"

"you said you're not brave, but you are. A lot braver than most people, to be honest." "Trust me, I'm not," she said with a snort. "I'm a homebody.

I like my safe little world back home. I went almost catatonic this morning after the bombing."

No, she didn't get what he was saying. He leaned forward, conveying the intensity of his conviction with his body language, his gaze.

"Courage isn't about words or beliefs. It's about actions. Going ahead with this even though you're afraid, especially after what happened to your father and the bombings today?

That's brave. That's what real courage is. You need to remember that and give yourself credit." A startled smile crossed her face, as though he'd surprised her with the compliment. Maybe because she was starting to see that she was stronger than she realized. She rested her chin on her upraised knees, in that moment looking impossibly young and vulnerable.

"Thanks." "For what? It's the truth." Jesus, he wanted to climb onto that bed with her and slide his hands into that thick mass of curls, then kiss the hell out of her. He knew exactly how she'd feel, all those soft curves cushioned against his body.

He wanted to touch that fine, smooth skin, taste it, mark it with his teeth. His muscles knotted with the need to go to her. But he couldn't cross that line, and if she responded with even a fraction of the heat, he thought she would, he'd want a hell of a lot more than a make out session with her.

He ruled in his wayward libido with a silent reprimand, mentally cursing the suddenly tight fit of the crotch of his pants. What the hell was wrong with him? In the space of a few minutes, he'd gone from trying not to be a hard ass to wanting to jump on her.

He'd never had this sort of immediate, animal reaction to a woman before, let alone one he was charged with protecting. If he wanted to do his job properly and keep his position as team leader, he'd better keep his head straight.

Neither of them spoke and a silent tension filled the space between them. He broke it by clearing his throat and shifting topics. "So. Any questions you want to ask me?"

She tilted her head thoughtfully for a moment. "Yeah. How do you handle it?

Things like this morning, I mean. You were so calm. It was unreal."

He shrugged. "Training and experience. Panic only makes things worse.

Over time I learned to slow my thought process down under stress, so I was able to make clear decisions, but don't beat yourself. You handled yourself just fine out there, and you're an untrained civilian."

"Well, I knew I had a kickass ex-SEAL there to shield me with his own body."

Her smart mouth made him smile, but he sobered quickly. "Not just me, hon." The endearment was out before he could stop it, though he wouldn't take it back even if he could have. "Any of the other guys would have done the same thing in my place.

Anyone thinking about hurting you is going to have to get through us first. And that's not going to happen." She smiled now, somehow making him feel warmer inside, and the set of her shoulders relaxed. "I believe you."

He was glad he'd at least been able to set her mind at ease on that count. Couldn't be easy, coming here and seeing the bombings after her father had been murdered. He was about to ask her more about him when the phone on the night table rang.

Carmela jolted a little and leaned over to answer it. She frowned at the response she was given and sat up straight, swinging her legs over the side of the bed. "Yes, go ahead." The sudden tension in her body was palpable. On alert, Charles leaned forward to rest his elbows on his knees, watching her closely.

A gasp escaped her, and her head snapped up in alarm. From across the room

Charles could see the color drain from her face. He was on his feet and at her side before she responded to whoever was on the other end. Setting a hand on her shoulder, he sank down beside her on the edge of the mattress, close enough that their thighs touched.

"Yes," she said at length, her voice a near whisper. Whatever the news was, it was bad. She didn't say much, mostly listened to whoever it was, but Charles relaxed slightly when she reached up and set her hand atop his on her shoulder, entwining their fingers. Her skin was ice cold.

When she finished the conversation and set the phone down beside her, he squeezed her hand in reassurance. Whatever was going on, at least she wasn't alone.

"What happened?" he asked.

"It was someone from the State Department," she answered duly, her eyes fixed on the beige carpet at her feet. "They've been investigating my father's. death." She swallowed and tightened her hand around his. "Apparently, they found evidence linking the Mafia official with the Interior Ministry to the company responsible for my dad's security before he was kidnapped." Her pale green eyes swung to his, devastation and disbelief clear in their depths.

Charles's muscles tightened in reflex, already fearing the worst. Her next words merely confirmed it.

"The Mafia and the company's owner made a deal to get a cut of the ransom when they took him hostage. They were working with the Sicilians the whole time."

Chapter 6

Carmela's Enemies

In the safety of his apartment, Joseph sipped on a mug of hot coffee while he worked up the nerve to get in touch with his shadowy TTP contact.

After two days of digging, he had nothing of consequence to report about Carmela Bonanno. Except for what he'd learned in the online article he'd read less than an hour ago. Since it was in English and as far as he knew his contact didn't speak it; Joseph hoped this early information was enough to satisfy him.

At any rate, he was out of time. He had to report in tonight. Setting the mug aside, he typed a message to Paul and waited for a response. Three minutes later, a sharp ding announced a reply.

Did you get the phone I asked you to?

Yes, he answered.

Log off, erase the data, and call me on this number immediately.

Pulse thudding in his throat, Joseph did, wondering about the sudden urgency.

They must be on to something big. What did they want from him, though? It made no sense for them to keep involving him unless they had other plans for him in the future. Were they grooming him for upcoming operations or something? Testing his loyalty? His palms turned damp as he dialed the number on the throw-away phone and waited for the call to connect. The man answered in Pashto before the first ring ended. "What have you found?

Joseph swallowed and glanced around the tiny apartment, glad he'd pulled the shades down. He kept his voice low, just in case. Had to be careful of the thin walls in this building. No telling who might overhear him, or if they could understand Paul.

"I wasn't able to find her exact location, but I know she's in New York, or at least she was yesterday." There were too many hotels in the city for him to check individually. He'd started with the upscale ones since they seemed the most likely candidates.

She hadn't been registered as a guest at any of them. Possibly she'd registered under a different name, or maybe she was staying under someone else's reservation.

"You've had two days," the man reminded him in a flat voice.

Yes, and he'd been working for most of them, getting that project finished up for that bitch.

"I did find out where she's going, though," he added quickly.

"We already know the location of the school."

Of course, they would. He scrambled for something else to say, settled on another bite he'd read. "She's going to be at the opening ceremony."

"Ah." Joseph could hear the delight in that single syllable. "When?"

He checked the online article again to be sure before answering. The printed newspapers wouldn't be out for hours yet. "Tuesday morning."

"During a holy week," the man said in disgust.

"Yes." Her timing couldn't have been worse. Or better, for the Americans. A western woman imposing her unwanted views on the population of Christians in the U.S. during the holiest week would only fuel their anger.

"It doesn't say anything about what time the ceremony will take place, but I would assume in the morning."

"Obviously."

Joseph decided it wise to shut up. He waited on the other end of the line, bouncing one knee up and down.

On screen, Carmela's smiling face looked back at him from where she stood beside the Secretary of Education. She looked young, almost innocent. He glanced away, uncomfortable.

"As you know, eliminating the woman is our number one priority at this time," his contact continued. "We have sworn to kill her and anyone working with Fair Start Foundation here in America. God willing, we can eliminate the men protecting her also."

She had a security detail. They hadn't told him that. Made sense after what had happened to her father though. "Yes," he said, mostly just to show he was listening. It unsettled him that the TTP had withheld information. How did they know she had protection and what else were they keeping from him? They needed someone who lived in the city who spoke English as well as Italian.

That's what they'd told him when they'd first enlisted his help. Yet all these months later he still didn't know what they really wanted from him. Maybe he was better off being oblivious.

"Our soldiers are ready to enforce Bonanno's will. If it is His wish, you will hear of their brave sacrifice in the coming days. I'll be in contact if we need anything more from you."

It was on the tip of his tongue to ask what they had planned, but he thought better of it. The less he knew the better and if anything did happen up in Swat on

Tuesday morning, he'd hear about it soon enough. "I understand. Peace be upon you." "And upon you. Be sure to dispose of the phone right away."

"I will." Hanging up, Joseph fought back the wave of guilt that assaulted him.

The image of Carmela's face was burned into his brain, and he didn't like it.

He rose and took the phone across his apartment to the galley kitchen to dismantle it, wiped the dampness from his palms and chided himself for his cowardly attack of conscience.

The woman had it coming. She and others like her had to be stopped. It wasn't like he was responsible for what the Mafia did to her after that night. It wasn't like he was the one harming her. He was merely standing up for what he believed in. For what was right in the eyes of the Mafia.

Annoyed, Joseph started a fresh pot of coffee and took the phone apart.

Going from sunrise to sundown without any food or drink for an entire month was hard but a small and necessary sacrifice. He intended to enjoy another hot beverage while he could.

After a restless night without much sleep, Ray answered Carmela's door for her when someone knocked at seven a.m. She glanced up from the desk where she and Ray had their laptops running and piles of papers spread between them to find Charles standing between the jambs.

Her welcoming smile faded, and her heart tripped when she saw his tight expression. Even though she'd only known him two days, she already knew that look meant trouble. "What's wrong?"

Walking to the desk, he pulled a copy of the morning paper out of his back pocket, unfolded it and set it in front of her to see. "This isn't exactly the low profile we're looking for," he said, keeping his tone even despite his obvious irritation.

Carmela peered down at the article. It showed a picture of her with the Secretary of Education, and the article was based on an interview he'd apparently given after she'd left yesterday. Her mouth dropped open, and her eyes widened in denial before she looked back up at Charles.

"I didn't authorize this! I didn't know they were going to print it. Oh, shit."

She slumped back in her chair, feeling sick to her stomach. "I had to attend the meeting, it's part of my duties and it would've been rude for me to decline the invitation because they wanted to offer condolences about my father in person. I was careful not to give any specific details about timelines or anything like that. "

Not that it mattered, since it was mostly there in front of her in black and white anyway. She rubbed a hand over her forehead. Wouldn't be too hard for a motivated radical to figure everything else out if they saw the article. Oh no, Why did things like this keep happening to her?

Ray was silent for a bit, as though choosing his next words with care.

Maybe he was afraid she would have some sort of meltdown under this additional strain, she thought in irritation.

"This changes thing, especially after last night," he said. She ran a hand over her face and laid her head against the chair's backrest with a weary sigh. Ray stood next to her and laid a comforting hand on her shoulder. She appreciated the gesture, but it didn't make her feel any better.

"Yeah, okay. What do you need me to do?"

"Nothing." When she blinked at him in surprise, Hunter continued. "We'll go with the amended itinerary and you'll still leave with the others early tomorrow morning. For today, you'll stay here in the hotel. I think you could use the downtime anyhow."

Yeah, she could, because she was beat. Hadn't slept more than a couple of hours after that bombshell the State Department rep had dropped on her last night. It still horrified her, knowing her father had been set up that way. That his life and his work to improve girls' lives here had been worth less than the ransom his insurance company had paid out to the kidnappers to save his life.

Then they'd butchered him on film anyway despite the money. Just to make a statement. She swallowed a lump of emotion lodged in her throat. The situation with the Italian official and the owner of the contracting company was twisted beyond comprehension. The amount of corruption over here was staggering.

"You both good with that?" Charles finished, setting his hands on his hips. He looked intimidating as hell like that, the tightly leashed power radiating from him like heat from a furnace. It simmered in those light brown eyes, along with a hint of heated interest as he searched her face.

When she and Ray both nodded, Hunter reached out one muscular arm to pick up the paper. "I'm briefing both teams in a few minutes. We'll be going over details about tomorrow and I'll bring them up to speed on everything else.

I'll be on my cell if I leave the hotel, but if either of you need to go anywhere today, call me and I'll arrange an escort first." He gave her a moment to absorb all that before lifting both brows. "Any questions?"

"Not about that."

She was still pissed as hell about the article. How far did this corruption extend, anyway? Were they trying to set her up for the now too? "Did you hear anything else from Tom this morning? About what the State Department said last night? He told me he'd investigate it and see if he could find out more." Because they'd told her jack other than they were following up on the investigation.

Until she found out the real story, until she learned who was involved and those responsible were brought to justice, it would eat her alive. Charles slid his hands into his cargo pant pockets, his whole demeanor softening. She didn't want his pity, but his concern felt nice. "Nothing further that I've heard, but he'll be conferencing with the rest of us during the briefing.

If he heard anything, either you or I would be the first to know. Tom's good that way. He's got lots of connections to call on, so he'll be digging right now along with the State Department, don't worry about that."

Why shouldn't she? She was already worrying about another thousand things anyway. What was one more? She forced herself to nod.

"Briefing's about to start," he said, assertive and self-assured. "I'll check back in later."

"Okay," she answered dully.

He started for the door, waving at Ray to stay where he was. "I'll let myself out." His gaze cut to her again and she couldn't help but respond to the kindness she saw there. "Try to get some rest if you can. I promise you we're on top of everything. You've already come this far, right? You can make it through the rest."

Touched by his words, she forced a small smile. "Thank you." Her eyes followed him all the way to the door, and when it closed behind him and left her alone with Ray, she already felt less safe.

Ray lowered himself into the chair opposite hers. "You all, right? I can leave so, you get some more sleep. We can go over all this later."

"No," she said, straightening her spine and grabbing the list of staff members' names. It was hard to focus when all she wanted to do was investigate further into her father's murder. If the State Department had any idea who was behind it, they were keeping it to themselves for now.

"I'd rather have something to do to distract myself for the time being."

Charles was right. She was going to see this through all the way, and do it right. Fuck the Taliban and whoever had helped them capture her father. She wasn't leaving until the job was done.

Once this school opening was behind her, she was going to do whatever she could to help nail the bastards involved with her father's murder.

Back in his room down the hall from 's, Charles found the others all gathered around the small circular table where Gage had laid out all the necessary maps and documents. The two remaining members of his team glanced up when he entered. Hunter hadn't worked with either of them before or normally that would have made him edgy as hell, but so far, he had only the highest respect for their conduct.

Tom had promised to send Charles his best, and he had. Blake Ellis was an ex-Marine Scout/Sniper. Standing around six feet tall, he had medium toned brown skin and a quiet deadliness about him.

His hazel eyes met Charles's, relaying a calm professionalism he appreciated. He'd worked with Scout/Snipers in the field before and had found them to be some of the best in the world. Ellis's expertise allowed them much more operational latitude and flexibility, which Charles considered invaluable.

Next to Ellis stood Sean Dunphy, his spotter in various missions since coming to work for the Italians. Black haired, black eyed and tattooed, the ex-Force Recon

Marine was hell on wheels with a computer, among other things.

With nothing more than a laptop and an Internet link, he could do things Hunter could never dream of. His technological skills were rivaled only by his field craft and shooting. Charles looked forward to exploiting that entire skill set on the upcoming operation.

On the far side of the table stood the other team leader in charge of Ray's protective detail, thirty-six-year-old Neil Braithwaite, a former Army captain. He straightened next to his three guys and nodded at Charles. "Morning'." "Morning," he answered, and pulled out his phone to dial up Tom on speaker. "We're already here," he said when his boss picked up.

"Okay, go ahead," Tom said.

"All right, then let's get down to business." Charles looked around the table, meeting each man's eyes. "We had a few developments overnight that need to be addressed.

First, Carmela got a call from a State Department official confirming that the owner of the illegitimate contracting company her father hired, and an unknown Italian official were working with the TTP to capitalize on Mr. Bonanno's capture and subsequent ransom." Gage already knew all this, but the hard set of his jaw made it clear how disgusted he was about it.

Charles shared the sentiment. The whole Bonanno debacle and subsequent riots had wound up costing Scottie's life, and Charles wasn't going to get over that any time soon.

One of the men from the other team let out a low whistle. "For real?"

"For real," Tom answered for Charles, his voice carrying through the phone.

"I'm checking with my sources and haven't been able to uncover anything else yet.

As far as we know there's no new chatter yet about credible threats against

Carmela, but that could change considering the second development this morning.

Charles?"

All eyes turned to him once more. "On top of all that," he began, "a local paper published an interview with the Minister of Education and printed

Carmela's picture along with certain details about why she's here. The school's grand opening was mentioned, and we must assume the people interested in targeting Carmela and Ray know where it is.

Won't take an advanced degree for them to figure out when Fair Start's people are going to visit the school. So basically, the element of surprise is gone. The Italians are going to want to act on this if they can pull an operation together in time.

The only thing in our favor right now is there's been no chatter picked up about her or Ray yet." "Which means less than a handful of shit," Ellis remarked dryly, and the others muttered in agreement.

"Exactly," Charles said with a nod. "Given these new developments, both

Carmela and Ray are on lockdown until we leave for the valley. In the meantime, let's make sure we eliminate any potential threats for tomorrow."

With that, he and Gage got busy teaching the others about the lay of the land around the school, the structure of the region, location, and the blueprints of the building itself.

Entry and exit points, layout, the staff, Emergency evacuation plan and counter sniper positions were all checked.

"Ellis, this is your and Dunphy's responsibility," he continued, tapping a spot on the topo map he'd dragged onto the cluttered tabletop. "Neil, members of your team will set up positions here." He indicated another point he and Gage had marked the night before.

The other team leader nodded, rubbing the side of his jaw. "What about this trail leading off to the northeast?" He indicated a path on the satellite image beside the map.

"There're only eight of us, so we'll cover the most at risk areas and adapt on the fly if necessary. Which brings me to contingency plans."

It took another two hours to go over everything that needed to be covered.

Overnight he and Gage had tried to plan for every conceivable threat or problem, but the reality was they couldn't predict exactly what, if anything, would happen out there tomorrow. Could be anything from nothing to a suicide bombing. If they were lucky, all their preparations would go unneeded. If not, then they'd already prepared for the worst.

One benefit was that since most of them were ex Spec Ops members, they were well experienced in adapting during the chaos of battle.

After a few rounds of discussion for clarification and handing out assignments, the coffee had long since run out and he could tell the guys were anxious to secure their gear and get going.

Charles shook hands with everyone. The other team left, but Dunphy and Ellis hung back, clearly wanting to talk.

"What's up?" he asked them.

"We're driving her in with Gage, but we haven't formally met her yet," Ellis began. "You want us to introduce ourselves, go over the emergency contingencies and exit strategy with her?"

Charles hid his instinctive reaction to outright reject anyone else going to her right now. Keeping his distance from her was probably in everyone's best interest, but she trusted him, and Charles would be lying if he didn't admit that he liked how it felt.

"She's got a lot on her mind right now and I don't want to make it worse by giving her anything else to worry about. I'll tell her what she needs to know tonight before I head out."

After he did what he could to ensure, she had as many stress-free hours as possible to unwind. Yesterday had left more marks on her than just cuts and scrapes. The bombings had been a brutal reality check for her, let alone that late night news from the State Department.

"Roger that." Ellis and Dunphy filed out of the room to go over their gear.

Charles began tidying up while Gage checked the radios and batteries.

Briefing Carmela was necessary, so she knew what to do in case of emergency, and it couldn't be avoided.

When he finally told her, it would probably scare her shitless no matter how he worded it. He wished there was something else he could do to shield her from all this. He hated her being in harm's way over here.

She was kind and gentle and only trying to make a difference. Not many people would go to these lengths to step up and do something to better the lives of complete strangers halfway across the world, let alone someone who'd just lost her father in such a horrific way and is now facing a lethal threat of her own.

Knowing those militant fuckers wanted to kill her filled him with a deep, protective rage he had to keep locked down if he wanted to be sharp out there.

"Sure, you want to be the one to give her the heads up tonight?" Gage asked as he packed equipment into his mass.

"I'm sure." She was already scared, even if she tried to hide it. No, this had to come from him. He was head of her detail. Dammit, he wanted to put her mind at ease before he left. Tomorrow was going to be hard enough on her as it was without her losing even more sleep over things she couldn't control. He'd make it short and sweet, to the point, then get out.

Glancing over, he caught the flash of Gage's knowing grin before he masked it. "That's one hell of a bedtime story for her, Charles. I think you'd better stay with her awhile afterward, just to make sure you don't give her nightmares. Maybe tuck her in. I promise not to wait up for you."

He shot Gage a narrow-eyed look that warned him to mind his own business. "Hey. Long walk. Short pier."

Gage only chuckled and went back to packing his gear. Charles scowled to himself and stalked across the room to check his weapons. He already cared about her on a personal level, and if Gage could see it too, he was in serious trouble here.

His reputation was on the line with this job, as was his chance of winning a partnership with Tom. With a sigh he pulled out his cleaning kit and SIG.

Tomorrow couldn't come fast enough. At least then he'd be away from her, and able to do his job with a clear head.

Chapter 7

The School Visit

The four men with her in the vehicle seemed relaxed enough once they passed through the final military checkpoint in their journey, but Carmela's stomach was in knots as they drove deeper into the northern part of the infamous

New York.

Charles had come to her room late last night to give her a brief rundown of emergency and safety procedures for the school. He'd listed them quickly and calmly, stressed he was only reviewing them all with her as standard procedure, and when she didn't have any questions for him, he'd left.

Surprisingly, knowing the procedures ahead of time made her feel more secure and she'd managed to sleep until her alarm woke her well before dawn.

Once known as the Switzerland of the region, it was easy to see why. If she hadn't known it was New York, she'd half expect to see Julie Andrews come running over the hill at any moment, dressed in a nun's habit and singing her heart out.

The high mountain peaks soared skyward, yet untouched by the coming snows, and lush, deep valleys nestled amongst the foothills. Upstate New York lay over a valley, yet less than an hour ago they'd passed the largest ski resort in all the state of NY.

She shifted in her seat and gazed out at the scenery. Aside from the deceptive beauty she was all too aware that these were not the Swiss Alps. The New York military had a strong presence everywhere. It was the Italians who truly governed here, forcing the vulnerable civilians to do whatever they wanted.

It seemed bizarre but here in these rustic hamlets women were subjugated by men, forced into a state of near slavery and some isolated in their homes without being able to set foot outside without permission from their husband or elder. It was so hard to reconcile that reality with the breathtaking view outside her window.

"Another ten minutes or so," Gage announced from behind the wheel. She was in the back sandwiched between Ellis and Dunphy or Blake and Sean, as they'd told her to call them. She'd met them for the first time that morning when

Gage had come to get her just before three.

On the way here they'd stopped outside to pick up the English interpreter. The late twentysomething sat in the front passenger seat beside Gage, speaking only when spoken to and with the trace of a British accent.

All the men were dressed in camouflage gear and ready for business. The silence inside the vehicle didn't seem to be bothering anyone but her. Tension continued to build inside her, already bad enough that her stomach ached.

"There it is."

At Gage's words she leaned forward to peer through the windshield, heart beating fast and a nervous flutter in her belly. Seconds later, her father's legacy came into view. She'd only seen pictures of it until now. Seeing it in person put a lump in her throat.

By western standards the school wasn't much. Positioned in a clearing between two small villages, the one-story white cinderblock building sat in the midst of lush grazing land and held only three classrooms. It was still better than anything this area had seen for years, since the Italian's initial campaign against girls' education.

Her father had chosen this location with care, making sure the playground was built at the rear of the building for added protection against snipers or other threats.

Carmela squeezed her hands together in her lap and bit the inside of her cheek against the sudden rise of tears. This was the dream her father had died for. She wished he'd been here to see it made a reality.

You mean you wish he was here instead of you; her conscience held her responsible. Yeah, a little, but Charles's final instructions to her last night were hard to forget. Even though he'd made it clear the contingency plan was only in place for an emergency, the need for its existence still weighed heavily on her mind.

"Here we go." Gage's voice and demeanor were perfectly calm. She wished she had half his confidence about being here. The vehicle rocked and jostled on the rough road leading toward the school. "Looks like Ray's already waiting for you."

She peered out the right rear window past Blake's shoulder to see Ray standing out front of the school with a group of who she assumed were the staff members. He was smiling as he spoke to the middle-aged woman beside him.

Carmela expelled a slow breath, hoping none of the others noticed her anxiety.

They were all experienced soldiers and probably already thought she was weak and helpless after her reaction to the bombings yesterday, so she didn't want to prove them right.

Gage stopped a good distance from the school and pulled out his hand held radio that matched the one Charles had given her earlier, stashed in her pants pocket beneath the robe. She had her own channel he would contact her on if necessary. "Charles, we're in position."

"Roger that," his familiar voice came back, creating a pang of yearning inside her. It bolstered her courage to know that he was out there in the cold somewhere, watching over her to make sure she was okay. "All clear."

Setting his radio in his lap, Gage partially turned in his seat and offered her an encouraging smile. "Go ahead, hon. I'll see you later."

"Show time," Blake announced beside her. He and Sean jumped out first, followed by Tom. She gathered the unfamiliar long robe she'd changed her clothing to avoid inadvertently offending anyone with her western style clothing and blend in more and slid out of the vehicle, then followed the others toward the school.

Again, the warm temperature was a shock after leaving the air-conditioned interior of the SUV. Her battered feet were still sore, but not so painful that she couldn't walk.

Ray met her part way to the building with the woman he'd been talking to.

"Well, fancy meeting you here," he teased and introduced her to the woman, who turned out to be the headmistress of the school and spoke a tiny bit of

English.

Carmela murmured something in Italian, bowing her head slightly, extremely conscious of her cheek and temple. The woman replied the same in turn. Her face was weathered and worn, making her look much older than she probably was, but her deep brown eyes were clear and kind.

"Come," the lady murmured once the politeness were over, gesturing for her and Ray to follow. When Carmela glanced back, Blake and Sean were nowhere to be seen and Gage was driving away to some undisclosed location.

An awful sinking feeling took hold, like she had a bright red bull's eye on her back. Though Ray was right beside her, she'd never felt so alone. Pushing aside her worry, she entered the school with Ray and the headmistress.

As she'd expected the interior was cold and lightly furnished, with only a single bare bulb lighting each room. Still, it was clean and appeared to be well supplied. Each little classroom boasted a chalkboard along one wall and neatly arranged rows of desks for the students.

The air inside was much cooler than outside in the warm September sunshine. Carmela wrapped the shawl covering her hair and shoulders more tightly around herself as she walked through to the far side where the courtyard lay.

Outside, the sun chased away the worst of the lingering chill inside her. At the sound of hushed voices, she turned to find a group of girls assembled around the border of the playground. Twenty-two of them in total, the oldest not more than twelve or thirteen.

They wore very conservative and modest clothing and they all stared openly at her. Seeing them, knowing they were risking punishment from the Italians for being here, maybe even risking their lives, made goose bumps break out across her skin. Their bravery humbled her.

Raising a hand in greeting, she smiled and repeated the only phrase she knew in their language. "Bon nono." The words were hoarse, but they did the job.

Most of the girls broke into grins, no doubt because of her terrible accent.

However, their smiles faltered when Ray and Zaid walked up to join her. Carmela wondered if they were worried the men would report them to the Mafia.

"The students are very excited to be here today," Zaid translated to Carmela and Ray for the headmistress. "She says many of the girls walked for hours this morning to reach the school on time. Some came with their parents, but others left before dawn for fear of reprisal from local religious leaders."

Carmela smiled at them again, outraged that they should have to worry about repercussions for pursuing an education. How could girls so young possess that level of courage? It amazed her.

Jack gestured toward the group. "They have prepared a special song for you both today, to thank you for building this school and giving them the opportunity to learn."

It touched her more than she could say when the headmistress assembled the group and the girls began to sing. Their joined voices caused a rush of emotion that made her eyes sting. Wherever he was, she hoped her father could somehow see this. Beside her, Ray was beaming.

When the song ended, she and Ray burst into applause then each said their prepared speech on behalf of Fair Start while Jack translated.

"Well," Ray said to her when he finished. "Shall we let everyone start their day?"

"Absolutely." She wanted to give these girls the keys to the world, starting with an education.

The headmistress and her two other teachers called the students inside to begin classes.

Carmela and Ray split up. She stopped in each classroom and lingered as the primary grades gathered into the smallest of the three rooms to begin their first lesson. This was so different from most of the primary classrooms she'd been in back home. Here the room had a hushed, almost reverent atmosphere. Ranging from about five through nine or so, each student sat at her desk watching the teacher intently as she began to write on the blackboard.

Their rapt attention blew her away. She spent most of the morning observing lessons and passing out simple supplies like colored pencils and notebooks. In the upper intermediate classroom, she walked in on a long division lesson.

During a lull, with Jack's help Carmela asked permission to assist, and when the teacher learned Carmela was a math teacher from America, her eyes lit up.

Carmela went around the room to help some of the students. After they overcame their initial shyness about Jack speaking to them, they listened carefully to her instruction.

Straightening at one girl's desk, a sense of unreality hit her. Miss Patterson, teaching arithmetic in an outlawed school in the tribal region of the Swat Valley. Who would ever have thought that would happen?

By the time they broke for recess she felt much more relaxed. The small windows set into the cinderblock framed distant craggy peaks that towered over the valley. Hunter and the others were out there somewhere, keeping watch over them all. At least for today.

In the afternoon session she joined a primary class in their reading circle.

When Carmela was invited to sit in the circle, one little girl around six years old came over and climbed into her lap. The trusting gesture completely melted her.

When the student beside her took her turn reading aloud from the book, Carmela leaned over to look at the foreign script on the page.

Noticing her interest, the girl paused and placed her finger on a certain word. She said it aloud, watching Carmela closely.

Knowing she was being tested Carmela did her best to repeat the word, but her efforts were met with a scattering of giggles around the circle. Grinning, she dutifully repeated more words her tutor gave her. More giggles. The girl in her lap finally reached up a tiny hand to place over Carmela's mouth to stop her from butchering their language, and peals of laughter broke out.

Pretending to insult, Carmela pulled back and looked down at the little kid with a mock scowl. The girl smiled and ducked her head, snuggling into Carmela's shoulder. She was enjoying the cuddle, basking in a sense of pride and gratitude when the radio beneath her robe suddenly chirped.

"Carmela, come in." Charles's voice.

Ignoring the bolt of alarm that slammed through her, she gently moved the child off her lap and stood, careful not to let her fear show. When she was out in the hallway she retrieved the radio from her pants pocket. She'd just keyed it when Ray appeared in the hallway holding his own radio and met her gaze. His face was ashen.

Oh, God. Carmela's fingers tightened around the plastic handset. "Go ahead."

Whatever Charles was contacting her about, it couldn't be good news.

"Evacuate the building."

She sucked in a breath as a wave of terror broke over her. The children. She threw a worried glance at the primary classroom door. A threat? Outright attack? "What's happening?" she demanded.

"Just do what I told you to do this morning," he said in a clipped voice. "I'll come for you when it's safe."

With that final chilling order reverberating in her skull, she shoved the radio back in her pocket and re-entered the classroom.

Everyone looked up at her. Schooling her features into a calm mask, she put on a smile infused with a confidence she didn't feel. Jack appeared at her side, face grim. "Tell them we have to do an emergency drill, for practice," she said quietly. He translated and the teacher's face froze in fear before she shot to her feet and urged the girls to follow.

Carmela helped gather them into a line and was getting into place at the end of it when faint cracking sounds came from somewhere in the distance.

A few of the girls stilled and whipped their heads toward the windows. Then more cracks, these ones sounding closer, and Carmella finally realized what they were.

Gunfire.

Oh shit, oh, shit, they're coming.

"Tell them it's okay," she whispered urgently to Zaid as fear threaded up her spine. This wasn't okay, it was straight out of her nightmares.

"Everyone must stay calm, and the girls need to see that we've got it under control. Ray's in the hallway with the other class and the headmistress is leading the third. Now let's go, quick." Her heart was already thundering in her chest. An unknown number of evil militants were about to attack the school, and only eight armed men stood between them and these innocent children.

They moved fast to evacuate. The girls were clearly frightened despite the adults' efforts to keep them calm. They knew what gunfire meant better than anyone. Some were crying by the time they reached the exit and stepped outside into the afternoon air. The sun was already descending in the sky, leaving shadows crawling across the valley floor.

Not daring to look behind her, Carmela's eyes fixed on her target, the emergency bunker.

Across the expanse of lush green grass before her, the signaling hillside seemed impossibly far away. A warning prickle began at her nape, as if someone had her in their sights and was taking aim at her. More shots erupted from the hills behind them. The lead group broke into run. The long line of students stretched out before her, racing after Ray as he led them across the thick green grass.

The volume of fire suddenly increased. It rang out from the surrounding hills, echoing in the tense stillness. A few girls cried out in panic and confusion, whirled around to see what was happening. Carmela's heart twisted at the raw fear she read in their faces.

The six-year-old she'd been cuddling earlier tripped on the hem of her robe and fell headlong on the ground while her classmates raced past her. She scrambled to her knees, whimpering in terror.

Carmela ran over and scooped her up, holding her tight against her body. The little girl clung to her in desperation, crying against the side of her neck in muffled sobs.

Anger and terror warred inside her that these radical assholes could terrorize helpless children this way. Whispering reassurances to the girl and hoping her tone would help despite the language barrier; Carmela ran behind the others.

Charles and the rest of the team were still out there. Were they okay?

Rushing toward their only protection until the gun battle was over, she sent up a silent prayer that Charles and the team would reach them before the Mafia did.

Chapter 8

Joseph Esposito got Caught

Through his high-powered binoculars, Charles tracked the students' steady progress across the grassy plain. Carmela was bringing up the rear, carrying a little girl. When she at last reached the emergency bunker and disappeared inside it, some of the tension in his shoulders eased. Good girl.

"They're secure," he said in a low voice to Gage over the squad radio. "Let's move." Grabbing his rifle, he climbed to his feet and prepared to make the fifty yard run across the open space to a clump of bushes he'd chosen for his next cover.

Currently making their way down the hillsides on two sides of the valley wall, the Mafia fighters seemed to be converging. So far Charles's team had spotted fourteen in total. That didn't account for any others hidden from view or possible reinforcements coming in from other areas.

Charging over the grass to his new position, he dropped to one knee and took another looks around. "I'm in position. Dunphy, give me status." The spotter's steady voice came through the earpiece. "Four tangos moving down a trail to your ten o'clock."

Charles's gaze immediately swung over there. Through the binos he could make out the shapes of the enemy approaching, thin men dressed in long black tunics, baggy pants, and turbans. They were still too far away for him to get a clear shot. "I see them. Gage?"

Six security team members now formed a protective perimeter around the school, with Ellis and Dunphy concealed in their sniper hide on the far hillside to keep an eye on the enemy's movements.

"Heads up, we've got company inbound. The cavalry has arrived," Dunphy said dryly. The sound of a vehicle's engine reached him seconds later, then an Italian military truck rumbled over a distant hill, no doubt alerted by the gunfire. "That didn't take long," Charles muttered.

"So, why am I not happy to see them?" Gage remarked.

"Because they can never make up their minds which side, they're fighting for?" suggested Braithwaite, the other team leader.

"What he said," Hunter agreed. "Okay, those assholes up there are way too far away to hit anything, but it looks like they're not going to take their ball and go home anytime soon. Gage, you, and I'll link up with the Mafia given them trouble."

"Roger that."

"Ellis, you and Dunphy keep an eye out and let us know if things are about to get hot."

"Roger," the sniper replied.

Keeping his weapon at the ready in front of his body, muzzle down, Charles rose to a crouch and hustled south to link up with Gage. From the left distant hillside, the Italians let loose with a flurry of useless shots.

Gage was waiting for him at the RV point. "They have my permission to keep wasting ammo like that all day long," his second-in-command said in approval.

"Hell yeah."

The Italian truck was a short jog away. Together they approached the six soldiers climbing out of the back. Gage's Italian wasn't quite fluent, but it was a hell of a lot better than Charles's and it sure came in handy at times like this. All the soldiers had their fingers on their trigger guards and wore resentful expressions, as though they blamed Charles and his crew for this latest incident.

The officer in charge, a kid who looked like he was in his early twenties, called out to them and Gage started talking.

The look on the Italian officer's face was priceless. His eyes widened and his expression went blank with the fact that a redheaded westerner was speaking to him in his own language.

With the translation it took a few minutes to inform them of what was going on and establish jurisdictions. The Italians agreed to engage the Italians if they attacked and Charles was authorized to protect the school and its grounds, including everyone hidden away in the bunker.

"Got movement at your two o'clock."

At Dunphy's announcement Hunter instinctively glanced over his shoulder at the foothills. Those bastards were coming closer, edging down the trails that led to the valley floor. He turned back to Gage. "Tell him I've got a sniper and spotter in position and does he want them to take a shot if they have one."

Gage translated and the man said something else, brows lowered in a disapproving frown.

Gage made a frustrated sound before turning back to Charles. "Goddamn," he muttered. "He says not unless we're under direct attack." As he spoke more sporadic firing broke out behind them.

The guy seriously wanted to argue about rules of engagement when the lives of twenty-two children were at stake? What was this, Article 17 peace keeping?

"I guess those are just friendly warning shots then?" he said angrily, leveling a glare at the officer.

"Must be," Gage muttered. He tried again, saying something else to the man but was met with an emphatic shake of the head that was recognizable in any language.

Charles didn't look away from the man's gaze, not about to be told what to do by this little shit who may or may not be an ally in this fight. "Tell him I will order my men to engage the enemy if I see fit."

Gage translated while Charles kept up with the staring contest. Yeah, chew on that, asshole.

Apparently tired of the negotiations, the officer waved them away impatiently and began issuing orders to his men. "Guess we're done here," Gage said with a smile in his voice.

"'About time." Walking away, Charles got on the squad radio and informed every one of the new rules of engagement, stressing that they should return fire if they felt it necessary to defend themselves.

"We clear?" They all checked in with an affirmative. "Ellis, Dunphy, stay where you are. Everybody else fall back into defensive perimeter around the school."

He could hear the Italian soldiers talking on the radio behind them, no doubt calling for reinforcements. Just as well, since they only had a few hours of daylight left until the sun sank behind the mountains.

Charles doubted the Italians would stay and fight through the darkness, but he couldn't rule out the possibility.

"Looks like they're planning to make things interesting over there," Dunphy spoke. "Both groups are joining in the center now. Might be getting ready to attack."

So much for hoping the added military muscle would scare them away. Or maybe they assumed the army would help them fight against him and the rest of the American infidels desecrating the valley with their presence. "Get into position," Hunter ordered everyone.

There was no adequate cover now except the school itself and they made good use of it. The entire group took up positions around the building, facing out toward the enemy coming at them from two sides.

"Dunphy, what are we up against?" Hunter prompted.

"AKs and a few RPGs."

Great, RPGs. "Any new players?"

"Negative. Still fourteen. Going to lose sight of them in a minute when they move behind that hill."

"Copy that." He raised his binos to check on the Italian soldiers, only to find they were still by their truck, apparently not moving until reinforcements arrived. Meaning, ROEs or not, Charles and his men were on their own for the time being.

Tense minutes ticked past as the enemy approached, unseen behind the screen of hills. Charles and the others remained in position, keeping watch on the far hills. Then it came. An eerie wail, increasing in volume and strength, one

Hunter had heard it many times before.

Bring it, you bastards.

"Three groups now," Dunphy reported. "Coming at you from three different directions. Ellis and I have a clear shot on the group at the far right."

"Copy that," he answered. "Fire at will."

"Roger."

Lying flat on his belly next to the east wall of the school, Hunter raised his rifle and took aim in the direction of the coming attack. His heart rate slowed as it always happened in a firefight, his body calm, and his finger on the trigger of his M4.

The fighters in the center group suddenly burst out of a gap at the valley's mouth, closely followed by the one on the left, then the right.

"Hold your positions," Charles ordered. "No one gets over us." They all knew what was at stake if they didn't hold their ground. Dozens of innocent lives depended on them repelling the attack. Including Carmela's.

As an image of her face formed in his mind, he forced it away and sighted down the barrel of his weapon.

The enemy bore down on them in a suicidal rush, yelling their war cry. They began shooting in that weird haphazard way they had, from the hip, spraying rounds all over the place in the hopes of hitting something.

A few rounds worked into the cinderblock wall at the front of the school, sending up tiny sprays of white. He stayed off the radio, letting his men do their jobs. They'd gone over this plan before, and each man knew what to do.

His finger tightened on the trigger. Another ounce of pressure was all he needed to fire. His gaze locked on the man at the front of the center column. He was running flat out toward the school, mouth wide open in his bearded face as he hollered; his AK spewing rounds. Some of the shots thudded into the ground yards ahead of where Charles lay.

He held his fire, waiting for the enemy to come into the kill zone. Five seconds. Four. Three. Two. One.

He squeezed the trigger, firing two shots that hit the man's chest. The

Taliban fighter dropped his weapon and crumpled, unmoving. Charles's men began to engage the enemy in their designated sectors, methodically picking the attackers off when they came into range.

The air was filled with the rattle and echo of gunfire. Hunter took aim at the next fighter, but someone beat him to it, hitting him in the torso and sending him tumbling to the grass.

A new burst of gunfire suddenly broke out on their far left. The Italians, finally getting into the fight. Charles stayed flat on his belly and waited for the remaining targets to come close enough.

"Three tangos down here," Dunphy reported, confirming Ellis had already taken out three of his own targets. "Looks like reinforcements are coming down that trail. Four so far."

"Team leader copies," Charles replied, readying to fire his weapon at the next enemy. Bullets slapped into the cinderblock beside him, showering him with dust. His vision zeroed in on the closest man's chest, sighting down the length of the rifle barrels.

"RPG, incoming!"

At Dunphy's warning, Charles and Gage simultaneously flattened against the ground and covered their heads a second before the round whistled over them and hit the north wall of the school with a loud bang.

The ensuing explosion blew apart the cinderblock and shook the ground. Charles grunted as the blast wave rolled through his body and chunks of debris rained down around him.

"Tango down. Someone else is trying to load the tube again."

"Take him out," Charles ordered, crawling on his elbows to get a better vantage point. The surviving enemy were still coming at them, running headlong through the hail of return gunfire. He saw three more drops. One crawled away clutching at a wound in his belly.

"He's down," Dunphy reported a moment later, "and so's the RPG. Ellis did it with one round."

One shot, one kill. This was why Scout/Snipers rocked. "Nice." Charles fired again, hitting another enemy fighter high up in the shoulder. His AK flew up into the air as he fell and crawled back toward his line.

More Italian fighters fell, cut down by the lethal fire delivered by his men.

One more man in the lead of his group toppled face first into the grass and suddenly everything got quiet. The eerie yells died away into silence and no more shots rang out. The survivors turned and ran for their lives, dragging the wounded with them.

Charles counteracted the adrenaline rush flooding his system with a few slow, deep breaths, bracing for a possible counterattack. "Dunphy, report."

"The three reinforcements are retreating and there're only six unwounded shooters left. We don't see any others hidden in the hills."

"Copy that. Update me if anything changes." Having Ellis take more of them out when they seemed to be retreating went directly against the ROEs, and with the Italian's army here as witnesses it would cause a serious shit storm.

Even though Charles knew those TTP bastards would likely be back another day when the school wasn't as heavily defended, that wasn't his concern now.

All he cared about right now was getting enough room and time to get to

Carmela and the students.

After a few minutes passed with no further sign of an attack, Charles got to his feet and surveyed the area before getting back on the squad radio. "Execute exfil plan Charlie, over."

In answer everyone got up and hauled ass to their pre-assigned positions.

With the enemy withdrawing, now was the perfect time to evacuate Carmela and the others. No telling if the Italians were regrouping for another round, and there was no reason to stay and find out.

As far as Charles was concerned, they were the Pak military's problem now. His priority was to get those students and staff to safety, then get Carmela and Ray the hell out of this valley.

Joseph left work that evening in a cheerful mood and opted to walk over to one of his favorite cafés for a hot cup of tea before catching the bus home. The entire day had gone by without a single visit from Mafia and he'd made good headway on the next project in his queue.

On top of that, he was looking forward to finding out if there'd been an attack on the girls' school today.

He took a shortcut down some side streets on the way from his office to avoid the crowds. The sun was just starting to set, casting a rosy glow over everything its rays touched. Calls for prayer rang out from the mosques.

Being near the end of Easter, everyone was in high spirits about the approach of the celebration and looking to fill up on a good meal before the ritual fasting began again at sunrise. When he arrived, his favorite coffee shop was much busier than usual.

After standing in line for almost fifteen minutes to get his vanilla chai tea and a slice of spice cake, he made his way back onto the crowded sidewalks and kept a leisurely pace as he ate his treat, then stopped to sit on a bench for a while. He deserved this reward for everything he'd done this past week.

He lingered over his fragrant cup of tea for almost half an hour, until the sky turned purple and soft and shadows began to swallow the streets. The restaurants, cafés, and shops in this area of town were bustling with activity. He walked for a while. When he got tired of battling the crowds, he hit an alley that led to another side street, polished off the last bite of moist, cake and washed it down with a satisfying sip of hot tea.

Enjoying the relative quiet on this route, he breathed in deeply and sighed. Life was good. At the next corner he took a left away from the busy part of town. His bus stopped all along this road, but he didn't feel like waiting for it with a big group of people.

Right now, all he wanted was to savor his solitude and get home to check the news and see if his TTP contact had left him an update of some kind.

A block from his destination, he noticed a black SUV driving up the street toward him.

He tossed his garbage into a trash bin on the sidewalk and continued up the street. The vehicle slowed as it neared him. A little weird, since the traffic light was still a few dozen meters away, but he figured maybe they were going to let someone out. When it pulled over to the curb and stopped ahead of him, he paused, a trickle of apprehension sliding through him.

The vehicle's windows were blacked out and the plates weren't marked. The passenger door popped open and a powerfully built man slid out wearing a dress shirt and an expensive-looking leather jacket. He stared directly at him, and Joseph took an instinctive step back, pulse accelerating.

The man stepped away from the vehicle and Joseph noticed a slight bulge beneath his jacket, just under the armpit. A gun?

"Joseph Esposito" the commanding voice demanded.

Run. His feet and hands turned ice cold. He took another step backward, ready to whirl around and make a run for it. Who was this guy? What did he want?

"Are you Joseph Esposito?" the man repeated in Urdu, in a tone that made it clear he wasn't used to asking twice.

Joseph struggled to find his voice. "Y-yes."

"I need you to come with us." He didn't make a move toward him or reach for his gun, but the threat was implicit all the same. Run, and the man would take him down. Maybe with one bullet.

Joseph swallowed hard, pulse drumming in his throat. These guys had to be from the government. "What do you want?" What did they know? Had they hacked into his e-mail accounts? Had they somehow listened in on his conversation the other night? His mouth went dry.

The man angled to the side and opened the rear passenger door, giving him a clear view of the holstered pistol beneath his left arm, and not by accident.

Joseph did not want to get into that vehicle. "Who are you?"

The stranger's face hardened. "Get in." Or else I'll make you regret it. His voice and body language made that clear.

Joseph cast a desperate glance up and down the street, finding it almost empty. A few other cars passed by without noticing his troubles. He wasn't close enough to an alleyway to try to escape into the shadows.

Feeling like his legs were made of lead, he took a tentative step forward, watching the man's hands. If he made a move to draw his gun, Joseph would take the risk and run.

The man didn't move anything except his eyes as he tracked Joseph's approach to the vehicle.

At the back door he paused again. There was no one else inside, save the driver who stared straight ahead without looking back at him. A hard hand between his shoulders pushed him into the vehicle.

Hesitantly he slid inside, and the door slammed shut behind him. He flashed out a hand to try the door handle, but it wouldn't open. They'd locked him in.

The sense of panic increased tenfold when the man with the gun climbed into the front passenger seat and the driver shot them away from the curb. His heart beat so fast he felt sick.

"Who are you?" Joseph asked again.

"Your escorts," was all he got.

"Where are you taking me? What do you want?"

"You'll see soon enough."

Fear curdled in his belly. They didn't speak to him all the way across town and into the industrial section of the city.

At a section of warehouses, they passed several mechanical shops and garages. Then the driver took another turn into the parking lot of a darkened building that appeared abandoned. He pulled up to the rolling bay door and shut the engine off.

Joseph had only a moment longer to worry before the man in the passenger seat was at his door.

It opened. "Step out."

He did, his breathing now fast and shallow. The windows of the building were dark and there was no one else around. No one to hear him if he screamed for help.

Too late for that. The thought made his knees go weak.

"This way."

Watching the man's hands as he shadowed him, Joseph had no choice but to follow the driver to the rolling bay door. It rolled up with a loud metallic rattle to expose nothing but a gaping maw of blackness.

"Go inside."

He stopped. "Alone?"

"You won't be alone for long." Something in the man's tone made a shiver crawl up his spine.

Joseph unwillingly entered the bay, senses on alert. The steel door rolled shut and he was swallowed by darkness. He whirled to his left when a light flicked on overhead, bathing the room with a harsh blue-white light. There was no one there.

"Joseph."

He swallowed a squeak and spun around. A well-built middle-aged man dressed in a business suit stood in the far doorway. He had short black hair that thinned on top and a neatly trimmed goatee.

"Please, sit." The man indicated a metal chair placed in the center of the cavernous room.

Joseph's stomach rolled. My God, were they going to interrogate him?

Torture him in here until he gave some sort of confession. Sweat broke out across his face.

One side of the man's mouth turned up in amusement. "Sit."

Shaking inside, Joseph sat, never taking his eyes off the man. He didn't dare speak. Who was this terrifying man and who did he work for? Some government agency?

The man spoke to him in perfect English. His voice was low and calm, as if he did this sort of thing every day. "You've had a lot of interesting conversations over the past few months."

Joseph lightened. Oh no, they knew. He'd been so careful to hide his tracks, he wasn't sure how they'd found out. Who were these guys? Military? ISI? Or maybe they were working for the Americans. Either way, he was in serious trouble and didn't know what to do.

The man walked toward him, each footstep ringing off the concrete floor and echoing through the empty space. He stopped a few feet away and folded his arms across his chest, looking down at Joseph with an unreadable expression that increased the shaking inside him. "Nothing to say to that?"

He wasn't going to speak a word without having a lawyer here. Unless they started torturing him. His stomach pitched in a violent roll. Would they kill him?

"No matter," the man continued, his bearing shouting of time in the military or some other position of power. "We know who you've been talking to. We know everything about you."

Joseph twitched restlessly in his chair. Unable to take the strain anymore, he blurted, "What do you want?"

The man's black eyes sliced over to him. "To deliver a message."

He couldn't imagine what sort of message this man had for him. Thinking frantically of what to say, he opened his mouth to speak but the man cut him off.

"The operation today was a failure."

He snapped his mouth shut. So, there had been an attack at the school?

"Your friends did not fare well, I'm afraid. They not only failed to take the school or inflict any casualties, most of them were either killed or seriously wounded in the attack."

Despite the growing fear, a wave of disappointment washed through him. He managed to find his voice, unsteady as it was. "I don't understand what that has to do with me."

The man's cold smile was terrifying. "Don't you?"

No. At least, he hoped not.

His interrogator took another step closer. Joseph automatically leaned back in the chair. "The Mafia thought are important enough to consult with, so naturally that caught our attention. You not only speak perfect English, but your cover is ideal.

No criminal record, graduated with honors from university, working at a sought-after engineering firm here in Islamabad, and you're eager to help TTP's extremist agenda.

"I can see why they saw you as useful." He tilted his head slightly, measuring him with those deep-set black eyes. "Just as I'm sure you will be of great use to us."

The words sent a chill racing up his spine. Joseph now understood what this meeting was about. He'd just gone from being a casual observer on the sidelines of this war to being thrown between the front lines in no man's land, and there was no escape.

Joseph swallowed and closed his eyes. He was nothing more than a hostage now. Replaceable and he didn't know which side would be the one to sacrifice him, his friends, or his enemies.

Chapter 9

The Struggling

The sound of the gunfire was terrifying, but it was the sudden silence that filled Carmela's veins with ice. A deathly stillness now engulfed the underground shelter as everyone held their breath.

Only a single dim emergency light shone in the far corner, casting shadows on the rear walls. The front half of the enclosure was swallowed in blackness, increasing the sense of claustrophobia.

Carmela grabbed the little girl, Aisha, to her chest, struggling to stay calm in the suffocating tension. Everyone was totally still, afraid to move. She cut a glance ahead at Ray, who stared up at the trap door that led to the emergency shelter that had been built at her father's insistence.

The end of the firefight meant one of two things. Either Charles and the others had destroyed the threat, or the Mafia had overwhelmed them and were coming to kill them next.

Carmela swallowed hard. There was no place for them to go. Nowhere to hide but here. Hold it together. The girls are looking to you for a sense of security.

Her radio wailed, startling her and several others around her. "Carmela, you copy?"

The sound of Charles's voice made her sag in relief. She set Aisha beside her and fumbled with her robe to get the radio out. Her fingers were icy as she keyed it to respond. "I'm here."

99

"We're coming to get you. Be ready to move fast."

"Okay." Did that mean the Mafia was still out there? She knew better than to ask.

Everyone was staring at her with anxious eyes as she communicated the message to Jack. He translated for her, and the adults got the girls organized. It seemed like a long time before someone finally pounded on the top of the trap door.

Carmela had no idea what they'd find on the other side of it. Some of those explosions had been big, large enough to shake the ground and rain dust and dirt down on them in the shelter.

Ray unlocked the door and an instant later someone wrenched it open from above. Squinting against the sudden flood of light, Carmela recognized Charles standing in the opening, bathed in the sun's dying rays.

Relief punched through her system at the sight of him, a gorgeous, lethal warrior here to save them. He dropped into the opening with the alertness of a cat and took in the scene with a single sweeping glance before his gaze came to rest on her.

"Are you okay?"

She swallowed. His face and clothing were covered in dirt, but no blood that she could see. The hot ball of tension in her gut eased slightly.

"Yes. Are you?"

"Fine." He motioned to Jack to come forward. "We're going to bring the girls out in groups, starting with the oldest ones. A teacher will escort them with some of our men to their vehicles waiting half a klick from here.

They'll make sure they get home to their families okay."

And then what? she wanted to demand. The military would escort them home and just pull out again?

These people needed protection, not an escort. She barely held the words back. Now wasn't the time for an argument like that and she knew it was the government's fault, not Charles's.

As everyone started moving toward the exit, Aisha tightened her arms around

Carmela and whimpered. "Shhh," Carmela soothed, rocking her slightly from side to side. "It's all right." It had to be all right. She wouldn't be able to live with herself if anything happened to these girls because of her or the foundation.

"Carmela."

She whipped her head up to find Charles staring at her, face grave. "There are things out there the girls are better off not seeing," he said.

"Do what you can to distract them, or at least shield their view north of the school."

Bodies. He meant there were dead bodies out there. But whose? She wanted to ask if all his men were okay but didn't get the chance because he was already helping the first teacher climb the steel ladder to the trap door opening.

Carmela kept the group moving toward him, filing into a line. When it was

Aisha's turn, her little arms suddenly slight around Carmela's neck like a vise. Giving her a reassuring squeeze, Carmela shifted the child from her hip to her front until Aisha's legs wrapped around her waist, then moved toward the ladder.

Charles was waiting for her at the bottom of it.

"I'll be right behind you," he told her, looking her straight in the eye. His calmness took the edge off the panic swirling in her chest. Aisha's palpable fear pushed her into action.

Go. Hurry.

She began to climb, thankful for the initial boost of Charles's strong hands on her back.

At the top she struggled to get her footing with the long robe and Aisha taxing her. One of the men from the other team noticed and grabbed her by the forearm to haul her upward, then gave her a push toward the others. The headmistress emerged behind her, then Charles cleared the opening and secured the hidden door before turning back to them, rifle held in front of his body in a practiced grip.

"Head west with the others," he called out, his gaze moving restlessly across the surrounding terrain. She couldn't help but look around, relieved when she didn't see anyone charging at them, brandishing a weapon. Walking faster, she kept one hand on the back of Aisha's head to prevent her from seeing the killing up ahead and broke into a jog.

She saw the damage to the school first, the bullet strikes and what looked like shell holes pock marking the front. Then she saw the bodies filled across the grass in the distance and the bile rose in her throat. She tugged her gaze away from the horrific sight and ran on, keeping pace with the line of girls ahead of her.

Other security team members guided them along the route, keeping constant watch on the distant hills as the students passed by. The lingering fear in the air was tangible.

Up ahead in the distance she finally caught sight of the military trucks Charles had mentioned. Soldiers were cooled out across the grassy plain keeping vigil for any further attacks.

Beyond the barriers they'd put up behind the trucks stood a growing crowd of civilian onlookers, probably attracted by the commotion.

The whole time she kept Aisha's head safely tucked into her neck to shield her. When they got closer to the military barricade, she saw some of the students at the front running to adults in the crowd, being surrounded in hugs and Carmela realized they must be the parents.

She couldn't even imagine how terrified they were from hearing the gunfire and knowing their children were in jeopardy.

Slowing to a walk as she neared the line of soldiers, she gently pulled Aisha's head away from her and pointed toward the crowd of adults. The girl scanned them with an anxious frown on her tearstained face. She must not have recognized anyone because she turned back and buried her face into Carmela's neck once more, her little body trembling with fear and shock.

A wave of anger swept away the shakiness. Whoever those dead men were on that field behind them, Carmela sincerely hoped they burned in hell for what they'd done and for what they'd wanted to do today.

Finally, she reached the group along with the main body of students. Chaos erupted around her as frantic parents and villagers reunited with the children.

Shouts and cries rose, frightened wails from the girls and their female relatives. Carmela stood away from it all and rubbed Aisha's back, watching the villagers to see if anyone had spotted the little girl.

Charles came up beside her.

"She alright?" he asked, looking down at the top of her scarf-covered head.

"No, she's still terrified." *And so am I.* She felt like she was living a waking nightmare.

Hopefully it looked like she was holding it together, at least on the outside. "I don't think her parents are here yet. She looked around but didn't react to anyone." *They would come for her, right?*

"We must move. It's not safe here." Before she could argue he took her upper arm and pulled her toward some of the soldiers, flagging Jack along the way. "Tell them her parents aren't here and that she'll need an escort home," he told the translator.

The soldier said something in response to Jack's words, then gestured to

Carmela to give him the child. Hesitantly she started to pull the little arms away from the nape of her neck but Aisha cried out in protest and shook her head, clinging even tighter.

Heart breaking, Carmela threw Charles a pleading look. "I can't leave her. I can't."

His mouth thinned and she was sure he would argue, but instead he gave in with a reluctant nod. "Bring her with us then. We'll take her to the next checkpoint but we're moving out now.

I don't want anyone hanging around here until the military clears out the valley."

"I'm not leaving her with a bunch of soldiers," she protested, horrified. She knew she'd promised to obey his orders without question, but she wasn't budging on this one, no matter what he said. "I must stay with her until her family comes for her."

"We'll worry about that later. Let's go." He grabbed her arm again to tow her past the soldiers and down the hill. "Jack !" he yelled. The interpreter finished up the conversation he was having with a soldier and hurried after them. Carmela fought to keep up. Charles glanced down at Aisha with an uncertain frown. "Will she let me carry her?"

"I doubt it." Not without terrifying her even further.

"Can you run for a bit with her?" he asked.

"Yes." She'd do whatever she had to, no matter how wobbly her legs were.

With the initial wave of energy gone, the muscles in her legs felt like mush. And oh no, just how close were the remaining enemy that they had to keep running?

What about all the parents and children? "Where's Ray?"

"With his team." He tugged her toward him again, less gently this time.

"Come on. I'll go slow but stay close and tell me if you can't keep up." With that he broke into an easy lope that was the equivalent of a fast jog for her.

She struggled to keep pace, balancing Aisha as they made their way down the slope toward the road blocked off by more military vehicles. Charles got on the radio to someone, issuing more commands.

She was panting by the time they reached the roadblock, her back and face soaked in sweat despite the cool air. Someone screamed Aisha's name.

The girl's head snapped up and Carmela spun around.

A young woman was racing toward them, her face crumpled with fear and grief. Aisha shoved at Carmela, so she let her go and watched the little girl run into the woman's waiting arms.

Carmela swallowed back tears when the woman caught her daughter and fell to her knees there on the dirt road, sobbing as she rocked her.

"We've got to go," Charles said impatiently, dragging her forward.

Carmela resisted, reluctant to leave them until she was sure they would be okay. "How will they get home? How do we know they'll be safe?"

"The military and police will handle it. We must go," he repeated. This time he jerked her forward hard enough that she had no choice but to follow. The sound of Aisha and her mother crying followed them down the hill to where a familiar black SUV was roaring toward them.

Breaking into a fast jog, Charles towed her toward it and yanked open the back door for her when it stopped. She barely had time to register that Gage was at the wheel before Charles slid in beside her, pushed her across the leather and slammed the door shut.

Jack jumped in the front passenger seat. The tires spun as Gage hit the accelerator.

"Is she, okay?" Gage asked.

"Yeah, but let's get out here," Charles muttered.

"What's going to happen to them all?" Carmela demanded, twisting around to look out the rear window at the dispersing crowd. She was cold and shaky, her heart only beginning to slow.

"How do we know the Mafia aren't planning more attacks later on in the villages?"

"They won't mount another attack this soon, and they rarely operate at night.

There're soldiers and police scattered all through the valley. They'll handle it,"

Charles said, laying his rifle on the floorboard between them.

"We need to make sure they're—"

"The only thing we need to make sure of is that you're out of this valley and

Be safe at the hotel," he snapped.

She bristled at his curt tone but didn't bother arguing because she knew it wouldn't get her anywhere. This didn't feel right though. Fleeing and abandoning the villagers to their fate after what had happened seemed wrong on every level, regardless of her inability to help them.

Still shaken, she fumbled to get the seat belt into the buckle. A large, strong hand closed over hers. She glanced up at Charles. The breath caught in her throat at the sudden leap of male interest in his eyes. Held by the magnetic pull of that gaze, she couldn't look away.

He broke eye contact first. "You're frozen," he said with a frown. "Gage, turn up the heat back here." He reached over the top of the seat to grab a blanket from the back and wrapped it around her.

"No, it's fine—"

"Just shush," he said in exasperation, taking her hand between his and rubbing. The heat of his skin took her by surprise as much as the gesture of concern did, but then he shocked her even more by settling an arm around her and pulling her to his side. Huddled against all that vital, masculine strength, she felt more confused than ever.

They both could have been killed today. Her attraction to him was wrong, especially here and now, but she couldn't stop her body's reaction to his nearness. It was a simple biological response to surviving a deadly situation.

What she really wanted was his arms around her, holding her tight to his chest, but wasn't about to act on it. She decided to make the most of the comfort he offered and closed her eyes, savoring his warmth and strength.

After a few minutes the trembling in her muscles stopped.

They drove toward the hotel in silence. She suspected the men stayed quiet to calm her down as much as to hide the details of what had happened in that gun battles.

The truth was she was dying to know what had happened. They passed through more checkpoints on the way to the hotel. Gage handed over their passports and other necessary documents and they drove into the city to drop Jack off without incident.

Charles surprised her again by staying with her and allowing her to remain cuddled to his side rather than take Jack's seat up front.

After passing one more checkpoint on the southern edge of the city, Gage finally got them on the highway back to the city and she took her first deep breath since the start of the firefight.

The five-hour drive seemed twice that long. At one point Carmela sat up and pushed the blanket down to her lap, rubbing her tired, burning eyes. Her mind was spinning with all that had happened, unable to shut down no matter how exhausted she was.

What would happen to those families now? What could she do to help them?

"Get some sleep," Charles said to her quietly, reaching out to place one hand on the back of her head and pull it down against his left shoulder. She didn't resist, grateful for the strength. The cumulative lack of sleep and continual stress had done her in. It weighed down her eyelids and she dozed off and on for the rest of the trip.

She woke disoriented and with a kink in her neck as Gage brought the SUV to a stop in front of a small hotel.

"Wait here," Charles told her and climbed out. He returned a few minutes later and opened the back door for her, handing Gage a room key. "See you up there." He reached out for her hand and helped her from the vehicle. They used the stairs rather than the elevator and exited into a hallway on the fourth floor.

In her room, Charles followed her. He let the door close behind him and stood near it, watching her as he took off his body armor and set it on a chair.

She watched, heart hammering, trying not to read anything into it. Next, he removed his holstered sidearm and laid it on the reading table next to the chair.

Realization dawned. "Are you staying?"

He nodded but didn't look at her. "Just for tonight. We're trying to get you on a flight home tomorrow.

After everything that's happened, I'll feel better staying here." He paused, finally met her gaze. "Unless you'd rather I didn't?"

"No, it's okay." She'd feel way better with him in the same room even though it was bound to be a little awkward. They were in for a long night but at least with him here she had a shot at sleeping, and the mention of going home made her feel sad.

God, she wanted to go home so badly but the thought of leaving now made her feel guilty. She also felt a sudden pang of dread about never seeing Charles again.

Her conflicting emotions confused her.

He wasn't interested in her that way, had made it clear he didn't even want to be friends. They had nothing in common. He was a hardened soldier; she was a teacher and wannabe humanitarian.

Charles had another side to him too. A few times already he'd shown her glimpses of a startling tenderness she wouldn't have guessed him capable of.

Now she craved more of it, with a strength that surprised her.

"Gage went to grab us something to eat," he said, heading to the vanity sink just outside the bathroom to wash his face and hands. "Be tough to get anything decent in the morning."

Since he didn't seem to expect a verbal response, she only nodded. After another few minutes of silence, however, she couldn't keep quiet anymore. "So are you ever going to tell me what happened out there?"

He looked up from checking his sidearm and hit her with that direct gaze of his. "What do you want to know?"

She stared at him, incredulous. "Am I breaking some kind of protocol by asking?"

"No, I'm just not exactly sure what you're asking for."

Okay, he didn't seem to be deliberately trying to misunderstand her or piss her off. She sighed.

"When did you first spot them coming?"

"Ellis did. About thirty seconds before I contacted you on the radio."

"And they just started...attacking?"

"Pretty much."

God, the man was so nonchalant about the whole thing. "Were any of you hurt?"

"No. That RPG round made things interesting for a few seconds though."

Carmela chewed on her bottom lip and folded her arms across her chest. He looked so strong and invincible sitting there, but she knew he was just a man, made of the same vulnerable flesh and blood as she was.

"I'm glad you're okay.

I was worried." Worried didn't even begin to cover it.

Surprise flashed in his eyes for a second before they warmed with what almost looked like affection. "No need. We had it covered."

"And you did it well, thank God. I'll make sure I tell Tom because I'm sure you won't tell him anything more than the operational details."

He shifted his attention back to his sidearm as though uncomfortable with the idea of her singing his praises to his boss. "That's not necessary."

"I think it is."

This time when he glanced up his eyes strayed from her face down the length of her robe-covered body and suddenly the room felt way too small. Every place his eyes touched, her skin started to tingle, her body coming to life as if waking from a long sleep.

Since that could go nowhere, she turned away and pulled the robe over her head, leaving her in her pants and T-shirt. When she continued to feel Charles's gaze on her, she told herself she was imagining things.

Gage showed up a few minutes later with some takeout and their bags and left, saying he had things to take care of. Without pause, Charles grabbed a small kit from his duffel and glanced at her over his shoulder. "Mind if I grab a shower first?"

"No, go ahead." When he disappeared behind the bathroom door and the sound of the shower started up, she pulled off her head scarf and shoes, dumping them on the floor.

After cleaning up at the sink outside the bathroom she pulled back the covers on the bed and sat down. The silence closed in, making her restless and jittery. The time alone gave her too much to think about. She sighed in relief when Charles came out of the bathroom a few minutes later in a cloud of steam, dressed in jeans and a black T-shirt, his short dark hair slicked back.

So very hot and so very unattainable, she thought wistfully. Though he'd certainly, star in her fantasies for a long time to come.

They ate together without talking until the silence began to feel stiff.

Watching him in between bites, she again marveled at his composure. Didn't anything bothers him?

Unable to stay quiet any longer, she laid her fork aside and blurted, "How do you do it?"

He looked up at her, white plastic fork poised halfway to his mouth. "Do what?"

"Cope with all…this." She waved a hand around to convey she meant everything. "Compartmentalize terrible things so they don't affect you."

Something flickered in his eyes at the last part, and he looked back down at his container of rice and veggies.

"Training and experience, mostly. I learned quick that dwelling on things doesn't do any good because it won't change any of it."

The decidedly cryptic edge to his tone made her certain there was a story behind the words. A thousand thoughts flooded her mind, none of them good.

By comparison he'd gone through much worse than her today and yet he acted as though nothing out of the ordinary had happened.

"Got any tips?" she prompted with a half-smile when it didn't seem like he was going to elaborate.

He lifted that light brown gaze to hers, and she saw the flash of empathy there.

After a second, he set his food down and leaned back in his chair, muscles shifting beneath the snug fit of his shirt. "None that would help much. You did good today though."

She sighed and rubbed a hand over her forehead. "I didn't do anything." That was the problem. The guilt was clawing at her, eating her alive from the inside.

She hadn't done enough to ensure those girls were safe, or their families. There must have been something else she could have done.

"Yes, you did. You stayed calm when you needed to, and you helped get those girls to safety. You comforted that little girl when she needed you. That's what you need to remember about today."

None of that eased her conscience any. She raked a hand through her messy hair and shot to her feet, needing to pace to relieve some of the anxiety coiling in her stomach. "I feel like I abandoned them, Charles. Here I am safe in a hotel room with a personal bodyguard when they're back in their villages hoping the

Mafia won't come after them for sending their children to our school."

"You didn't abandon them," he argued, his voice calm. "Those parents all knew the risks of sending their daughters to the school—" She shook her head in denial but he kept on going. "—and the government is responsible for protecting its citizens. Your foundation built a school to give those girls a chance in the future, which is more than anyone else has done for them in their lifetime.

Now it's up to the local police and military to keep them safe."

"Who may or may not be a Mafia sympathizer," she pointed out glumly.

He was silent a moment, watching her. "You can't save the world, Carmela.

Believe me, I know."

She stopped pacing and looked over at him, something in his tone pulling at her. "I'm not trying to save the world. But I damn well feel like I should be doing something other than hiding out here with you."

He stood so fast she took an instinctive step back. It was on the tip of her tongue to apologize for snapping at him but the absorbed look on his face made her stay silent. He erased the space between them with two strides, until he stood close enough for her to smell the shampoo and soap he'd just used in the shower.

His nearness and the heat radiating from him made her dizzy, scrambled her thoughts.

During all that dark stubble his lips looked incredibly soft. That black shirt was stretched taut across his chest and shoulders, emphasizing the firm planes of muscle.

She'd felt them against her on the drive back to the hotel. Now she wanted to run her hands over them, feel his hard body pressed full length against hers. His size and nearness woke every feminine cell in her body.

Staring up at him, she watched his pupils dilate in response to her arousal. An instant wave of heat submerged her.

Though he had to feel the tension simmering between them, Charles laid both hands on her shoulders and squeezed, the contact setting off tiny shocks in her belly.

"You did what you came here to do, and you helped get those girls to safety today. You don't have anything to feel guilty about."

His words banked the fire building inside her. Oh, but she had a lot of things to feel guilty about. Because right now all she could think about was how scared she'd been today, and how much she wanted him.

"You could've been killed today because of me."

His gaze softened and the hint of a smile played at the corner of his mouth. "I could've died from a fall in the shower just now, too."

She shook her head, frustrated that he was making light of it. "I put you in the position to have to fight off those militants."

He lifted the hand resting on her right shoulder to brush a lock of hair away from her temple.

She sucked in a quiet breath as his fingers grazed her skin, sending shocks along her nerve endings. "The job did that, not you. I knew the risks when I signed on. I've faced worse things than we did today. And yet here I am, safe and sound."

The touch was so gentle, almost a caress. She couldn't help but lean into it.

His eyes darkened from caramel to amber. The air between them felt electric, crackling with tantalizing possibility.

She wanted to touch him, be held in those strong arms, have him pin her beneath him on the double bed behind her and strip everything away with his hands and mouth until she was naked and his for the taking. She wanted to stop thinking, seize the moment and feel alive.

To hell with waiting. She placed her hands on his wide shoulders, reveling in the strength and solidity of him beneath her fingertips. Swaying forward, she rose on tiptoe to kiss him, unable to fight the unbearable hunger a second longer.

Chapter 10

Carmela Couldn't Resist

Charles saw the kiss coming in plenty of time to avoid it if he'd wanted to.

He didn't and it was impossible for him to keep his professional distance any longer.

Still jacked up from the battle, seeing that hungry, hopeful look in Carmela's eyes sealed the deal. He settled his hands on her waist, his attention narrowing to the way her lashes fluttered closed as she leaned up on tiptoe, the tempting curve of her lips rising to meet his and the arc of raw sexual energy leaping between them.

The tentative weight of her hands on his shoulders sent a ripple of heat across his skin and made his cock harden. That she was leaving in the morning made it easier to ignore just how bad an idea this was. But he wanted her too badly to stop it.

Threading his fingers into the curly mass of her hair, he squeezed, bringing her head back before their lips touched and eliciting a tiny gasp that made the sexual fire inside him burn hotter. His way, the grip told her, and he loved the way she stilled and watched him, waiting.

Three heartbeats, four, then he lowered his head and kissed those soft, cool lips. The feel of that tender flesh parting beneath his made him desperate to get inside her, any way she'd let him. Forcing back the need to rush, to take, he allowed her to explore him with tiny brushes of her lips until she surprised him by reaching up to grip his head between her hands and pull him down to deepen the kiss.

He took over with a low growl, gripping the curve of her hip with one hand to pull her tight against his suddenly overheated body. Fisting his other hand in her hair, he angled her head to glide his tongue across her lower lip with the last of his restraint. She made a soft sound in the back of her throat and opened, allowing him in.

Charles took her mouth, licking and caressing, holding her in place while he tasted her. She kissed him back just as wildly, wriggling in closer until every sweet curve was plastered to him.

His throbbing cock wedged against her abdomen, making him want to rip away the offending cloth between them and plunge into her to ease the relentless ache.

Christ, no woman had ever set him on fire this fast.

Still clutching his head, Carmela rubbed against him in a full-length caress and moaned into his mouth. The plaintive sound burned right through him. He dropped both hands to her ass, picked her up and walked her backward to the wall where he pinned her with his weight and fisted both hands in her hair. Her legs immediately came around his waist, squeezing tight, fighting to get closer.

He stroked his tongue into her mouth, so slowly she whimpered and bowed up against him.

Hell yeah.

He did it again, and again, absorbing her cries. Those soft, needy sounds drove him crazy as she met each caress of his tongue with a raw hunger that shook him. She was burning in his arms, and he was more than happy to put out the flames for her right after he encouraged them as high as they'd go.

He kissed the corner of her mouth, over her chin to her jaw and up to her earlobe. Capturing it between his teeth, he nipped gently as he brought one hand up and trailed his fingers down the smooth column of her throat. He could feel her pulse pounding beneath his fingertips, hear the ragged breaths she took as she tipped her head back to give him better access.

Settling his mouth over her pulse point, he licked at it, absorbing the shiver that sped through her, and lowered his face to nuzzle just inside the collar of her shirt where her neck met her shoulder.

She hissed in a breath and pressed her breasts harder against him, goose bumps rising across her skin. He loved the response. Holding her against the wall he continued to taste her, nibbling, and sucking a path up her neck. Her hands pulled his head in close, her hips pressing against his erection in erotic circles.

Charles moaned against her smooth skin. More, he wanted more of her, to taste every inch of her and hear her scream his name.

Flicking his tongue against a spot he found that made her shiver, he reached down to cup her right breast where the distended nipple beaded against her shirt.

He molded the soft weight of her in his palm before brushing his thumb softly across the hard peak.

She moaned and struggled to get closer, pulling his head up to meet her kiss. The pounding between his legs was agonizing. He wanted to take her shirt in his hands and wrench them apart, tear it open to expose the lace he could see through the thin material. Wanted to peel the bra cup aside to feel her naked breast in his hand, pull that tender center into his mouth and suck until he had her begging.

The way she rubbed against him told him she was at least halfway there already. He couldn't wait to slide his fingers into her hot center, his tongue in her mouth while she exploded around him then took him with her.

His cell buzzed in his pocket. He blocked out the sound of the incoming text message, too lost in kissing the hell out of her, plucking at the sensitized nipple and loving each ragged sound he dragged out of her. It buzzed again and this time he barely noticed.

He gripped the neckline of her shirt, about to tear it apart when loud rattling startled him into jerking his head back. Carmela gasped and opened her eyes, staring up at him with a lust-glazed expression. Her mouth was swollen and wet from his kisses.

The solid hold on his head didn't ease up. The phone kept jangling. A annoying ringtone he now regretted choosing for his boss's number.

Fighting back the driving need to strip her naked and finish what he'd started, somehow, he found his voice. "Sorry, I Must answer."

She nodded and licked her lips, watching him with unfulfilled hunger in her gaze.

With a reluctant sigh he eased back and let her feet drop to the floor. When he was sure she wasn't going to fall, he pulled out his phone and stared at the rigid peaks of her nipples while he answered. His jaw clenched. "Phillips."

"Just got off the phone with someone else from the State Department," Tom said.

"They know something about the attack today, I know they do. They just won't tell me what it is."

Taking a deep breath, trying to find his center after Carmela had tilted his world on its axis, Charles rubbed a hand over his face and turned away from her.

"Okay, so…"

"So, I need you to help me go over their heads and find out what they know."

He wasn't following, probably because his brain was oxygen denied since most of his blood was still pooled between his legs. "And you want me to do that how?"

"This is big, Charles. Way bigger than I first realized. There's a leak someplace.

It must be."

Ah, shit. He'd wondered about that. "Got it."

"I need you to get Gage to call in a favor at the NSA."

That wiped any remaining traces of lust from his brain. "Oh, Christ. Why me? Why can't you tell him?"

"He'll listen to you. He and I'll just get into an argument, and you know I wouldn't be asking this of him if I wasn't desperate for answers. Do it and get back to me ASAP, yeah?"

Not like he had an option on that one, did he? "Yeah. Bastard."

"And proud of it. Get on it." Tom disconnected without waiting for a reply.

Charles hit end and turned to face Carmela.

Her cheeks were flushed but her eyes had cleared. She also had her arms folded over her breasts, which was a damn shame. "I have to go see Gage for a few minutes."

She nodded, looking uncertain. "Is everything okay?"

He didn't see any reason to cause her more worry. "Yeah, everything's fine.

Got to have this talk in person though.

Are you okay?" He meant with what they'd just done and what they'd almost just done. And most definitely with what he wanted to finish when he got back.

Her smile was strained, a little forced as if she was suddenly unsure of herself. "Yeah."

He'd make it up to his after talking with Gage. "Lock the door behind me. I'll be back in a little while." With lingering sexual frustration putting his mood in the shitter, he made the trip down and across the hall, rehearsing how he was going to word this.

Gage was going to be pissed as hell no matter how he said it, and he'd prefer to end the conversation with his face intact.

At his knock Gage opened the door and stepped back to let him in with an expectant look on his face. "What's up?"

Charles stopped in the middle of the room and met his gaze, deciding it best just to put it out there. "Tom needs a favor."

He was a smart son of a bitch, Gage's expression immediately turned suspicious. "Apparently he needs a messenger, too." He eyed Charles with a raised brow, his southern boy drawl laced with a hard edge.

Yeah, this wasn't going to go well. "He thinks there's an Intel leak somewhere in the chain and he wants us to investigate it. Starting with you contacting Claire."

At the mention of that name, Gage's face went eerily blank. "You're shittin' me."

Charles shook his head. "No, man, I'm not." He held up his phone, screen out to show the ignored text message if he wanted to read it.

Gage's eyebrows crashed together in a glower as he set his hands on his hips.

"He has other contacts. He can start with them instead."

Charles barely refrained from scrubbing a hand over his face. "Gage. Just call her. See what she can find out."

Gage's jaw clenched, his eyes simmering with resentment at being placed in the position he now found himself in. "Fuck."

Well, at least it wasn't a Fuck no, or a Fuck you, followed by a sucker punch to the face. "Want me to...?" He pointed over his shoulder at the bathroom, raised his eyebrows.

"No, I'll go," Gage muttered, eyes shooting daggers at him as he stalked past and threw the bathroom door shut with a bang that rattled the framed picture on the wall beside it.

Releasing a breath, Charles dropped into a chair by the table that matched the one in Carmela's room, wishing he was still with her instead of here. If Tom hadn't called, he'd be buried inside her as deep as he could go right now, absorbing more of those sweet little cries as he took her to heaven and back.

He swallowed a groan at the thought and focused on the matter at hand. How the hell, long was this going to take, anyway?

No yelling from the bathroom. That had to be a good sign. Unless Gage was still working up the guts to dial.

While he waited, he texted Tom. He's calling now.

Sighing, Charles leaned his head back and closed his eyes. Would be real interesting to see what came of this.

Gage had faced the attacking line of Mafia fighters that afternoon with barely a rise in his heart rate, yet at the prospect of this phone call, his hands and feet were cold and his heart knocked against his ribs.

He scowled at his phone. Talking to Claire always made him feel like he'd swallowed a mouthful of hydrogen cyanide, the acid burning him alive from the inside out.

Pushing out a hard exhalation, he stared down at the screen of his phone. He still had her number programmed in it, because apparently, he was a fucking closet masochist. Or a goddamn hopeless romantic, he wasn't sure which. Either way, when it came to her, he was fucked.

Well, hell. Stalling wasn't going to help, was it? He hit the call button and raised the phone to his ear, part of him hoping she wouldn't pick up. It was early back on the east coast. Maybe she'd slept in or was in a meeting.

On the fourth ring he was just starting to get his hopes up about getting voicemail when she answered.

She'd seen his number and picked it up anyway. That had to mean something.

"Hello?"

Gage closed his eyes. Her voice.

In all the months they'd been apart he'd never forgotten the sound of it. Low for a woman and slightly husky, it was pure sex. One syllable from her, and he was thinking of the countless hours they'd spent tangled naked together in sweat dampened sheets, that sultry voice praising whatever he was doing to her aroused body, crying out his name in ecstasy as she came around his fingers or tongue or cock...

Dammit. Now his tongue was stuck to the roof of his mouth. His suddenly dry as sand mouth. "Hey, it's Gage," he managed.

"Yeah, I saw your name come up." The cautious note in her voice made it clear that the past six months without speaking to each other hadn't made her memory of him grow any fonder. But at least she'd answered rather than let it go to voicemail.

The tightness in his chest expanded, making his lungs feel overinflated.

"So...how are things?"

"Fine. Gage, what did you want to talk to me about?"

She'd always been a straight shooter. He scrubbed a hand over his closely trimmed hair, leaned against the edge of the vanity. "I'm calling in a favor." *Tom is so going to pay for this.*

"What kind of favor?" Now her tone was suspicious.

"We've run into a situation here—"

"Where's here?"

"New York."

A pause. "Go on."

"There've been some...problems on this job and Tom thinks there might be a

Leak."

"You're working for Tom?"

That would be the thing she zoned in on. They'd met through Tom at a security conference in DC. Nine hours after that he'd shown up at her hotel room door and things had burned out of control between them ever since. "Yeah. Have been since the spring."

"You never told me."

Yeah, because we haven't spoken a single word to each other since March. "Well, anyway, with everything that's happened on this job Tom thinks there's something going on between Italians officials and the TTP. They're getting help somewhere. We just don't know from whom."

"And that's where I come in." She didn't sound happy about it. Not that he'd expected her to.

He pushed out a breath. "Yeah." This entire situation depressed him.

How the hell had they come to this? He'd bought a ring for Chrissake, had the whole romantic proposal mapped out in his head before she'd suddenly brought his world crumbling down on him in a pile of rubble.

Not so long ago they would have done anything for each other. Now they could barely have a civil conversation.

"Is this official, or off the record?" she asked.

"Off the record."

She made an incredulous sound. "Are you serious? I could lose my job for something like that."

"I'm not asking you to do anything illegal," he said quickly. "Anything you could find out would be a big help. We'd all appreciate it."

He could almost feel the anger deflating out of her on the other end of the line. "What's happened over there?"

She had security clearance, maybe even a higher one than him, so he didn't see the harm in telling her the basics. "I'm part of the detail for Bonanno's daughter."

"What? Holy shit, Gage, that story is still all over the news. The Italian have threatened to kill anyone associated with... Wait, were you there at that school in the Swat Valley today?"

"Yeah." He mentally winced. She hated what he did for a living, the danger he was sometimes in. It was one of the biggest reasons for her breaking up with him.

"God, it's all the newscasts over here are talking about, along with the Bonanno case. Are you okay?"

Nice to know she didn't want to see him dead, at least. That had to count for something. "We're all good, but we need answers. The daughter, Carmela, got word last night that the State Department is investigating her father's case.

They said they have Intel showing a link between an unnamed Italian official and a known TTP operative. According to them, Bonanno, and his security team were murdered for shares of the ransom money."

She was silent a moment. "I'll do what I can, but I'm not making any promises. Digging into this without the proper authorization isn't going to be easy, let alone keeping anyone at the agency from finding out."

"I understand. Thanks." He wanted to say so much more. I miss you. Every day. Why the hell did you walk out of my life like that? He would also rather die than set himself up for another hit from her.

Another pause. "Tom made you call me, didn't he?"

He smothered an ironic chuckle, hating the lingering estrangement between them. "Yep. Well, he made Charles order me to."

"Charles is there?"

"Yeah, he's team leader on this job." And he'd proven his worth yet again today out in the middle of that firefight. Their team was solid, even with Ellis and Dunphy being newcomers and Gage was glad to be a part of it.

Especially since gainful employment over here meant he didn't have to be home staring at the walls of his empty apartment and being constantly reminded of all he'd lost.

"Carmela is lucky to have you guys."

He had no idea what to read into that response or what to say in reply.

"Thanks," he mumbled lamely.

Claire expelled a long breath. "All right. I'll see what I can do and get back to you. Or should I contact Tom?"

For some reason the hopeful note in her voice on that question was the hardest to take. He clenched his jaw. "You can contact Tom if that's more comfortable for you."

"That's not what I said," she argued. "I'm an adult, Gage. I know how to leave personal feelings out of my professional relationships."

Great. So now he was a grudge and a professional relationship in addition to being her ex. Tamping down the angry response ready to burst out of his mouth, he shifted gears and went with shock tactics instead. "So, what are you wearing right now?"

A snort, followed by a grudging chuckle. "Wouldn't you like to know."

"Depends on what the answer is." He'd rather know what she was wearing underneath whatever she had on, though he could guess. She had a fondness for lace and satin and sexy thong panties because they didn't leave lines beneath the cozy ass-hugging skirts and jeans she liked to wear, and a fine ass it was, too.

"You're such an idiot," she told him, this time without any bite.

He smiled sadly, feeling that yawning ache opening in his chest again.

He'd made so many mistakes he could never put right and now he had to live with the knowledge that he'd lost her forever. "I know."

"Well. I'll be in touch. Bye, Gage. Take care of yourself." She disconnected before he could reply.

Gage lowered his phone and stared at the picture of her on screen that came up with her contact info, the one he'd taken on a ski trip last year with her and his daughter. Her light brown hair spilled around her shoulders, dotted with snowflakes, and those gray eyes sparkled with life and laughter as she smiled up at the camera.

Gage shook his head at himself. Every time he'd convinced himself he'd moved on, something drew her back into his life. Like Janelle reaching out to her about something instead of him, or the order from Tom tonight. He was starting to think he'd never get over her, no matter how much time went by.

He made himself delete the image before putting his phone back into his pocket.

Feeling almost as shitty as he had on the night Scottie was killed, he walked out to face Charles.

He was spread-eagled in the chair doing something with his phone and looked up when Gage came out of the bathroom. "Well?" he asked.

"She said she'd see what she can do."

Charles smiled. "You still got the old charm going, huh?"

He didn't have shit and was reminded of that daily. "What's the story with Carmela?"

"Tom booked her on an eleven-hundred flight tomorrow. She'll be glad to get out of here and go home."

Maybe, but Gage wasn't blind. She and Charles had been striking sparks off each other from the first moment they met. "You are staying with her tonight?"

Charles looked down to play with his phone some more, a sure sign he didn't want to answer. "I told her I would."

Gage didn't envy the guy a night with her, especially since the job to protect her was officially over tomorrow and all that was left was to put her on that plane in the morning.

"Well why are you still sitting there then? Get in there and make sure she gets her money's worth."

Charles's head snapped up, the blaze of anger in his eyes disappearing when he realized Gage was only teasing. A grin spread across his face as he got to his feet. "Will do. I'll check in with you later."

"Yeah. Don't forget to use protection, son," he added when Charles hit the door. Charles answered with a raised middle finger as he walked out, leaving Gage alone with thoughts and memories he'd rather not face. It was going to be a long ass night, but at least one of them wouldn't be alone.

Chapter 11

The Love Nest

When Charles opened the door, Carmela came up onto one elbow on the bed and pushed the hair out of her face. He slipped inside, flashed a smile.

"Everything okay?" she asked, not fooled by the smile.

"Yeah. Gage was looking into something for us. It's all good." He nodded at her phone on the nightstand.

"You talk to your family?"

"My mom. She was really upset."

Carmela was thankful her mother wasn't involved in this side of the foundation so she hadn't been subjected to any of this.

"Understandable."

She nodded, wishing she'd taken the time to have a shower instead of just changing into her sleep shirt and yoga pants.

"I texted my brother too. I told them I'd let them know when my flight is leaving."

"Eleven hundred tomorrow."

Oh. She frowned, confused by her conflicting reactions. She wanted to go home more than anything, but she couldn't help feeling responsible for those girls and the thought of never seeing Charles again set off a stab of pain beneath her ribs.

On top of that there was the unrelieved arousal that hadn't gone away since he'd pinned her to the wall and kissed her into a state of mindless need.

Never in her life had she experienced that kind of melted heat before.

She shifted her legs to ease the unsatisfied ache between them.

"What about you, are you going back to the States?"

He set his phone on the small table where he'd left his sidearm, and spoke without looking at her.

"I'll be here a few more days at least. Might be home by next weekend though."

It was obvious he didn't plan on picking up where they'd left off against the wall. Did he regret what they'd done? If he was worried about her reporting him to Tom or issuing a complaint, that was beyond insulting.

Of all the things she'd experienced on this life changing trip, those few mind-blowing minutes with Charles was the only one she didn't regret.

"And where is home, by the way?" she asked, feeling the need to maintain a civil conversation.

"Georgia Sea Islands. St. Simons."

He said it with such pride that she smiled.

"I've never been there but I've heard it's beautiful."

"It's heaven on earth, as far as I'm concerned."

For a former SEAL it must be, living right on the edge of the ocean.

"You don't have a Georgia accent though."

His lips quirked as he faced her. "That's because I grew up in Nebraska."

She sat up fully and looped her arms around her knees. "My dad was from there." "I know."

He looked away from her when he said it and something in his tone bothered her. Maybe he'd read it in the file Tom must have given him about her and her family's background.

Since she didn't want to think about her father right now, she changed the subject. There was so much she wanted to know about Charles and he certainly seemed to have dropped the "no friends" rule with the kiss.

She just wished they hadn't been interrupted because she didn't have the guts to make a move on him a second time. If he wasn't reciprocating now that he realized how much she wanted him, then clearly she'd overestimated his interested in her.

She pushed the embarrassing thought aside. "Did you always know you wanted to be a SEAL?"

Stretching out on the small sofa that was about two feet too short for him, he laid his head on the armrest and stared up at the ceiling.

"No. After high school I had no clue what I wanted to do, beyond leaving Nebraska. I joined the Navy and they put me through college."

"You have a degree?"

He turned his head to look at her, amusement on his face. "Yes, Miss Yale grad, I do. And a Master's in business administration."

She hadn't meant to sound so surprised; it was just that she didn't understand why he was working as a contractor and putting his life at risk rather than using his education for a safer career.

"If you have all that, why did you become a SEAL? No disrespect intended," she added quickly, "I'm just curious."

He crossed one ankle over the other, his long legs dangling over the far end of the sofa. His expression was thoughtful.

"It was the toughest challenge out there and I'd always wanted to serve my country. The SEAL Teams gave me the chance to be part of something bigger but I promised my mother I'd wait to report to BUD/S until I finished my undergrad degree."

"But you're still not using your degrees even though you're out of the

Teams. Why?" She couldn't understand why he'd continue taking on such a risky job when he had so many other, less dangerous options available to him.

She'd seen him in action enough to know that he was highly skilled and an expert at what he did, but he had to know he couldn't do this forever.

"It's hard to explain."

"Not as hard as going through BUD/S, I bet."

He cracked a grin at that and rubbed a hand over his jaw. "Once you're part of something like that, it's hard to quit. Leaving the Teams was hard enough without giving up the rest of it. Our skill set is unique and there are only so many careers where we can put them to use."

"Did you quit? The Teams, I mean?"

He shook his head, not seeming offended by her questions. "I knew I wouldn't be able to stay in the Teams forever. It's hell on your body. I blew out one of my knees for the second time on a training mission and started my

Master's while I was laid up after surgery. I knew I couldn't keep up with that lifestyle for much longer and needed to look at my options. I always thought I'd apply to the FBI once I got out, but I never did make it back to active duty after that surgery."

That would have devastated a lot of men in his position. "That must've been hard. I'm sorry."

He shrugged, his gaze shifting over to her. "I don't regret it. That Master's degree's going to help me get a partnership in New York. And the money I make as a contractor is damn hard to pass up, especially when I get to do what I love and what I'm good at."

Yeah, she could certainly understand that part of it. The man never ceased to amaze her. "You mentioned your mom earlier. Are you close with her?"

A fond smile spread across his face, softening the harsh lines of his face and warming his eyes. "Yeah. She raised me on her own, so it was just the two of us.

It makes me appreciate the work your foundation is trying to do even more.

Without a college degree my mom would've wound up on welfare in the projects and we both would've been stuck there. Instead, she busted her ass working two jobs and went to school at night to earn her degree.

It took her seven years, but she finally got her accounting degree and moved us into our first house when I was eight."

An impressive lady, and even better role model for her son. Carmela shook her head in bemusement. She'd found out more about the man in the past five minutes than she had during the whole three days she'd known him. "Good for her."

"I don't know how she did it, but I'm proud of her. She's amazing."

"Kind of like her son."

That made him grin. "Glad you think so." He sat up, clearly done with that sort of intimate conversation. "You get enough to eat?"

"I'm good." Just tired, worried, and extremely sexually frustrated. And really confused about why you're over there and I'm over here.

He nodded, searched her eyes. "Think you can sleep now with me here?"

It shouldn't have mattered, but knowing he'd changed his mind about wanting her hurt more than she cared to admit.

"I'll try." She reached over to switch off the bedside lamp, lay down and closed her eyes, trying to ignore his nearness and the persistent ache in her chest. "Thanks for everything, Charles," she said quietly, knowing it was a ridiculously inadequate thing to say to someone who'd saved her life twice in the past two days.

"Nothing to thank me for. I'd do it all again in a heartbeat."

All of it? His choice of wording made her want to groan, because right then she was dying for more of the pleasure he'd shown her. She curled up onto her side and pulled the covers up beneath her chin, fighting the sting of tears. She told herself it was just simple exhaustion.

"Good night."

"Good night."

Sleep wouldn't come. She'd known it wouldn't. Not with images of the bombings and the girls' frightened faces flickering through her head.

Charles's quiet breathing reassured her she at least wasn't alone, yet somehow, she felt lonelier with him stretched out on that couch across the room. She turned from one side to the other, even pulled the pillow over her head to block out the tiny bit of light coming from the bathroom. No matter what she did she couldn't relax.

"That mattress has lumps in it or something?" Charles asked finally after an unknown amount of time had passed.

She rolled to her back with a sigh. "Sorry. Am I keeping you awake?"

He gave a half chuckle. "No. I'm not much of a sleeper these days."

"I used to be up until a few weeks ago. I miss it."

In the dim light from the bathroom, she watched Charles sit up and set his elbows on his knees.

"I'm not going to lie to you, sweetheart."

The endearment caught her off guard and warmed her at the same time.

"Going through what you have, seeing the things you have, it's not going to be easy. You can't just shut it off when you want to. It'll take time for you to figure out how to cope with everything that's happened, and that's normal, and you should talk to someone when you get home."

"Oh yeah, my therapist and I will be spending lots of quality time together once I get back," she assured him. "I started seeing her right after my dad was killed." Even saying it still made her throat constrict. "You, on the other hand, handle everything so well. I wish I knew your secret."

He went still for a moment, an almost haunted expression flickering over his face. "No secret. Trust me, I've got my own demons to deal with."

She wanted to ask what that mysterious comment meant but thought better of it, not wanting to ruin the fragile bond they'd established. "Here. You come take the bed and I'll sleep on the couch," she offered, throwing off the blankets and swinging her legs over the side.

Tomorrow she'd have lots of time to sleep on the plane. Charles would most likely be working all day again.

"I've got a better idea."

Her head snapped up when he rose suddenly and approached the bed. In the thin slice of light revealed by the open bathroom door she could see the broad silhouette of his shoulders, the shadowed planes of his face as he advanced on her.

The breath backed up in her lungs as all the oxygen seemed to get sucked out of the room. She shifted around while he rounded the bed to climb on the other side and laid down facing her, head propped in one hand so their faces were less than a foot apart.

Before she could ask what, he was doing he reached out a hand and brushed a curl away from her cheek. "You look scared to death," he said softly, amusement coloring his deep voice.

She flushed, though he probably couldn't tell in the dimness. "I just don't know how to read you. I thought you'd changed your mind about...earlier."

"No, but I like catching you off guard," he admitted. "And I bet I can help you fall asleep."

The way he said it, the words laced with such sensual heat and promise, made her nipples harden and her abdomen clench. Oh yeah, she wanted him. She was leaving tomorrow; this was her only chance. "What have you got in mind?" she whispered, heart pounding in anticipation.

In answer he curved his hand around her nape and eased her head closer until she could feel the warmth of his breath on her face. "I'll show you, but you have to close your eyes first."

She searched his eyes in the dimness, found nothing but arousal and a frank male hunger that made her toes curl. As soon as she allowed her lids to fall, he began trailing kisses across her forehead and down the bridge of her nose. The unexpected tenderness surprised her.

Needing to touch him, she slid her hands down his chest to the hem of his T-shirt and under it to the naked flesh beneath. Oh God, the feel of him, all hot, hard male in prime condition.

She stroked her palms over his skin, across the firm, sculpted planes of his chest and abdomen. He let her explore, seeming content to cover her face with kisses so sweet she found herself tilting her head back in a silent request for more.

"Lie down," he whispered against her lips, feathering across their edges. She allowed him to turn her fully onto her side, facing him. "Keep your eyes closed."

More heavenly kisses feathered over her jaw, teasing her lips, then finally centered there. She opened instantly, sighed in satisfaction at the feel of his tongue sliding inside to tease and caress hers.

During the previous kiss she'd felt the urgent lust raging through him, but this one was slow and seductive. Need drove her closer to his body and she felt the thick ridge of his erection press against her pelvis.

One rock of her hips and she was rewarded by a low groan, a hard hand sliding from her hair to the small of her back and lower to grip the curve of her hip. He squeezed, his long fingers kneading her flesh in a rhythm that made her want to purr.

Carmela stroked his tongue with hers and ran her hands over him, luxuriating in all that male power at her fingertips. When his palm slid up from her hip to cradle her breast she gasped into his mouth, the puckered nipple gathering even tighter against his palm.

Tingles radiated out from his touch, heat pooling low in her belly. The thin cotton of her sleep shirt prevented her from feeling his hand on her bare skin. She wanted it gone.

Twisting up, she reached down to drag the shirt off. He stopped her, catching her hands in one of his and again brushed his thumb across her throbbing nipple.

Ruins of fire swept through her, centering in her core, making her wet and ready for him.

A shiver rippled through her. Charles kissed her deeper, letting her feel more of his need before he took the hard point between his thumb and forefinger and squeezed gently.

Her back arched of its own volition and a high-pitched gasp escaped from her tight throat. She was melting, drowning in pleasure and she never wanted it to end.

Before she could plead for more than he was giving her, he pulled the hem of her shirt up just far enough to expose her breasts. Cool air caressed her naked skin as he leaned in. The scrape of beard against her tender skin was erotic as hell, and when he cupped the weight of her in his hand and dragged his tongue across the sensitive center, she couldn't hold back a soft cry.

Grabbing his head, Carmela arched her back and pulled him closer. He obliged with a low sound of satisfaction and took her into his mouth. Her eyes fell closed under the lash of pleasure.

She was so hot and wet. Unbelievably sexy. He sucked at her with slow pulls of his mouth, letting his tongue flick over the sensitive tip. In the space of a few heartbeats the pulse between her legs transformed into an all-consuming pressure, demanding release.

She wriggled against his mouth and fought the restraining hold he had on her hip, scissoring her legs in a useless effort to press her mound against him and find some sort of relief.

A loud striking made her jerk, and her eyes fly open. Charles stilled against her, her nipple still in his mouth. It took a second for her to realize it was her phone ringing.

As much as she loved her family, she didn't want to talk to anyone right now. "Probably just my brother," she panted, muscles tight with strain, feeling like she'd die if he stopped what he was doing. "Just ignore it."

Charles obliged her and did something devastating with his tongue. Her delighted sigh was just melting into silence when another phone in the room began to ring. This time it was his. Charles cursed and released her so fast she landed on her back.

By the time she sat up and pulled the shirt down over her breasts, he was across the room and answering his phone.

"What? Are you sure?" she heard him ask, and a ripple of unease went through her at the tension in his voice. With a feeling of dread, she picked up her phone to check the call display. Tom.

When he hadn't reached her, he'd obviously called Charles right away. And that had to mean more bad news. With her arousal extinguished under a bucket of ice water, she hurriedly straightened her clothes and watched Charles.

He was pacing beside the bed, ran a hand through his hair. "Jesus. Yeah, hang on." He raised his head to look at her. "Pull up your e-mail."

Grabbing her phone, she did, fighting back the fear slithering inside her.

Someone pounded on the door. She scrambled to her knees, wondering what the hell was happening.

Charles flipped on the light, checked the peephole, and pulled it open to let Gage in. He strode in, his gaze connecting with hers. The worry she saw there made her gut shrivels.

"Did you get it?" he gestured to the phone in her hand while Chares continued to speak to Tom.

"No, I'm just checking my e-mail now," she said shakily. What the hell was going on now? It seemed to take hours for the program to load.

By the time her messages came through, Charles and Gage were near her, looking over her shoulder at the illuminated screen.

"Click on the one from New York and open the attachment," Charles told her.

"Okay." Her heart thudded against her breastbone. She enlarged the image and stared at it, realizing it was some sort of map. Everyone seemed worried as hell about it. "What is it?"

Face grim, Charles set his phone down between them and put Tom on speaker. "Tom?"

"It's addressed to you, Carmela," Tom answered, "and we need you to figure out what it means, fast."

"Why, what's going on?" It scared her even more when Charles reached out to take her hand and squeezed it.

"It's part of a ransom note," Tom said. "An Italian spokesperson is claiming they've taken a family from the school hostage."

No! As horror swamped her, she could barely feel the pressure of Charles's fingers around hers. Tom kept talking.

"Whatever this diagram means will lead us to their location, and they want only you and one person from your security team to go there. They've threatened to kill the hostages if you don't show up there in the next three hours."

Chapter 12

Aisha's Father

Oh, fuck him, this was the last thing they needed.

Charles evaluated Carmela's reaction to the news. With everything that had happened he kept waiting for her to crack under the strain, and so far, she'd hung in there better than he ever could have expected.

Even so, he couldn't help but feel like this was the tipping point and he couldn't stand the thought of watching her break. With this new strain, he was very afraid she might.

Her mouth was pinched, her forehead creased with an anxious frown as she stared at her phone. She squeezed his hand so tight her fingers were white. The room was deathly silent in the wake of Tom's announcement.

"Is it Aisha?" she demanded, a quaver in her voice.

"We don't know yet," Tom answered.

A muscle jumped in her jaw, her gaze still on the phone's screen, then she gave a sharp shake of her head. "I can't tell anything from that picture, it's too small. Give me my laptop." She reached an arm toward where it lay beside the sofa Charles had tried to sleep on earlier.

Gage went over to grab it and set it on the bed before her. Both he and Charles gathered closer while she booted up the computer and pulled up Tom's e-mail.

The image on screen was a map of some kind, drawn with what looked like pencil. Even on the laptop's larger screen it was still too small for them to make out the writing or symbols all over it. She enlarged it again.

"Now it's blurry. But if I shrink it any more than this, I can't see much of anything."

"Kind of looks like Italy," Charles commented, pulling back to angle his head. Although other than the basic shape of it, the remaining marks and blurry symbols didn't make any sense to him.

"Tom, you said they sent this through the company's website contact form?"

"Yeah, about twenty minutes ago. They included a number for you to call them at when you arrive at the location."

The one marked with a big star. He glanced at Carmela, who was chewing her bottom lip as she studied the screen. "Any ideas?"

She shook her head, still staring, and he turned his attention to Gage, who gave him a hell if I know look. "Any English or Italian in there?" Charles asked him, referring to what might be writing or symbols on the map.

"Not that I can tell," Gage answered, bending even closer. "Numbers maybe?

The writing's awful."

"I think it's a triangle," Carmela suddenly murmured. All three of them bent their heads closer to squint at the map and the lines set amid the other symbols.

"I see it," Charles said at last, mentally connecting the three biggest dots.

"What are those down at the bottom, numbers?"

Carmela enlarged the image again to read them better despite the blur, and gasped a moment later. "It's trig."

"Huh?" he asked, squinting at the numbers. As in, trigonometry?

"And algebra," she confirmed, sounding convinced. "They've given me the distance between two points on the map and the degrees of this angle..."

She muttered something else to herself then nodded. "It's a math problem to calculate the length of this line." Her finger traced a route from a dot in the middle of the map to the star on the left.

Holy shit, it really was trig. She pointed to another line running west/northwest from a dot on the right, her lips moving as she took in all the info. "Give me a sec."

Rummaging through her laptop case she came up with a scientific calculator and began plugging in numbers, mumbling about sines and tangents. Hunter was no slouch with math but she was too quick for him to follow as she punched various figures into the calculator.

"It's one hundred forty-four from this point to this one," she announced, tapping the screen, and looking up at him expectantly.

"A hundred and forty-four what? What kind of measurement?" Gage asked, scooting closer to get a better look.

"Klicks," Charles answered, heart suddenly beating faster as everything clicked into place.

The others looked up at him expectantly, hoping he'd cracked it.

"If this is Italy, where would this point be?" he asked Gage, pointing to the dot on the right.

Gage studied it for a second, frowning as though he wasn't convinced the image even was a map of Italy. "England, most likely."

Charles nodded. "So, what's a hundred and forty-four klicks almost due west of here?"

"Finale," Gage said, sounding surprised and a little impressed.

"Yeah, and that means we're running short on time." Charles sat back, mind whirling. Whoever had sent this knew Carmela was a math teacher. They were smart enough to include exactly enough information for her to figure out the puzzle.

"This is way too advanced for an Italian spokesperson," he said to no one in particular.

Tom's sigh came through the speaker phone. "It's from someone working for them. I'd guess someone with a college degree."

Carmela glanced up at Charles. "The go-between for the Italian and the

American official the State Department told me about?"

He took her hand again and stroked his thumb across her cold knuckles, trying to ease the anxiety he sensed in her. "Not sure, but they were specifically targeting you with this. We'll have barely enough time to get there even if we leave right now." Each passing second wound him tighter inside.

These assholes were part of the cell responsible for Carmela's father's death and the subsequent riots that had led to Scottie's death. Charles wanted them taken out. If that meant having to take Carmela along to draw them out of hiding, he'd do it as long as he could be there to guarantee her safety and make sure she didn't get too close.

"Can we bring back up to this meeting?" he asked Tom.

"Negative, they were very clear that it must be just Carmela and one other person to the destination.

I'm designating you, and the others will go as backup. When you hit the outskirts of New York, call the contact number. They've threatened to kill the hostages if local authorities get involved. All we need is their location.

The Italians will handle the rest. I've already been in contact with them. SWAT team is on standby, waiting for word from us."

There were a lot of things Charles had to say about that, and he couldn't say any of them in front of Carmela without freaking her out even more. Though she had to realize by now how corrupt things were over here.

"So how are you going to keep them out of it?" Anyone from the police to the ISI could be involved in this plot.

"Can't, because they're already working on it. I'll update them again when you contact the hostage takers in Italy. With all the international pressure on them about the wave of riots and now the school attack, the Italians are desperate to break up this cell. Just get us the location, then get out."

Meaning Tom had already been getting pressure from the ISI for Intel about this cell and if he wanted Titanium Security to keep operating in country, he had to comply no matter what the risks were.

"That's how it is?"

"Unfortunately, yeah."

Wait, so they were all fine with using Carmela as bait? Taking her to New York to make the call and make everything look legit was one thing.

Expecting her to go with him and verify the actual address was quite another.

Charles set his jaw, the protective male in him rejecting the idea outright. She wasn't just the main target to him anymore. He cared about her, more than he'd ever thought possible in such a short amount of time, and he wanted to shelter her from any more danger or ugliness.

What if she was their only shot at nailing this cell?

He struggled to let the hardened professional side of him take over, mind racing. "Even if they can't go in with us, I'll need the rest of the team close by for Intel and backup."

"Damn straight. They'll go along and hang back at a spot you designate until you get a hard location. Once you verify it, you pull Carmela out and get out of town," Tom said.

Good, because under the circumstances Charles wouldn't have allowed anyone but him to take her back to the states, and he had no intention of letting her anywhere near the meeting location, no matter what Tom or anyone in the ISI wanted. But could she withstand this?

He searched her face, read the apprehension in her pale green eyes. This was asking more of her than anyone had a right to. He knew she realized that this was so much bigger than her. That this might not only save the lives of the hostages, but take out the cell that had attacked the school and murdered her father.

"Can you do this?" he asked her, feeling torn. Part of him wanted her to say no, refuse outright, but another part wanted these fuckers caught and dispatched to hell where they belonged, and right now she was their best shot at making that happen.

She wanted it too. He could see the vengeance burning in her eyes.

"These are the men who killed my father?" she asked, looking for reassurance.

"Yes," he and Tom said at the same time.

She swallowed, her eyes searching his as if for guidance. "If I don't go they'll kill the hostages, right?"

"Most likely," Tom answered for him. "We don't have much time for you to make up your mind. Best start heading there before we lose any more leeway. As soon as we get off the phone, Gage and I'll contact the State Department and anyone else I think is necessary."

"What about the police?" Carmela asked. "How are we going to keep them from tipping off the kidnappers with their own investigation?"

Tom spoke up again. "Don't worry about all that. Gage and I'll handle everything while you're en route. Are you going?"

Charles watched Carmela wrestle silently with her decision. He empathized with her position. Until ten minutes ago she thought she'd be on a flight home in a few hours.

Now the responsibility of innocent lives had been dumped straight into her hands, but more than that she now had the chance to personally help bring her father's murderers to justice.

The possibility of the hostages being Aisha and her family, or any other family from the school would eat her alive with guilt. All of that combined was one hell of a motivating force, even for an untrained civilian.

"No one here's going to judge you for not going if that's what you decide," he said quietly, needing her to believe him, his conscience forcing him to give her an out.

As much as he dreaded the thought of her leaving him in the morning, he hated the idea of her being in further danger. Yeah, he was good at his job, but even he couldn't guarantee her safety if they did this.

Going into New York blind with no immediate backup was a huge risk. Yet, he still wanted the cell enough for her to do this and trust in him to watch her back. What did that say about him?

"It's my fault," she whispered tightly, her face stricken. "They want me and now they're threatening more innocent people to draw me out."

"It's not your fault. They're not going to get you," Charles said fiercely, gripping her shoulder. "You think I'd let you go near wherever the meeting point is when we've got a confirmed threat against your life? No way." It pissed him off that she'd even think it.

"Then what are we going to do? Call the kidnappers and wander around the city until we find them?"

"Once we get an address, we'll get close enough for me to verify the location and let the locals do their thing. Tom and Gage will work out the logistics while we drive."

Pulling free of his grip, she took a shaky breath and stood, resolve stamped all over her expression as she faced him and Gage. "I want this cell destroyed. I want them to pay for what they did to my father and everything else."

"I know you do." They all wanted the cell eliminated. The reasons didn't matter now; they were united in the cause.

She gave a decisive nod. "Let's go."

"Roger that. Tom, we're on our way." He didn't ask her if she was sure or give her a chance to hesitate. If he did, she might second guess herself and every minute spent here cost them. As it was, they'd have to haul ass to get to New York by the deadline.

Gage left to get his own gear together. Hunter put on his tactical vest and grabbed his weapons while Carmela changed in the bathroom. Less than a minute later she reappeared in the black robe with a scarf covering her dark curls. Her face was pale, but her eyes burned with conviction.

Hold that thought, sweetheart. She was going to need every bit of the fire burning in her gut to see this through. Shit, he admired her. He held out another vest for her. "Put this on under your robe."

She did, reducing a little at the stark reminder of the danger ahead. Wrapping his fingers around hers when she finished, he squeezed tight in reassurance and led her out to the parking lot.

Ellis and Dunphy were already standing next to the first of the two SUVs, both engines running.

"Gage brought us up to speed. We are following you?" Ellis asked.

"With Gage, and just until we hit the outskirts of New York," Charles answered.

"No idea what's going to happen once we call the number we were given, but once we reach the city, hang back until I contact you.

We've got..." He checked his watch. "One hour sixteen minutes to get there. Tom will keep you updated if

I can't."

With that he ushered Carmela around to the passenger side then came back to slide behind the wheel. Gage burst out of the hotel's front door and jumped into the other SUV just as Hunter pulled away from the curb. "Gage, you read me?" he asked, checking the radio link.

"Loud and clear," he responded in Charles's earpiece.

Charles took a right out of the parking lot and hit the gas, weaving his way through traffic to get to the highway entrance.

"Pull up the GPS for me," he said to Carmela. "Once we get to New York, we'll need a map. Try and memorize the general layout if you can." He'd been there more than a few times, but he still didn't know his way around the city well. The place was a tangle of alleys and crowded neighborhoods easy to get lost in, which also made it the perfect place to hide.

No doubt because the hostage takers had chosen it.

Rather than using the vehicle's GPS, Carmela used her cell phone. The image on screen showed them as a little moving arrow and gave the remaining distance to New York State. His main concern now was the clock, which was ticking down too fast.

The tense silence in the vehicle broke when Carmela spoke.

"So, what's the plan when we hit the city limits?" she asked, rubbing a hand against the folds of her robe as she enlarged the map and studied it.

"We make the call and wait for further instructions, find out where these assholes are and what they want from us and make a decision then."

If he was right and they expected Carmela to walk into their trap, they had another thing coming.

"They're going to target me though, right? I mean, it's me they want dead."

A fierce protectiveness rose inside him at the tremor in her voice, so strong the hair on his arms stood up.

"I won't take you anywhere I think might be a trap, and I'm sure as hell not letting you get close enough to anywhere that might make you a target for anyone. We'll wait at the edge of the city and let Tom update everybody involved first.

By now the local authorities will be starting their own hunt. If there's any kind of sting set up once, we get the location, they'll handle it."

She nodded, lips pressed together, gazing still on the map. "Are you going to call the number, or am I?"

"You'll have to, so they know we've complied with that part of their demands. We must make everything look as legit as possible, in case they have eyes on us somehow."

He and Carmela would have to hope that whoever was behind the messages couldn't trace her call to a specific cell tower in New York, or they'd be walking targets.

She didn't answer, turning her head to stare out the passenger window. He hated that he had to pull away emotionally from her, but he couldn't worry about her that way right now and do his job.

Right now, it was all about putting on his game face and focusing everything he had on the unfolding mission.

The sound of the purring engine filled the interior as he pressed down on the accelerator and merged onto the highway, weaving his way around slower moving traffic. Ellis stayed right behind them in the other SUV.

He drove at a steady clip, well above the speed limit, not caring about the risk of being pulled over and very much aware of the minutes ticking past.

Carmela remained silent and tense beside him during the drive and there were no updates from Tom or the others. When they were within a few minutes from New York, Charles handed her his cell phone.

"Mine's encrypted. Make the call."

Pulling out the number she'd written down, she dialed and put the phone on speaker. She swallowed audibly before the call connected and the phone began to ring.

A man picked up within seconds. "Carmela Bonanno?"

"Yes. Who is this?" Her voice was surprisingly steady.

"Are you in New York?" he asked in heavily accented English.

"Just arriving now." She cast an uncertain glance at Hunter, and he nodded for her to continue. "What do you want?"

"You," the man said flatly, and Charles bit back a growl. "You will come to the address we give you, or the hostage dies."

Only one hostage?

"Who is it?" she demanded, and he had to give her points for maintaining her cool when she had to be scared shitless.

"The man whose daughter you rescued today."

Those big green eyes flashed up to him as she answered, the stricken look on her face punching him in the heart. "Aisha's father?"

"You have twenty-two minutes from now. If you alert the authorities, he will die. Do not try anything. You are being watched." The line went dead.

Fuck. Twenty-two minutes to find and verify the location of the Italians, on foot in this city? He pulled them out of traffic and put the SUV in park close to a police checkpoint, alerting Gage over the radio. When Charles opened his door seconds later, Gage was already there.

"Stay here and wait for an update," Charles told him. He rounded the hood and took Carmela by the arm to lead her to the checkpoint as he called Tom and gave him the heads up.

The first of three heavily armed policemen took their ID. His face tensed in sudden recognition and he quickly got on the radio to someone. Another officer squared off with Charles. "You will wait here."

Like hell he would. If the local police already knew who they were then they knew what was going down and Charles wasn't going to deal with any bureaucratic when so much hinged on this.

Carmela's life was in danger just by being in the city. Here he didn't trust anyone outside of his team, including the police and military, because he'd already learned that lesson the hard way. Every potential leak increased the chance of losing the cell.

"I've got twenty minutes to find out where they are. Move the hell out of the way."

The guard bristled at Charles's tone and shifted his grip on his weapon in silent warning. "You will stay where you are until we receive further orders."

Carmela's fingers bit into his biceps and he forced himself to tone down the aggression.

"Let us through, now." This was insane, and whoever was on the other end of that radio had to know it. He hit a few buttons on his phone and raised it to his ear. "Tom, we're being hassled at a checkpoint. Get us clearance or we're going to miss the deadline."

"Working on it," Tom muttered, and disconnected.

They lost three more minutes waiting for the higher up to grant permission for them to pass through. A supervisor appeared and started firing questions at Charles.

He was thinking about taking on all three of them when his phone buzzed with an incoming text. Instead of a message from Tom, the screen showed an elaborate mathematical equation along with a name, the word Address, and You are being watched.

"Shit," he muttered. The supervising officer fell silent as Charles passed the phone to Carmela. "Can you crack this?" It was something right out of an engineering textbook, full of confusing brackets, square roots, exponents, and all kinds of other fun stuff. The kind of thing it would take an hour and five pages of notes for him to solve.

She grabbed it from him, frowning in concentration as she studied it. "I need a pen and paper."

"Give her a pen and paper," Charles barked at the officers. Face slack with surprise, the man closest to them rummaged through his pockets and came up with a pen and note pad and thrust them at her.

Charles watched her work, awed at the speed and skill she showed in unraveling the equation under such intense pressure. Her lips were moving, her right hand scrawling lines of numbers across the paper as she used a calculator app on her phone. She flipped the page and punched more numbers into her smart phone, kept going.

He shifted his posture, impatient to get moving. Jesus, how long did the hostage takers expect it to take her to answer it?

As she worked, the guards kept arguing with Charles. Carmela was on her fifth page of the solution when she began scribbling frantically. Charles could tell she was getting close. He held up a hand to make the guard shut up, not wanting anything to interfere with her concentration.

"Six hundred ninety-one," she announced a moment later.

"You're sure? "Charles urged.

"Positive." Her voice rang with conviction.

Charles grabbed the pad from her and force it in the officer's face, repeating the street name from the text message, and the number Carmela had given.

"Where is that?" Carmela was already punching the address into her phone, bless her. The man pointed to the northwest and shook his head. "Two kilometers.

Very crowded."

"Let us through now," Charles growled. Verifying the location was critical and they were short on time, especially if the Italians were thinking about making a move before he could confirm it was the right address.

The supervisor relayed the address to whoever he was talking to, then waved them through with a brief nod. "Go."

Gripping Carmela's upper arm, Charles took off in a fast jog and called Tom as he ran to give him the info. "Heading there now," he finished, and hung up.

Carmela hurried along beside him, checking her phone. "Left at the third street we come to."

God, he loved her brain. He'd never seen anything so sexy in his life as her solving that bitch of an equation under those circumstances. "How the hell did you solve that thing?"

"BEDMAS."

"What?"

"Brackets, exponents, division, multiplication."

"Yeah, I got it. Christ, you're smart." He shook his head in wonder and hustled her along the uneven pavement, dodging cars and carts and people.

Due to the Easter holiday, the city was crowded even at this time of night.

The residents were packing up their groceries because the store owners were closing shops for the day. He and Carmela now had only sixteen minutes to make it to their destination.

"They've got Aisha's father," she said in a shaky voice.

"I know." He kept up the demanding pace, aware of her panting breaths and the way she began to lag. Slowing his speed to a fast walk, he kept pulling her onward. "We'll stop once we're a couple blocks away," he told her.

"What? We can't, the time limit"

"You're not going to that address, Carmela."

"But if the police storm the place the hostage takers will kill him! Aisha's father is probably their only source of income. They might starve this winter without him."

"You're not going," he repeated, his tone making it clear he would tolerate no further argument.

"You said we had to make it look legit," she shot back, her voice ringing with frustration despite her obvious fear and fatigue.

"Yeah, to make them think you're going to comply with their demands. I brought you so we could find out what we need from the kidnappers, buy time to update the authorities and let them get a plan together to take these guys down.

Which we've done. Now we'll get close enough so I can verify we've got the right place, but not close enough for them to see you, because you're bait, not a sacrificial goat. Big difference."

Charles's instincts were already buzzing, telling him they were being watched. He kept their route erratic to make them a more difficult target, zigzagging along the streets. He could feel the eyes on them, people staring from windows or alleyways as they passed.

Any one of them could be an informant. Any one of them might have a bead on them with a weapon right now, and if there were any snipers in position, he'd just have to hope the shadows were thick enough to hide them.

Chapter 13

The Search

Carmela's heart banged against her ribs as Charles finally slowed to a walk.

"Stand tall and look straight ahead, like you belong here," he whispered.

God, she was having trouble catching her breath, and he wasn't even breathing hard.

It went against every instinct to do as he said instead of constantly looking around to scan for threats, but she knew he was right. Giving off that sort of nervous energy would only look suspicious and make her stand out more.

Right now, the only things giving her the courage to see this through were having Charles right next to her and feeling the strength of his hand around hers. Wanting justice for her father and putting her own life on the line to see it done were two very different things.

The map on her phone showed the address as being just a few blocks from where they stood. Here amongst the back alleys and quieter residential streets the night seemed hushed and gloomy. The narrow street they were on was dark, lined on both sides by rundown buildings that stretched three and four stories tall.

Lines of drying laundry hung suspended between houses, casting eerie, swaying shadows below. The hot, muggy air smelled of cooking food and the underlying stench of rotting garbage.

Her breathing slowed, though her heart kept beating a frantic rhythm the closer they got to the target location.

Charles stayed deep in the shadows cast by the buildings, hiding them from any curious or hostile eyes. It made the back of her neck crawl to think that someone might be following them. She tightened her grip around Charles's hand, and he squeezed back in silent reassurance. He wouldn't lead her into danger, and he wouldn't let her down.

Somewhat up the street he tugged her into a little alcove tucked beneath a boarded up door and pressed her back against the peeling plaster wall with one arm, positioning himself in front of her. "Put your phone away," he whispered, staring out into the dark alley.

The map showed them to be a block and a half from the target. She quickly dimmed the phone and shoved it into her pocket beneath her robe, worried that she might have drawn unwanted attention to them with the illumination from the screen.

Charles kept her pressed to the wall and leaned forward to peer around the corner. He searched up and down the alley before speaking again. "Stay put. I'll be back in a minute."

He was leaving her here. Without thinking she reached out to grab his arm, then caught herself and forced her hand down. She was being ridiculous. As long as she stayed still it was likely no one would even see her. With one last look about, Charles darted around the corner and vanished from view.

Suddenly everything around her seemed more sinister. The shadows were deeper, the darkened windows in the buildings across the alley staring down at her like suspicious eyes, the rushing sound of what she assumed had to be rats searching for food was overly loud to her pulsing ears.

Doubts began to creep in. What if they were in the wrong place? They were already suspicious that this entire thing was a setup, so they had to assume the kidnappers were manipulating them into a bad situation.

Her T-shirt stuck to the skin between her shoulder blades and her palms were damp. When she heard someone coming toward her from the opposite end of the alley she barely resisted the urge to peek.

Instead, she huddled deeper into the cover the alcove provided, hardly daring to breathe until the man passed with a huge basket slung over his back. He didn't even look her way.

"Hey."

She jumped and swallowed a cry. Charles stood at the edge of the building and she hadn't even heard him coming. She grabbed onto the hand he reached out for her. "It gets busier from here and I don't want to leave you this far back. We'll go up another block and I'll check again."

She licked her dry lips. "How much time left?"

"Six minutes."

God.

She hurried after him, anchored by the firm grip of his hand. He'd been right, the neighborhood got much busier the next block over. The moment they turned the corner she could see lights on in some of the upper floor apartments and people moving around inside.

A few people walked on the street ahead of them but so far no one else was following. Someone might come by at any moment though. She was careful to stay in the shadows, making sure she followed Charles without looking around or changing her posture.

At the end of the block, he led her to another hiding spot behind an abandoned wooden cart.

"Okay?" he whispered.

"Yeah," she answered, the word barely carrying over the still air.

"We're less than a block away now. We're just going to go a little farther to check it out quick and come straight back. If they've got eyes on us, I don't want you exposed, so hug the walls and stay where it's darkest."

She nodded, wanting to just get this over with and get the hell out of here.

She fell in step behind him. They were halfway up the street when a sharp bang up ahead broke the relative quiet. Then frenzied shouting. Charles froze. She drew up short behind him, holding her breath. She stayed where she was, ears straining, alarmed when Charles whirled around to face her.

In the dimness she made out just enough of his face to see the rage in his expression.

"What?" she whispered, heart flying into her throat.

"The Italians jumped the gun," he said tightly.

No. She opened her mouth to ask if that meant what she thought it did when a thunderous boom rent the air.

Carmela cried out and hunched into a ball as the terrible wall of noise ripped through the night, the pressure of the blast vibrating against her ear drums in a relentless wave. Glass shattered in the buildings around them, the ground shaking with the force of the shockwave.

A bomb.

The seconds that followed, a vacuum of silence stained out everything but the roar of blood in her ears. She felt the pressure of Charles's hands around her upper arms, the urgency in his grip as he hauled her to her feet.

People were flooding out of their homes in their sleepwear, yelling and gesturing forward the blast, their expressions filled with anxiety.

"Come on," Charles growled, yanking on her hand.

Her legs were uncooperative. She stumbled along in his wake, casting a terrified glance over her shoulder toward the explosion. An eerie yellow and orange glow lit the sky behind them, plumes of smoke boiling up into the dark sky. She could hear people around them screaming, shouting, the too familiar sounds of confusion and terror closing around her.

"Run, "Charles snapped.

The sharp command cracked like a whip through the haze surrounding her. She put her head down and ran, focused only on keeping up with Charles.

At the end of the third block, he paused to glance back. With a curse he steered her around the corner, pushing her forward with a hard hand between her shoulder blades as he got on the radio to Gage. "SWAT team went in and triggered a bomb.

Either a hidden tripwire or someone remote detonated it."

Carmela shuddered and kept going, driven by the desperate urge to escape and that rigid hand at her back.

"Someone's tailing us," Charles added.

What? She almost turned around to look but Charles pushed her around the next corner in a sharp left turn and kept talking to Gage.

"We'll keep moving east but you may have to lead us out... Roger that."

"Someone's after us?" she demanded, terror stealing more strength from her legs.

"We're okay. Just keep running."

He didn't need to tell her she was slowing them down. She knew. He could've left her in his wake but instead he was sticking with her. Pushing herself harder, she dug down for an additional burst of speed and raced down the nearly empty streets.

Behind her she could hear the distant wail of sirens. Someone was after them but all she could think about was that if they'd gone to the address like the hostage takers had insisted, they'd both be dead right now.

Don't think about it, just run.

Charles maneuvered them in a zigzag pattern, whipping them right then left, then back again until it all became a blur. She made it another nine blocks before the initial burst of panic faded and sucked the strength out of her muscles.

As though he sensed it, Charles brought her up short and dragged her back against him, retreating into the deep shadows between two closed shops and flattening himself against the rough bricks.

She stood with her back pressed tight against his chest, gasping for breath, sweating and trembling. He brought one hand up to cover her mouth and she grabbed at it until she realized he wasn't trying to cut off her air, but conceal the sound of her panting.

Braced against him, she was too scared to close her eyes, instead staring dead ahead at the street in the gap between the buildings.

Charles kept his hand over her mouth and brought the other one to his side.

She glanced down in time to see him holding a pistol at waist level. His arm was like warm steel across her belly. She barely registered the feel of it there before he rolled her behind him to shield her with his body in case the threat materialized.

She tugged her gaze back to the alley, helpless to do anything but wait. It seemed to take forever. Several people passed by a few moments later, including a younger man dressed in jeans and a dark hoodie. Was he, their tail?

Charles didn't move. He gave no indication if the threat was past or not.

Tense seconds ticked by after the man in the hoodie disappeared.

Carmela could feel Charles's heart beating against her back, his muscular frame coiled and ready to spring.

After a full minute, he lowered the hand holding the weapon and tucked it back wherever he'd drawn it from. Risking a look at him, she tipped her head back to search for his face. Charles slowly removed his hand from her mouth, and she took her first full breath since ducking in here.

He bent his head until his mouth brushed her ear, his voice barely carrying.

"There are probably others. We're going to move quickly and quietly until we meet up with Gage and the rest of the boys. All right?"

She managed a nod, feeling slightly nauseated. Her silenced phone began to vibrate in her pocket. Charles's head snapped downward, telling her he'd heard the quiet buzz. She hesitated.

"Check it."

Almost afraid to, Carmela pulled it out and looked at the screen. Incoming call from an unknown number.

"Pick up."

Everything in her told her not to. Her hand shook slightly as she answered, keeping her voice as quiet as possible. "Hello?"

"You were warned not to contact the police!"

Her skin turned cold and clammy, a hard knot lodging in her throat at that angry male voice. "I didn't." "This is on your conscience."

With that chilling declaration the man on the other end stopped talking.

Carmela shot a helpless look over her shoulder at Charles when the screams started. She didn't speak Italian, but even she understood the plea for mercy in the other man's voice through the phone. His chilling screams were cut short with an angry growl, and then a wet gurgling sound filled the line, replacing everything with absolute silence.

"Now his blood is on your hands," the captor roared.

Carmela dropped the phone and covered her mouth with her hands, backing away from it like it was a coiled rattlesnake. She shrank back against Charles and squeezed her eyes shut, horror and denial blotting out everything else.

No. No, she couldn't take this. Couldn't be responsible for Aisha's father's death.

Cursing, Charles pushed her to the side and slammed the heel of his combat boot down on her phone, shattering it.

In the echoing silence that followed, Carmela couldn't breathe. Couldn't see through the blinding haze of tears spilling down her cheeks.

"Move." He pulled on her arm, but she resisted, feeling frozen inside, still staring at the phone, her mind wanting to refute what she'd just heard. They'd just killed Aisha's father, slit his throat, she was certain, because of her.

Charles swore again and got in front of her, took her face in his hands and tilted her head back until she was forced to look into his eyes.

"We must keep running. They just traced your cell phone, Carmela. They're hunting us right now. Our only chance is to get out of here and get to the trucks before they find us."

The words barely penetrated the paralyzing numbness. How could they get out? They'd managed to trace her cell. Maybe the police were involved. Maybe the entire police force was in on this and one of them would shoot them at the next checkpoint they approached.

She realized with a start that they were moving again, though she hadn't been conscious of doing so. They rushed past a confusing flurry of colors and sounds.

She was distantly aware of her legs moving, of her heart throbbing, her shallow breaths echoing in her head.

Shaking herself, she swiped at the tears covering her cheeks and picked up her pace, driven by survival instinct alone. With every step she was aware that they were the prey, that the predators were in the shadows, closing in on them. A strangled sob caught in her throat, the edge of hysteria nipping at her.

"We're okay," Charles said calmly, guiding her through the confusing tangle of streets. "Gage has us on GPS, he's guiding us out. Just a few more minutes."

She held onto that hope and broke into a jerky rush, struggling to keep up with his longer strides.

They weren't running; she couldn't have anyway, and running would draw more attention. The streets in this part of town were full of people running out of their homes, trying to figure out what the explosion had been.

Carmela stumbled on a stone and went down, knees hitting the paved street, her free hand scraping along the stones. Charles hauled her to her feet.

"Come on, sweetheart. Almost there."

The sweet talk and gentle tone he used threatened to close her throat up.

She choked on another sob and kept going, all her senses sharpened.

"Where are you?" Charles asked Gage in a clipped voice. She didn't hear Gage's response but Charles's next words sent yet another wave of terror breaking over her.

"Be ready with cover, just in case. We've got more company."

Jesus! No more. She wanted out of here, out of New York entirely. She wanted to go home and be safe, back where things made sense. Despite her quivering thigh muscles she forced her uncooperative body into a jog.

"Good girl," Charles praised. "Almost there." He lied. Covering the remaining distance seemed to take forever.

By the time they finally reached the checkpoint, she was done caring about anything but getting to the SUVs. She could see them parked just beyond the barricade, the rear door of the first one swinging open. The armed guards seemed to part when they saw them coming.

Carmela's field of vision narrowed to that open door as she put on a final burst of speed. Charles pushed her in front of him and turned and she didn't look back.

No one tried to stop her, which was good because she would have attacked them with everything she had.

She cleared the barricade and raced for the truck, catching sight of Gage's face in the driver's window. He was watching her, tracking her progress. Hard footfalls behind her told her Charles was there. She ran for that open door and dove into it. Her palms and knees met leather.

Strong hands grabbed her hips and shoved her forward across the seat. The door slammed shut, the tires squealed as Gage hit the gas. The weight of Charles's arm across her back was both protective and reassuring. Out. They were out. Safe, and Aisha's father was still dead. Her system finally hit overload. Cheek pressed tight against the leather seat, Carmela curled into a ball and dissolved.

Chapter 14

Being Selfish

Charles kept a hand braced on Carmela's back as Gage took a sharp right and floored it. He secured her to stop her from sliding across the seat, felt her shuddering with the force of her sobs. Those heartbroken sounds cut straight through him, more unbearable because she was trying so hard to hold them back.

Ah, shit. Just…shit. With Gage in the vehicle, they had no privacy but he couldn't take watching her hurt like this. Charles rubbed a soothing hand over her back in a gentle circle, not knowing what to say. There was nothing he could say to make this any easier on her.

At his touch, she curled further into herself and turned her face away, burying it in her arms to hide from him, as though ashamed of him seeing her crying.

Something sharp twisted in his chest and a burning pressure took hold of his lungs. Holding his hip close to hers, he slid his hands beneath her shoulders and pulled her upward. She resisted, throwing one arm out and attempting to rush away from him.

"No, come here," he said softly, ignoring her wordless struggle. Those little hitching gasps were killing him.

He drew her up and dragged her straight into his lap, her legs resting along the seat. Carmela immediately brought her knees up and curled into him, sliding her arms around his back to grip fistfuls of his shirt, her face jammed into his shoulder.

Biting back a curse, he wrapped one arm around her ribs and buried his other hand in her hair to hold her close. He might not be able to make it go away, but he could at least hold her and let her know she wasn't alone.

Pressing his cheek against her hair he sighed deeply, having no clue what else he could do for her except get her on the first flight out in the morning.

Up front he heard Gage talking to someone on the phone, probably Tom.

"We're on our way back." A pause. "Charles, any injuries?"

"Negative." At least, not physical ones. The kind they could do something about.

"They're good," Gage said. Then, with a bite to his tone, "No, Charles's busy right now. He'll have to call you back."

Charles appreciated Gage's judgment. Tom was likely climbing the walls right now, wanting Intel and answers, but Charles didn't care. Carmela had reached her limit and his only priority now was taking care of her. Let the police and ISI work on this case for a while. They were the ones who'd fucked everything up anyway.

Carmela took a shuddering breath and held on, still cuddled into him like a terrified kitten. It hurt him to see her so scared and broken. A few days ago, he would have put some space between them. He'd have put her in her own seat and buckled her in it, then left her to cry it out alone.

There was no way he could do any of that now. He held her tighter instead.

Maybe it made him a selfish bastard, but he didn't want to let her go.

Couldn't. Not while she so clearly needed him. He was still jacked up from the adrenaline rush and holding a soft, trusting woman while coming down from that high was a hell of a lot better than anything else he'd ever tried. It was Carmela in his arms only made it a thousand times better.

Though he was the one holding her, the truth was she eased him as much as he eased her. The interior of the vehicle was silent except for the hum of the engine and the little breathless sighs Carmela made as her tears faded. He didn't let go of her or ease the pressure of his hold, savoring this chance to have her wrapped up in his arms.

She felt so soft and fragile, and she smelled good despite the sweat drying on her skin. She wasn't for him, Charles understood that because they lived in different worlds, but being able to hold her like this when she was down and defenseless made him ache for something more.

His actions spoke way louder than words. He'd seen firsthand how caring and dedicated she was. Tonight, she'd showed him the hard core inside her in the willingness to come to New York, then the ability to come through under pressure. She'd earned his undying admiration in the process.

Charles pressed his face into her hair, breathed in the scent of her shampoo.

I'm right here, baby. I've got you. This trip was going to change her forever no matter how much therapy she had, and he hated knowing that. Most of all he hated the thought of losing her forever once she boarded that plane a few hours from now.

Carmela seemed to sag against him. Eventually her shifting breaths evened out, growing slow and deep, and her body turned careless against him as exhaustion took its toll.

Charles eased her into a more comfortable position and leaned his head back against the head rest, expelling a long breath.

"Is she out?" Gage asked quietly a moment later.

"Yeah." For that, he was grateful. She needed the rest and he needed the pardon to figure out what the hell to do about her.

He'd never been good with emotional stuff, and that was doubly true for when it involved a woman. He just didn't speak the language. It was easier for him to just lock it all in a box and walk away rather than walk through all that shit.

Being in touch with his softer side was Gage's gift, not his, and right now Charles was envious of that ability. Somehow Gage knew how to put people at ease and understood how to comfort a woman.

Ironic how those same qualities hadn't done him much good in his personal life, wasn't it?

Charles closed his eyes and focused on the feel of Carmela draped against him.

Gage should be the one back here with her. He'd know what to do, what to say when she woke. Then, Charles would have to rip the fucker's throat out for getting to hold her like this.

"For a homemade bomb, that was one hell of an explosion," Gage commented, his voice just loud enough to carry back to Charles.

He grunted and glanced down to make sure Carmela was sleeping before he answered. Her lashes were wet and stomped together, silvery trails streaking her cheeks. He wanted to wipe them away but was afraid to wake her.

"They called her cell phone."

He caught Gage's frown in the rearview mirror. "They trace it via cell tower?"

"Maybe. Or they could've hacked into Italians' database. Guy behind this is damn bright, and he sent the initial e-mail through the site."

"Or they might have help in the ISI or someone else in the government,"

Gage murmured. Yeah, or that. Of all the possible scenarios, that scared him the most.

If the Italians were involved on some level, who the hell knew how far the corruption went up the government chain of command? "The caller blamed the explosion on her for reporting the address to the police, then killed the hostage with a knife while she was listening." He'd never forget that look on her face.

She'd blamed herself for that death and there was nothing Charles or anyone else could say to convince her otherwise. Gage's frown transformed into an incensed scowl. "You destroy the phone?"

Charles nodded.

"The victim was Aisha's father, the girl she was protecting at the school." Gage swore under his breath. Charles stroked a hand over the tangle of Carmela's hair, feeling useless. She felt so much, cared too much. He had no idea how to help her through this.

"Since I've got my hands full, will you call Tom for me?"

"You lucky you. Sure." He connected to Tom using the hands-free device and gave him the update, keeping the call off speaker phone for Carmela's sake.

"He's still busy," Gage said a few moments later. "He'll have to call you back when we get to the hotel."

Charles half smiled at that because it was damn funny to imagine the look on his boss's face. Tom wasn't used to being told no, about anything, let alone by one of his own guys.

"Hey, ask him to arrange an earlier flight for Carmela when he gets a minute." He'd feel better with a last-minute change in case anyone from the cell tried to track her and had somehow found out about her original flight.

Gage repeated it to Tom and responded a moment later with, "He says he'd be happy to." Like hell he had. Charles grinned anyway. "So, where're we going to stay now?"

He asked when Gage ended the call. His second-in-command knew the city better than any of them.

"Well, they got our plate numbers, so depending on who's involved with all this, we could have a big problem. How do you want to handle it?"

"Let's switch vehicles with the boys before we hit the city limits, then split up and stop at a few different hotels before we settle on one.

You guys can ditch the trucks once you drop Carmela and me off. WE must get new wheels by morning."

"Roger that."

Carmela sighed in her sleep and shifted in his lap, setting off inevitable reaction with his dick. He was keyed up, his body all too aware that she was the perfect release. He stayed still, tormented by the feel and scent of her, and she settled under again. "So how come you keep passing up being team leader?" he asked Gage a few minutes later. He knew Tom had approached him with the offer multiple times and he'd always turned it down.

Charles watched in the rearview as Gage's mouth curved in a mocking smile.

"Don't want the responsibility that comes with that job, thanks. Guess I can't kick my master sergeant days because I still like being the team dad too much to let it go. Though I got to say, from where I'm sitting, the perks of being team leader looks good right about now."

He smiled into Carmela's hair, but it quickly faded. Time was running out to lock down this cell. There was a calculation coming, and he wanted Carmela to be far away from here when it happened. If he only had a few hours left with her, once they had some privacy, he was going to make every minute of them count.

Carmela stood beneath the spray of hot water from the showerhead, hands braced on the slick fiberglass wall, her forehead resting against the backs of her fingers.

A little over two hours ago she'd survived yet another bombing then listened to the sound of an innocent man's throat being slit. The same thing that had been done to her father, and maybe even by the same hands. Ever since his death she'd imagined a thousand times what he must have gone through, but hearing the real thing tonight across the phone line was too horrific to bear.

Blowing out a breath, she stretched the taut muscles in her neck. It was the middle of the night. She'd woken when the team had reached Islamabad to change vehicles, and after that it had been a blur of traffic and hotels as they searched for a safe place to stay. Hunter had checked them in and whisked her straight up to the room without saying anything to her.

There were no more tears to be shed. She'd cried them out in painful bursts on the drive back before crashing in Hunter's lap. Now she just felt hollow and alone.

She let the water beat down on her shoulders and neck, grateful for the warmth, grateful for being alive yet feeling guilty because of it. Charles was out there in the room right now, conferencing with Tom and the rest of the team.

She was done. There was nothing more to say now and the last thing she wanted to do was talk to anyone, even Charles. No matter what anyone said, Aisha's father had died because of her tonight.

She swallowed hard. It didn't matter that Carmela had risked her life by going to the city with Charles or that they'd tried their best to meet the deadline. It didn't even matter that the police were the ones who had screwed up and triggered the bombing.

The result was the same. Now, Aisha was left to suffer the same grief Carmela had gone through just weeks before. Only worse, because while Carmela's father had left part of his estate to her, Aisha and her family faced a long winter in that harsh valley with their primary and maybe only source of income gone.

Giving them money might slat off starvation for a time, but it wouldn't fill this new hole in their lives. She didn't know how else to help them.

Squeezing her eyes shut, she forced herself to take a steadying breath. The shower door clicked open behind her. She straightened with a gasp, immediately covering herself with her arms.

Charles stood in the opening, stark naked. He was staring right into her eyes, and his rigid expression made her breath catch. Before she could move, he stepped inside and shut the door behind him without breaking eye contact, taking up all the remaining space in the enclosure.

His heated gaze broke from hers to trail down her naked body, past her arms crossed over her breasts and down to her ass. When he dragged his eyes back to her face and she saw the melted hunger burning there, a sudden yearning roared to life inside her, so strong she turned and wound her arms around him.

He caught her to him in a fierce hug, burying his face in her wet hair. Carmela held on and concentrated on breathing through the sudden bombardment of sensation. He was hot, hard. It was as if her body was starved for his touch, every nerve ending in her skin suddenly hypersensitive. He was so strong. With every inhalation she breathed in more of that soapy, lemony scent that clung to him.

The feel of those steely arms around her, holding her close to his powerful chest, made her feel safe and cherished. But the way he held her made it clear he needed her just as badly.

This wasn't just physical, not for either of them. She felt his emotional response to her as clearly as if it were her own. Every touch, every snuggle was loaded with a need and tenderness that made her throat tighten.

Tangling her fingers in his wet hair, she tilted her face up and sought his mouth with hers. His hands clenched in her curls as he kissed her, sliding his tongue inside the moment she opened for him.

The kiss was hungry and desperate, yet she could feel the gentleness in him, the most primal part of him held back. His big body played with tension; his muscles locked tight.

She rubbed against him, gasped at the sensation of her nipples rubbing against his naked chest. She wanted him to let go and give her everything, melt the freezing core of ice inside her.

In response Charles growled low in his throat, a raw sound that vibrated over her skin and made the hair on her arms stand up as it spiraled through her. In a single, fluid rush he backed her up against the slick wall and pinned her there, then blazed a path of kisses down her jaw to her neck.

She sucked in a breath and threw her head back, shoving his face harder against her. Delicious shivers spread in the wake of his mouth as it traveled to the tender juncture of her neck and shoulder.

Sparks of heat cascaded across her skin. The scrape of his beard and teeth were like a whip, driving her closer to the release she needed. His big hands slid up from her hips to cup her breasts, lifting and pushing them together for easier access.

Arching her back, Carmela offered herself to him, head falling back when his hot, moist mouth closed over one aching center and sucked. A high, thin cry broke from her throat.

He took his time despite the desire driving him, working her with his mouth until she began to tremble, the ache between her thighs becoming an urgent pounding she was desperate to ease.

She twisted in his grip, loving the erotic contrast of all that strength holding her in place and the tenderness of his lips and tongue on her body. He was worshipping her, and he wanted her to know it. Her throat ached as she cradled his head to her, little cries of pleasure slipping out.

Charles went to his knees in front of her and released her breasts to slide his hands over the curve of her waist and grip her hips. He squeezed her flesh and pressed his face hard against her abdomen, conveying his own need and desperation without a word.

Carmela stroked his hair and started to kneel with him when he raised his head and stopped her with a stare so melted the breath backed up in her lungs. Her knees wobbled.

Straightening, she leaned back against the wall and gazed down into his eyes, letting him see her consent. He shifted his gaze to his right hand, watching with an absorbed expression as it travels back and forth over her damp skin just above the trimmed strip of hair that covered her mound.

Under the power of his stare the ache between her legs intensified. Her heart pounded and she bit her lip as she waited for him to touch her where she needed him so badly.

His expression was intent, absorbed as he studied her most intimate place. She was too turned on to blush or feel embarrassed by his inspection. The muscles in her thighs and belly were pulled tight in anticipation of that first touch.

When he brushed his fingers over her folds and found the wetness there, he groaned and lifted that amber stare to hers.

"Charles," she whispered unevenly, the pleasure twisting like a knife inside her until she was on the limit of begging. He locked his gaze on hers and leaned forward to kiss just above where his fingers caressed. Her breath hitched, her heart slamming against her breastbone.

The desire was overpowering, simultaneously drawing her body tight and sapping the strength from her muscles.

With a wicked sparkle in his eyes, he parted his lips and touched his tongue to her softness. The hand on her hip contracted when she whined and shifted her hips forward. More.

She tightened her hold in his hair in a silent plea and this time he stopped teasing. Closing his eyes, Charles settled his mouth over her and stroked his tongue across her aching flesh. Soft. Slow. As if he wanted to make this last for hours.

Her quiet cry of desperation and pleasure echoed in the shower stall. The muscles in her legs trembled so much she was afraid they'd give out but Charles's solid grip on her right hip held her still as he made her mindless.

She could hardly breathe, overwhelmed by the uncontrollable wave rising inside her. His tongue was like velvet against her most sensitive place. The pleasure was immediate and huge, each erotic caress sending her further up the crest gathering inside her.

Then he moved away from her most sensitive place, lower, and slid his tongue into her. In and out in firm, rhythmic strokes until her knees shook and she was tugging on his head to bring him up to where she truly needed him. He followed the motion, gliding that wicked tongue up and over her pulsing clit.

Shockwaves of sensation radiated everywhere. Her head fell back, eyes sliding closed as he continued to cherish her with his mouth. She was panting, mewling for more when he eased two fingers into her core and hit a spot that made her see stars.

"God," she moaned, holding on top of his head for fear he'd stop. In answer he made a low sound of reassurance and sucked gently at the rigid bundle of nerves as he stroked her inner hot spot.

Carmela gripped his hair and pushed closer to that maddening tongue, needing him so badly she couldn't stand it. Her body was shaking now, a rapid tremor she couldn't control. His tongue was so soft and warm, so patient, his fingers hard and demanding inside her.

The combined caresses built the worrying ache to an almost painful level, leaving her swollen and sore. Desperate.

She rocked her hips against his face, demanding her pleasure now, refusing to let him stop. A quick twist of his head and his mouth was gone, his fingers pulling away. "No" she cried in protest, but the words were lost in a passionate kiss as he rocketed to his feet and took her mouth.

He fisted one hand in her hair, the other gripping her bottom, lifting her against him so she could feel the imprint of his erection against her belly. She tasted her own essence on his tongue along with his near desperation, and forgave him for tormenting her. Wrapping one leg around his hip, she reached one hand down to caress the scalding length of his cock, curling her fingers around him.

Carmela shook and groaned into her mouth, then pulled back to nip at her lips. "Turn around." His voice was deep, rough. Breathless, she lowered her foot and did as he said, bracing her palms against the wall and tossing her wet hair back to look at him over her shoulder.

His expression was almost wild as he devoured the sight of her awaiting his possession. To tempt him further she spread her legs and arched her back to tilt her ass up.

His sharply withdrawn breath was a reward, but it was nothing compared to when he seized her hips and his fingers bit deep into her flesh, holding her still.

Then he leaned in and nuzzled the side of her neck, right where he knew she was most sensitive, and scraped his teeth over her skin. She pressed back against him and rubbed her ass against his cock.

With a low growl, he reached over to the small shelf and snagged the condom she hadn't realized he'd brought in, then rolled it on. Setting one forearm against the wall, he turned back to her and laced his fingers through hers.

"Want you," he whispered against her ear, wracking another shiver out of her.

Unable to speak, she turned her face toward him and wanted his mouth.

Charles cradled the side of her face with his free hand and kissed her so thoroughly she couldn't breathe before pulling away. With gentle pressure on the back of her skull, he urged her head forward until her cheek rested against their joined hands, then gripped her hips and pulled them back, opening her to him completely.

She felt the hot, hard pressure of him against her folds and closed her eyes, dying for the moment when he entered her. He only pressed an inch or two inside her and stopped. Carmela groaned at the delicious teasing, the heavy stretching that somehow both soothed and intensified the pounding inside her.

She tried to press down and take more but he stopped her with an implacable grip on her hip and leaned in to deliver an open-mouthed kiss into the curve of her shoulder, his front plastered against her back.

Melting, she sighed and relaxed in his arms. The moment she did he bit down on the place he'd just been kissing and thrust deep.

Carmela shook and squeezed her eyes shut as a husky cry ripped out of her.

He was huge inside her, filling and stretching every aching inch of her with his hot, hard length.

Roaring in satisfaction, he began to pump in and out of her with a smooth, steady rhythm. He slid his hand from her hip around between her thighs to stroke her swollen clit.

She shuddered at the lash of pleasure. So good. Trapped between him and the shower wall, Carmela could do nothing but hang on for the ride. Her fingers clenched around his and her head fell back as pure ecstasy burned through her.

The tender stroke of his fingers matched each internal glide of his cock, turning her liquid with ecstasy. She dimly heard her own moans as they reflected off the enclosing walls and knew she sounded out of control but didn't care.

All that mattered was this. Charles dropping deep inside of her, holding her so close that she could feel every inch of his body against hers. The orgasm rose swift and hard, flinging her up until she was mindless with the need for release. She turned wild, fighting to hit herself onto his driving cock, make him fuck her harder as those skillful fingers rubbed her clit.

He pushes again. The climax slammed into her and sent her flying, fragmenting into a thousand sparkling shards of sensation. She could hear her broken moan of release as it beat through her, traveling throughout her body in endless ripples.

When they finally began to fade, she collapsed against the wall, trembling, too weak to move. The only thing holding her up was Charles. He was pressing soothing kisses across the tops of her shoulders, his hands and weight locking her in place.

Her eyes flew open when he began to withdraw. She was sure he hadn't come yet. Forcing her careless muscles to cooperate she pushed up a few inches from the wall and looked over her shoulder at him.

As if he'd been waiting for her to do just that, he seized her and turned her around to face him, those strong hands curving around her bottom to lift her.

Automatically she brought her legs around his waist and wrapped her arms around his robust shoulders, kissing him with every bit of longing and gratitude in her.

Charles gave a low growl against her mouth and positioned his cock at her entrance, plunging his tongue deep into her mouth as he drove home into her body.

She caught her breath at the forceful penetration, whimpered at the feel of him fixed so deep inside her and began to rock, her tired thigh muscles quivering in protest.

Charles took her with rough, urgent thrusts, plundering her mouth as well as her body. Beneath her splayed hands she could feel the acute tension in him, his muscles quivering with the need for release.

Wanting to ease him and give him the same pleasure he'd so unselfishly bestowed upon her, Carmela locked her ankles in the small of his back and began to ride him, rotating her hips in little circles. He sucked in a harsh breath and reared his head back, eyes closed, expression tortured.

Fascinated, loving the sense of power it gave her to pleasure such a powerful man, she covered his face with kisses and worked him with her body.

The muscles in his chest and shoulders stood out in sharp relief, his jaw clenched tight. He opened his eyes to stare at her, his gaze glittering with possession and lust.

"Carmela," he ground out, almost a warning. "Let go," she whispered, circling her hips once more, squeezing the rigid length of him with her internal muscles. "Let me see you."

His nostrils flared, his eyes darkening to a liquid amber a split second before he closed them and let his head fall back. His breathing was rough, his hands urging her to move faster, take more of him.

Sliding him deep, she held him there with all her strength and made three slow, tortuous circles with her hips. A low, shattered moan tore out of him. He arched up into her, his hands digging so deep into her as she knew he'd leave marks, and shuddered against her as he began to come. She rejoiced in every moment of it, wrapping herself around him as close as she could, her face tucked into the curve of his neck.

The hot water drummed down on them in a soothing, relaxing rhythm.

Breathing in his delicious, clean scent, she sighed when he finally relaxed and rested his head on her shoulder with a long exhalation.

It took a while for his breathing to slow and finally he pulled back to look at her. With one hand he reached up and stroked the strands of wet hair that had stuck to her cheek. His eyes met hers. They were soft with satisfaction and tenderness.

"You're so beautiful."

If he could say that while she was naked, and her eyes were red and puffy from crying and what little makeup she'd been wearing was long gone, then it meant a lot. When he smiled down at her before leaning in to kiss her lips gently, her heart rolled over in her chest.

Chapter 15

New Experience

Face buried in Carmela's neck; Charles fought to slow his thundering heart.

He'd never experienced anything like that in his life. He loved sex, always had, but this was so much more than sex it had rocked him to his core.

Sweet Jesus.

Whatever this emotional and physical connection between them was, he wanted more of it with Carmela. As much as he could have before he put her on that plane in a few hours.

Being with her was the only thing that truly eased the constant bombardment of guilt and restlessness he'd felt since the night Scottie died.

She was still wound around him, holding him deep inside her and he didn't want to break the connection. Carmela's legs and arms were trembling with fatigue, and he didn't want her to be uncomfortable for even a moment longer.

He eased out of her and gently unwound her legs from his waist, noting the wince she tried to cover when he set her feet on the shower floor. He paused again, to stroke his hands through her damp hair that clung to her cheeks and shoulders in little ringlets. Her eyes were half closed, her mouth swollen and wet from his kisses. He'd used her hard and selfishly just now, yet she still gazed up at him with that soft expression he was becoming addicted to.

"Are you okay?" Little late to ask now, but he still felt the need to.

She smiled, a slow, supremely satisfied feminine smile, and tilted her head.

"So much better than okay."

He was relieved to hear it, but her legs were still unsteady. "Come here," he murmured, and drew her under the spray. Holding her against his chest, he smoothed his hands over her hair, shoulders and back.

She rested her cheek against his breastbone and hummed in pleasure whenever he touched her. God, he'd never felt this kind of closeness before. She seemed to like it even more when he massaged shampoo into her hair, his fingers rubbing at her scalp. She was like a kitten, purring and moving against his hands, all soft and trusting.

It set off a pang inside him because he wasn't sure he deserved that kind of trust anymore. His best friend had trusted him with his life, and Charles had failed him.

Logically he knew it wasn't his fault. He just couldn't get past the guilt that said he should have done something more. That he could have done something more and Scottie would still be here.

Locking the thought down in an airtight box, Charles rinsed Carmela's hair and began soaping up her skin. He glided his palms over the wet silk of it, enjoying every moment of the easy silence between them and the hot water washing over their bodies.

She was half asleep against him by the time he washed all the suds away and shut off the water. He opened the shower door to snag a towel and wrapped her up in it before scooping her up and carrying her out to the bed.

She let out a soft laugh and wound an arm around his neck, her other hand tracing over the frog bones tattoo on his right shoulder. "I haven't been carried to bed since I was a kid."

"No? Long overdue then." None of the guys she'd dated had done this. What the hell kind of dipshits had she gone out with? The primal part of him loved being the first to do this.

After settling her against the pillows, he withdrew the towel so she could dry her hair and slid in beside her to draw the thick covers over them both. The clock on the night table read one forty am, its bright green digital display and the light coming from the bathroom giving just enough illumination for him to see her expression in the darkness. She looked happy. Satisfaction slid through him that he'd put that look on her face.

Tossing the towel aside, Carmela rolled onto her side and laid her head on the pillow, a little smile on her lips. "You're quite the romantic when you want to be."

Her comment coaxed an ironic chuckle out of him. "Yeah, romance isn't my strong point."

She reached out and laid a hand against his chest, rubbing the spot over his heart in little circles. "That's okay. You have more than enough of those already to make up for it."

His heart squeezed at the sincerity in her words. She was getting to him more and more with each passing minute, and though it made him self-centered bastard and it would hurt worse the longer he let this go on, he didn't want to put distance between them now.

A low buzz from behind him signaled an incoming text. Carmela tensed as he rolled over to grab the phone from the night table on his side. It was from Tom.

"You're now booked on a flight leaving at oh-nine hundred," he told her, replacing the phone and turning it back to her.

She was quiet for a moment, watching him in the near darkness. Then she inched closer to lay her hand on his chest again and he felt the tension melt out of his muscles. "I wish you could come back with me," she said quietly.

Ah, hell, there it was. He'd been hoping to avoid this conversation, not wanting to ruin the last few hours of their time together, but maybe it would be kinder to set things straight right now. He snaked an arm around her back in a possessive move, in direct conflict with his answer. "I can't. I'll be working over here for the next two weeks." He wanted to leave it at that, not have to come straight out and say this was all they could ever have.

She nodded and continued to rub those gentle circles on his skin. "So…you going to respond if I e-mail you after this?"

"Of course, I will." Jesus, he wasn't a total asshole, just…relationship challenged, and considering the logistics of things, couldn't offer her anything beyond the next few hours.

With a hard sigh, Charles edged nearer and looped an arm tighter around the curve of her waist, drawing her closer. "I've never been much good at long-term relationships, let alone a long distance one, and I don't want to hurt you by not being up front about that." She'd been through more than enough shit already.

"Okay, thanks for the heads up."

The ironic edge to her response made something tighten inside him. "Hey."

He slid his other arm beneath her neck, buried his hand in her damp hair to pull her face into his neck. She didn't resist, snuggling into his body, her curves melding into him and her breath washing over his skin in warm puffs. Sheer heaven.

"I never expected any of this to happen," he admitted finally.

"Me neither." She hooked a thigh over his, wriggled until she was pressed flush against him from neck to knees.

Yeah, he'd bet she hadn't. While he wouldn't say it, she was the only woman who had ever tempted him to want something long term. "Just so you know, I've never done this before."

Carmela pulled her head back slightly to look up into his face. "Done what?

Cuddle afterward?"

"No," he said on a laugh, then sobered. "Getting involved with the principal on a job."

"Oh." She dropped her head back down. "Will this get you in trouble with Tom?"

"I don't know." He didn't care if it did. Nothing on earth could have made him walk away from her tonight.

"I wasn't planning on saying anything to him."

"I'm pretty sure he knows already."

Charles was betting that's why Tom had just texted the flight details, rather than calling. It was his way of not condoning the relationship per se, but at least accepting it.

Carmela sighed softly and looped her arm around his ribs to stroke his back.

Up, down, up, down, in a gentle, relaxing rhythm. He was supposed to be the one comforting her, and instead she was soothing him. He fumbled for something to say. Should he bring up what had happened in New York and let her talk it out, or act like it never happened?

"I'm glad you're here with me right now," she whispered against his skin. "I feel safe with you next to me."

Ah, Jesus. Charles closed his eyes as the knife twisted harder between his ribs.

After tonight, he wouldn't be there to hold her in the dark when she had nightmares. And she would have them. By taking her to New York tonight he'd almost gotten her killed, and for what?

They'd lost the cell and the hostage. He nuzzled the top of her head, her damp curls catching on his stubble.

"Good. Think you can sleep for a while now?" He hoped so because she needed it. Plus, it would spare them any more of this intense conversation he didn't want to continue.

"Not sure. I'm tired, but I can't stop thinking. Does that happen to you?"

"Yeah." All the time.

"So how do you deal with it?"

"Depends on what's causing it. With practice you learn to block most of it out." He let his fingertips glide over the small of her back, exploring the delicate indent of her spine there.

She tipped her head back to rest her cheek against his shoulder. "Most of it," she repeated slowly. "But not all of it."

Shit. He avoided her gaze in the dimness, fighting the urge to pull away.

"No."

"And what do you do with the rest of it?"

He didn't want to answer that, but he wouldn't lie to her and shatter this fragile intimacy between them. "I'll let you know when I figure it out."

Carmela stared at him for several long seconds, then surprised him by leaning up to place a slow, soft kiss on his lips. His hand automatically tightened on her hair but she eased away before he could deepen the contact. Her left hand kept up that gentle caress over his bare back, sweeping from shoulder blade to hip.

She was quiet for a long time, the only sounds in the room their quiet breathing and the hum of the air conditioning unit beneath the window.

"I don't know what to do now," she said finally. "My whole reason for coming here was to finish what my father started, and instead…"

"Don't," he murmured, squeezing her tight and wishing he could stop the wheels in her head from turning. "Don't do that to yourself. It won't help anything."

She blew out a steadying breath, and when she spoke her voice was rough. "I didn't mean for any of this to happen."

"I know." He kissed her temple, tucked her in close to his body, wishing.

There was something, anything, else he could do to take the pain away. "It's not your fault, and it's not your responsibility anymore. You came over here and tried to make a difference, which is a hell of lot more than most people in your position would be willing to do."

Every time he thought about it, it amazed him.

Seeing that sort of conviction and courage from a civilian was damn rare, at least in his experience.

"I wanted to get those guys. I wanted them to pay."

He understood her need for vengeance perfectly. "And they will. I promise you."

A tiny nod against his shoulder. "Tom knew my father. Did you ever meet him? You never said."

Charles tensed, knowing he was on shaky ground. "No, I never met him."

"He was a good man; we were close. The media's made him out to be rich, reckless philanthropist who acted without thinking, and they're wrong. He wasn't like that.

Stubborn and too opinionated sometimes, but he wanted to make a difference. He lived his life trying to help others."

All he could do was nod and frantically search for a way to change the subject.

"I heard a lot about him." He knew everything about the man.

He'd made it his business to know everything.

Carmela's hand paused on his back. He heard her swallow. "I think what I hate most is that they tried to use him to turn people here against Americans."

Dammit, he didn't want to talk about this. The memories were too fresh. "I know."

"They used his death like a propaganda campaign, spurring riots."

"I know what they did, okay?" Charles pushed away and sat up, turned away from her and sat on the edge of the bed. The sudden silence was so complete that he could hear his pulse drumming in his ears.

"Okay," she said at last, her voice wary, as though she was afraid of upsetting him again. Then quieter. "Sorry."

Ah, Christ. He dragged a hand through his hair and down his face, regretting his lack of control. Letting out a deep sigh, he half turned to look at her. She was propped up on one forearm, the covers clutched over her breasts, her expression uncertain. He felt like an idiot.

"No, look, I'm the one who's sorry," he said, and swung his legs back onto the bed. He leaned his back against the padded headboard, took a deep breath and released it slowly before he continued. "You asked me earlier how I handled.

'The rest of it'. Well, not very well, as it turns out."

Carmela was silent, watching him so intently that he couldn't hide the truth from her any longer despite the potential landmine he was about to step on.

"A good buddy of mine was killed in one of those riots," he said at last.

Her swift intake of breath sliced through the quiet. "Oh my God. I didn't know."

"I realize that."

"What happened?" she asked softly.

"Did you hear about the attack on some foreign diplomats over here a few weeks back? It was all over the news."

She nodded. "Two of them died, along with…an American security contractor," she finished in a whisper, and he knew she was already piecing it together.

"Scottie Easton," Charles said. "My best friend."

Cool, slender fingers touched the clenched fist he'd placed on the sheets. At the contact he let his hand open, and she slid her fingers between his to intertwine them. Charles felt oddly soothed by the gesture. "You were one of the contractors there with him," Carmela finished.

He swallowed. "Yeah."

"I'm so sorry, I had no idea."

She said it with such sincerity, without the overtone of pity that most people would have. He relaxed his shoulders. "Thanks."

Carmela sat up and scooted closer to kneel at his side. The warmth of her body brushed against his. "So, you took this job a few days after being there when your friend died in the riots caused by my father's kidnappers."

"Pretty much, yeah."

She shook her head, searched his eyes. "Why? You must have hated the thought of working with me so soon after that."

A unwilling smile tugged at his mouth. "Well, I wasn't exactly overjoyed."

Charles's first impression of her certainly hadn't done anything to change that, either.

"Then why did you take the job?"

"Tom asked me to lead the team, and he never asks me for anything. I wanted the same thing you did when you came over here."

Her gaze was unflinching. "Justice."

Charles nodded, feeling such an intense bond with her that his heart pounded.

Lifting a hand, he reached out to smooth a stray curl away from her cheek. "I'm going to get it, for Scottie, and for you."

Carmela 2 leaned into his touch and closed her eyes. "It scares me to hear you say that because I don't want anything to happen to you. I don't want to lose anyone else I care about, never like that."

"I don't plan on being a martyr," he said, and stroked his thumb across her cheek, not knowing how to make her understand. "I must see this through. It's who I am."

He'd vowed it silently to Scottie at his funeral. The SEAL in him would accept nothing less than finishing the job. His skill set, his honor and integrity were all he had left from that part of his life.

Charles would rather die than turn his back on a fallen brother and everything he stood for. She swallowed and started to pull away, but not before he felt a trickle of moisture on the pad of his thumb. His heart constricted when he realized she was crying for him. "Hey," he whispered, reaching for her. "It'll be alright."

Carmela, embraced him and pressed her cheek to his, her breasts flush against his chest. "Charles."

"What, baby?" he whispered in her ear. He felt the answering shiver that passed through her in his intimate tone.

"I think I need you to distract me again."

With a soft laugh, he tilted her chin up to look into her eyes. "I'd love to."

Rolling her beneath him, he pressed her into the mattress and gently took her mouth, pushing away the emptiness for just a little longer.

Later, as she was curled against him fast asleep, he eased out of the bed when his phone buzzed with an incoming call.

The moment he saw Claire's name on the display, his pulse accelerated. Careful not to wake Carmela, he went to the bathroom and shut the door before answering. "Hey, beautiful, good to hear from you. You got something?"

"I think so. There's a guy whose name keeps popping up on the militant chat rooms and he's based out of Ronald. He might be linked to some of the known members of the cell, so it's probably worth a shot to track him down and at least check him out."

His heartbeat even faster. "Roger that. Who is he?"

"Not exactly sure yet, but he goes by the handle Joseph 911. I've got a hit where he accessed one of the chat rooms a few days ago, one at a residential address in Philly, and the other looks to be an engineering firm in New York. I'm sending you both addresses by e-mail."

"This is why I love you, Claire."

She snorted. "Yeah, well, your love could get me in some major shit if I keep digging. Speaking of shit, how's it going over there?"

"It's been…interesting. Never a dull moment, you know?"

A pause. "Everyone okay?"

"We're good. Anxious to get hunting though."

"I'll bet. Good luck. Sorry I couldn't get anything else, but like I said, digging any deeper would cause all kinds of grief for me."

"Understood. I appreciate you taking the risk for us." Though they both knew why she'd done it, and it wasn't for him. She'd done it for

Gage, break up or not, which was why Tom had wanted him to call in the favor personally.

"It's okay. You take care of yourself."

"You too."

The e-mail came in before he'd ended the call and he dialed Ellis. The sniper answered on the first ring, his voice betraying only a hint of grogginess.

Charles got right to the point. "I've got a couple of addresses for you to check out. I will start with the residence, then move to the workplace. If anything looks promising, let me know."

"Roger that, chief."

Charles hung up and called Gage next to give him the news. "Ellis and Dunphy are starting at the residence. Wouldn't be a bad idea for you to try the engineering firm while they're checking it out."

"You sure?"

"Yeah. I've got to get Carmela to the airport by oh-seven hundred. I'll meet you after I drop her off." Only four hours from now.

The sinking feeling in his gut at the thought of letting her go was far worse now.

Once he ended the call, Charles went back to the bed and carefully slid beneath the sheets.

Carmela was on her side facing away from him, still asleep. He eased forward until his chest was against her back, his thighs cradling the soft swell of her hips and her curls tickling his chin.

She sighed and shifted closer, trusting him even in her sleep. *I could get used to this.* Exhaling a painful breath, Charles wrapped an arm around her and held her close, both dreading and welcoming the dawn that was racing toward them.

Chapter 16

The Escape

Joseph paused during yanking a handful of shirts from the shelf in his tiny closet to wipe the back of one wrist across his sweaty face. Lord, he was soaked. He dragged a small duffel bag from the closet floor and shoved the clothes inside.

No matter how he tried to control it, he couldn't stop his hands from shaking. He hadn't been lying when he'd called in sick to work earlier. He was sick. He'd already thrown up once and his stomach still churned as if it might bring up the light breakfast he'd eaten just before sunrise.

That sick feeling in his gut was why he'd decided to run. The authorities were closing in on him, he felt it. Whether it was the Americans or Italians who eventually took him out was irrelevant at this point.

Joseph had no intention of suffering torture or imprisonment for his part in this operation. He'd already fulfilled his obligation to the organization behind all this and now he wanted out. How could he do that?

You can't. You know you can't. Ignoring the shiver that raced up his spine, he grabbed an extra pair of shoes and stuffed them into the bag for good measure. Once he left this apartment, he could never come back.

He now knew for certain that the TTP cell he'd been in contact with were merely chess pieces in this game. Whoever the man in that warehouse was the other night, he was no lowly militant warlord.

Joseph had done everything they'd asked of him, had led the Bonanno woman to New York, and so far, managed to avoid detection. Now his only chance was to flee while he still could.

He yanked the zipper on the bag closed and headed for the door. Behind him, his smashed computer lay in pieces across the desk and floor, along with its hammered hard drive and SIM card from his old phone.

A new burner phones now rested in his jeans front pocket. He took one last glance around the apartment and out the window above the kitchen sink. The sun was almost up. This time to escape was dropping by the second.

He was halfway down the block in the coolness of the morning air, on his way to a bus station when the muted complaint of a ringtone went off. He nearly jumped out of his skin when he realized it was the phone in his pocket. No one had the number. No one.

There in the middle of the sidewalk as the city came to life with the call to prayer rising from the towers at the local mosque, he cast a frantic glance around. They had eyes on him even now. He felt it.

The damned phone continued to ring in his pocket, the quiet note sounding as loud as an air raid siren to his panicked ears. For a second he considered not answering it, thought about throwing it in the nearest trash can or grinding it to pieces beneath his heel and making a run for it.

He knew it was far too late for that. If they already had his new number, they were close. He wouldn't make it as far as the other side of the city before they found and killed him.

For all he knew, a sniper could have him in his sight at that very moment.

As his heartbeat drummed in his ears, he dragged the phone from his pocket and answered with a husky voice, "Yes?" Frustration and anger pulsed through him.

What did he have to do to get out of this mess?

"Joseph," that familiar chilling voice said. "I'm disappointed that you think so, little of my intelligence. Almost as disappointed as I am to discover you thought you could run from me."

It was the man from the warehouse, and his tone was more sinister for its chiding edge. Fresh beads of perspiration bloomed across Youssef's forehead and beneath his arms.

A cold, sticky sweat borne of fear. "I did what you asked," he argued.

"You did, but unfortunately last night did not go as planned."

Joseph didn't know what that meant, but he knew it wasn't good. He'd seen the footage of the bomb's aftermath on the news last night and had wrongly assumed it meant everything had gone smoothly. His hand tightened around the phone. "What do you want?"

"Walk one block up and turn right. There's a black SUV parked at the curb, waiting to pick you up."

He couldn't help but shoot a glance over his shoulder, back the way he'd come. No, there was no telling how many eyes they had on him. He'd waited too long to make his escape and now he was little more than a five-dollar poker chip in a million-dollar game. Utterly expendable.

The thought made his bowels stir. "What do you want," he repeated, anxiety making his voice sharp.

"Another meeting. What happens after that is up to you."

The line went dead. Joseph stood trembling for a moment, his mind whirling for a solution to the problem, a way out. He found none, save darting into an alley and bolting to the nearest mosque for sanctuary. But he knew they'd find him eventually.

The walk to the SUV was agonizing, and when he got there, he found a big man dressed in khakis and a polo shirt standing beside the vehicle. His head turned toward Joseph, eyes concealed by black wrap-around shades.

Though he half expected to be gunned down with every step, Youssef approached and climbed in the back of the SUV when the man opened the door for him. He jolted when the door slammed shut behind him.

No one said a word to him on the drive across town, this time to a different industrial area. They parked in front of what appeared to be a series of deserted warehouses.

Given how early it was, it didn't surprise him that no one was around.

They escorted him into one of the buildings, bordering him on either side in a show of intimidation, and through it to a dark room at the back that smelled of dust and musty carpeting.

A lamp came to life on the edge of a desk and once again, he found himself face to face with the powerful, goateed Italian man at the center of all this.

"Sit," the man told him without explanation from behind the stainless steel desk, jerking his chin at a plastic chair on the opposite side.

The two guards left the room, and the sound of the door shutting echoed off the walls like a gunshot.

Joseph's knees gave out. He dropped into the uncomfortable seat and waited, barely daring to breathe in the tense stillness. The man regarded him with black, unblinking eyes that seemed to gleam in the dim lamplight.

He didn't make Joseph wait long to find out why he was here.

"Ms. Bonanno escaped both the bombing and Mafia last night," the man told him. "Because the local authorities acted rashly, some of them were killed in the blast along with our men guarding the hostage."

Joseph swallowed and didn't reply. This was bad. Very bad. A faint smile curved one side of the man's mouth during his neatly trimmed facial hair.

"So, you've proven very useful to us with your abilities so far. Now we need something else from you."

Joseph managed a weak shake of his head, his insides trembling. "I'm an engineer, good with numbers."

"And very good with computers," the man added. "Though not as good as some of my people are."

He straightened at the desk and regarded Joseph with a curious expression. "You realize at this point that we can't let you go, yes?"

Joseph felt the blood drain from his face, leaving him dizzy and sick. Hearing the words aloud set off a burst of denial and panic.

"How this plays out is your choice." The man reached down to open a drawer with a shriek squeal of metal on metal. Joseph's skin crawled as the man withdrew something and set it on top of the desk. A soft black case made of material, rolled up to conceal whatever lay inside. The man let his hand pass over the top of it, almost a caress. One edge of the material fell away to expose something silver and shiny in the lamplight.

It glinted against the black cloth, the sight of the stainless-steel surgical instrument making Joseph's heart rise into his throat. The man smiled faintly, as though he enjoyed Joseph's obvious fear.

"I can force your cooperation if I must," he continued in that deadly, silky tone.

"However, I'd prefer you continue to work with us by choice. If not..." He left the sentence dangling, the threat already open.

"What is it I have to do?" Joseph managed through bloodless lips.

"Find the woman. She's somewhere in New York, and you will locate her for us."

He removed his hand from the case of instruments, the sparkle of steel still visible. "You will also find their location for us. There is a team assembled and ready to launch the attack. We need her position first."

Those eyes hardened. "We think she'll be at a higher end hotel in the city because of the added security. Her bodyguards will be scrambling to get her out of the country as soon as possible, and we want to avoid having to make an attack at the airport because of all the extra security measures there.

You have only a few hours to complete the job, otherwise it will be too late. Either lead us to her, or you are of no further use to me."

He drew a finger along the line of exposed steel, and in that moment, Joseph knew he'd do whatever it took to avoid death at this man's hands.

"Now." He rolled the instruments up and placed the case back into the drawer. Again, the screech and grind of metal as he closed it, and Joseph couldn't help but draw back as the man rounded the desk.

"You'll need a ride back into the city." He gestured for Joseph to precede him out the door.

Joseph wasn't sure how he got to the SUV, because his legs were like rubber. The man slid in beside him in the back seat and lounged there with one arm stretched across the back of it as though he hadn't a care in the world. "Back to his place," he told the driver.

Joseph didn't dare tell him there was no point, that he had no way of starting his search there because he'd already destroyed his computer and smart phone. What was he going to do? They'd be watching his every move. If he left, they'd assume he was running and be killed.

The minutes ticked past with agonizing slowness. As they reached the outskirts of Joseph's neighborhood, the man next to him stopped scrolling through something on his phone and spoke.

"Your mother looked very tired this morning," he remarked. "Is she sick? Maybe her houseguests have kept her from getting enough rest."

Joseph's heart stopped beating as the man held out the phone and showed a picture of his mother. The shot was so clear it must have been taken with a powerful telephoto lens.

She was standing in the kitchen where Joseph grew up, cooking something for all the family members who had stayed with his parents last night. From the timing of the guests' arrival and the darkness outside the kitchen window, the photo had been taken before sunrise this morning.

Joseph swallowed back the grief and guilt that threatened to choke him. The threat was clear. If he didn't comply with their every demand, they'd kill his family.

"Please. Don't hurt her. She knows nothing of this. Nothing." She would be devastated if she found out. His father would disown him for the shame it would bring upon their family.

The man made a noise. "I would only harm an innocent woman as a last resort. You're the one who determines her fate, Joseph, not I."

A hot rush of tears blurred his eyes. He blinked them back and took a steadying breath. "My office," he blurted. "I need to go to my office to get what you need."

"Why?"

"The computer. I…my computer isn't working." It's in pieces on the floor. "I need to use their system to do a thorough search."

"If you think you can find help there, you're mistaken."

Joseph shook his head stubbornly. "No. I wouldn't." Not with his mother's life on the line as well.

The man searched his eyes for one long moment and Joseph was sure he was going to say no. Then he turned and spoke to the driver.

"You know where to go." The driver immediately turned right and took them toward the city, where the engineering firm was.

Joseph buried his face in his hands and prayed he'd be able to find Carmela before she left New York.

Outside the engineering firm, Gage shifted against the SUV's leather seat and attempted to stretch out some of the tightness in the middle of his back. He'd been parked in the firm's lot for over an hour now, and as it was early only a few people had come into work yet.

Ellis and Dunphy had called to say Joseph's apartment was empty, and from the damage he'd done to the computer, it looked like he had no intention of returning. At least they now knew what the fucker looked like. Dunphy had sent over a few pictures he'd snapped of the framed photos he and Ellis had found in Joseph's place. A young Italian, early twenties, clean cut family guy from all outward appearances.

Except it seemed he was aiding and aiding the TTP in his spare time.

Stifling a yawn, Gage checked his watch and settled the digital camera in his lap.

Almost five in the morning. He was strategically positioned to be able to see everyone who came in and out of the secure high rise, and he'd been using the telephoto lens to zoom in on anyone remotely resembling Joseph.

He'd just decided to give it ten more minutes when a black SUV pulled into the lot and parked in front of the building. Its windows were tinted dark enough that Gage couldn't see inside.

He leaned down in the seat, brought the camera up into position and aimed it at the passenger side in time to snap a few shots as the back door swung open. Bingo. Joseph Esposito.

Gage took a few high-speed frames as Joseph exited the vehicle. The guy looked like shit, pale and sweaty as hell. He turned and said something to whoever else was in the back. Who was he with? There was just enough room when Joseph eased back for Gage to zoom in on the other passenger in the back seat and take a few shots.

A middle-aged man wearing a button down Oxfordstyle shirt and dress pants. His goateed face was half hidden in shadow, but the bad angle was better than nothing. Joseph shut the door and started for the front entrance while the SUV drove away.

Gage took a couple shots of the plate and memorized it, then watched Joseph hurry toward the building. When the front doors closed behind him, Gage got hold of Dunphy to have him run the number and the photos, then texted Charles to let him know they had a lead on Joseph.

Gage sincerely hoped Joseph was their guy. He'd be more than happy to go in there and frog march the bastard out of the building in front of his coworkers before he turned him over to the Italians.

Right after he scared him so badly, he made Joseph shit his pants. His phone rang a few minutes later. Dunphy. Gage's heart rate kicked up a notch. "Got some news?"

"Vehicle's registered with a government agency, but I can't find out which branch."

"What about the other guy in the back?"

"Got a few possible hits in our system, but I can't verify him with my software. I need Claire to look at it."

The mention of her name would probably always make his gut tighten, but he knew they needed help on this. "Do it."

"Already done."

Gage tamped down the irrational surge of possessiveness he felt toward her.

She wasn't his anymore. When was his heart going to get that? "Let me know if she turns up anything."

"Will do. You want us to stay here just in case?"

"For now. I'm staying put for the time being, until we can figure out what he's up to."

"Roger that."

He hung up and sighed as he sank down into the seat to get comfortable.

Surveillance sucked at the best of times because it was boring, but especially when he was alone and had too much time to think about things best forgotten. Plus, there was nothing to eat.

Man, Easter really made you appreciate simple things like food and water when you were deprived of it all day long. The thirst was absolutely the worst part. He had a to-go cup of tea in the cup holder, but it had gone cold well over an hour ago. What he wouldn't give for a cup of coffee, hot, black and strong enough to float.

Eventually the sun's first rays finally peeked out around the edges of the engineering firm. Cars were starting to arrive more frequently now, all the employees filing into the building. None of them tripped his radar. Two minutes later, his phone rang.

Gage grabbed it from the center console, his heart giving a hard knock when he saw the text message from Claire.

Call me on my cell, ASAP. Urgent.

He frowned. Whatever it was, she didn't want anyone else knowing about it, and that worried him. Shit, what the hell had she found?

Chapter 17

The Discovery

Claire put on her screensaver. There was a picture of her, her brother and father to cover up what she'd just found, though the image of the man was now permanently burned into her brain.

Mathew Harris.

She sat back and ran an unsteady hand through her hair. Her heart was racing double time because of what she'd just discovered on file. Holy shit, Gage and the others had no idea what they were up against.

She had to warn them. Claire prayed Gage would respond to her text. Things were about to become critical for everyone involved and she didn't want him or the others to walk into the situation unawares. That wasn't the only thing that made her stomach twist.

By poking around in the system and coming up with Mathew Harris's name, she'd just flagged her activities to the entire NSA network, and probably a few more three letter agencies as well.

She stood and rubbed a hand over her face, took a deep breath and headed for her boss's office. Better to lay it on the line before they came to her, rather than have it look like she was trying to hide something.

As it was, her ass might be put on probation for this, or worse. Hoping she was wrong about that, she knocked on Alex's door and waited for permission to enter.

As always, he was on the phone, and waved to her while he finished up. He was former Special Forces, ironically a trait most of the men in her life shared, and still very fit for being in his early fifties.

He wore his usual pale blue dress shirt and black slacks, and his gray-streaked dark hair was short and neat. His silver eyes met hers as she sank into the chair in front of his desk and waited for him to finish up, which he did a few moments later.

Alex set the receiver back in its cradle and leaned back in his chair, crossing one ankle over his knee in a picture of relaxed poise. "What's up?"

Claire stifled the urge to wipe her damp palms on her dress pants, and licked her lips.

Either he didn't know what she'd done yet, or he was playing her to see if she'd come clean. She never knew with him. "I have a situation I need to report."

His posture and expression never changed. "Okay. Shoot."

Where to begin? "I was checking into something and got a hit that you need to be aware of."

Alex didn't respond, not so much as a flicker of an eyelid. She blew out her breath and plunged onward. "A friend contacted me and asked me to run some information about some chatter between an Italian civilian and the TTP."

"And this friend," Alex said slowly, "knew to contact you for this how?"

"I owed him a favor." Her face was bright red, she knew it was. "He's former SF and now contracting in Italy."

Alex grunted. He put his foot back on the floor, sat up and folded his hands on top of his desk. "So, you're here to inform me that you've been looking into something you shouldn't have."

"Partly, yes. But the information I found is going to be flagged in the agency database, because…"

"And you wanted to come clean before I found out on my own," he finished, one dark eyebrow arching.

God, it was near impossible to not squirm under the intensity of that gaze.

"Yessir. But there's more." She faltered as her phone buzzed in her pocket.

Gage. Had to be. She resisted the urge to grab it and check the display.

"Your friend?" Alex asked wryly. "What's his name?"

SF was a tight knit community. Despite their age difference, it was possible Alex and Gage had crossed paths at some point. "Gage Wallace."

Alex's gaze sharpened with interest. "I know Wallace. Solid operator. What's he working on that he needed Intel from you?"

Her phone vibrated again. Though she desperately needed to warn Gage, she didn't dare talk to him here. Instead, she gestured to the computer on Alex's desk. "I found a link a few minutes ago, a big one.

If you wouldn't mind looking up Mathew Harris, Italian." She reached down and silenced her phone without looking at it, sending a silent apology to Gage.

Alex's brows immediately drew together. He turned to his computer without a word, making Claire sure that he was already familiar with the name.

A few keystrokes and commands later, Alex turned his head to look at her in astonishment. "You mean him?" He angled the screen toward her so she could see Harris's face, a middle-aged Italian man with dark eyes and a closely trimmed goatee.

"Yes. I investigated it, and since the bombing last night in the city there's been chatter about another operation in the planning stages. It's set for this morning, but they don't mention where or who the target is." Though she could guess and she wanted to be sure Gage knew what was happening.

At least her voice sounded more confident than she felt. This information was important, and if she was smart, she could frame what she'd stumbled upon as a win for both her and the agency. She just needed to find a way to make this work in her favor.

Claire waited, bracing for a reprimand at the dark look on her boss's face.

"Start at the beginning," he commanded, his attention riveted on her, his posture radiating urgency.

Claire did, explaining about Youssef Khan and how he was linked to Harris, how The Italian Security was involved in everything. She mentioned Carmela and her father, and his kidnapping and murder. All the riots that had cost the life of the American security contractor Scottie Easton.

Alex's mouth was a thin line by the time she finished. "You realize who Harris is, right?"

She nodded. "I do now." It made her feel sick to think of Gage being involved in anything to do with that slimy asshole.

Alex grabbed the phone and dialed someone, barking orders about gathering a team. She pulled her phone out, saw Gage's text.

What's up? I'm out doing recon. Call me.

She'd call him the first chance she got. When Claire got up to leave the room, however, Alex pinned her with a hard stare and thrust a finger at her chair in a silent command to sit, so she sank back down.

A humiliated flush rose in her cheeks. In her three years with the agency, she'd cultivated a spotless service record and reputation. If she didn't spin her involvement in this situation the right way, this one favor to Gage had the potential to blow it all to hell.

Claire forced herself to sit still and await Alex's response. She'd known coming in here to expect a dressing down, but now she was afraid that her job might be on the line. It was her own fault for bending the rules, but then, there wasn't much she wouldn't do for Gage. Except let him back into her life, that is.

Alex made two more calls then stood and crossed to the front of the desk, holding her gaze. "Go to your station and show me everything you pulled up. I want to see the chat room evidence myself, and I'll need to talk to Tom Webster about Italian's involvement in all of this and what's going on."

Claire wasn't about to argue. She hurried back to her computer and started pulling everything up as people began to gather around. Alex quickly briefed everyone and divided them into teams before delegating various tasks, including contacting the State Department, Homeland Security, the CIA, and FBI. Claire's poking had disturbed one hell of a hornet's nest.

Each passing minute was its own separate agony. When everyone had broken up to take on their new assignments, Claire finally looked up at Alex. He was staring at her screen reading the e-mails from Joseph to his TTP contact, his eyebrows drawn together in concentration. From his time in SF, he was fluent in Italian, and it was clear he didn't like what he was reading now.

"Sir," she began, "I must contact Gage and let him know what's going on before they act on the Intel they've gathered."

Alex flicked her an annoyed look. "Get Tom on the phone and I'll brief him myself, then he can alert his team. As of this moment, you're on a short leash."

Her stomach clenched.

"What? But I just brought us a huge find with this."

"I know what you did, and I can see the bigger picture here, but you also know the rules. While I admire you for coming to me right away, I have to do my job and part of that includes making sure I can trust my staff to obey protocol. Understood?"

"So, I'm on probation?"

"Not officially." He slanted her a sharp look. "Not unless you make it necessary."

Meaning he'd be keeping a close eye on her from now into the foreseeable future. Lowering her eyes, she pulled out her cell phone and handed it to him.

"Yes, sir."

Damn you, Gage.

With all the other shit she was dealing with in her personal life, her career was one of the only bright spots in her existence, and now it might be in jeopardy.

Even when Gage wasn't technically in her life anymore, he still managed to cause destruction in it.

Yet through all the anger and embarrassment, the growing sense of fear was strongest. Hard as it was to acknowledge the amount of shit she might face from the NSA over this, Claire was preoccupied with Gage's safety.

She knew Gage. Hell, she'd spent her whole life surrounded by men like him, men who lived and died by the brothers-in-arms code. If the militants launched this next attack and caught the team unprepared, she knew without a doubt that Gage wouldn't hesitate to give his life to defend his teammates.

She also knew it would kill her if that happened.

"Claire."

She pulled herself out of her morbid thoughts to focus on Alex. He was still studying the chat room messages, his attention on the screen, her phone sitting useless in his hand. "Yes?"

"This is damn good work. You might have given us the break we need to nail this cell and Harris's whole network."

A trickle of relief slid through her, but the urgency to warn Gage remained.

"Thank you, sir. Want me to get Tom on the line for you?"

One side of his mouth curved up, his eyes still on the monitor as he handed her phone back. "Yeah."

Charles cracked one eye open when his phone buzzed on the nightstand.

Grabbing it before it woke Carmela, he snuck back to the bathroom to answer it.

Tom bulldozed straight ahead with the situation the moment he picked up.

"Gage got some photos of Joseph and some other guy he'd been meeting with, and sent them to Claire. Her boss just contacted me to say it's Matthew Harris, former head of intelligence for the ISI.

This guy was fired under suspicion of aiding the TTP eight months ago and dropped off on the face of the earth. This is the first time anyone's seen him since then."

Charles went from sleepy to wide awake in the space of a few heartbeats.

"Are you fucking serious?"

"Dead serious. Apparently, there's also some chatter about another operation to happen this morning, but as far as the NSA can tell, it looks like it's still in the planning stages.

We're pretty sure they don't know where you guys are yet."

Well, thank God for small favors. He grunted, checked his watch. "They planning to hit the airport?" Would make sense, since the cell had to know they were flying Carmela out of the country as soon as possible.

"That's my bet. I'm looking into departures from another airport, maybe Kennedy Airport."

"Yeah, okay." He ran a hand through his hair. Fuck, how far up the chain did this threat extends. If the TTP was getting help from the former ISI intelligence chief, then it wasn't a stretch to imagine other agencies and officials being involved as well.

Maybe putting Carmela on a plane back home wasn't going to make her any safer. He wasn't sure what else they could do for her now though.

"What about stateside when she gets home? She'll need a protective detail there until we can verify the threat against her is neutralized."

"I'll get on that later. You sure no one had eyes on you when you checked in last night?"

Charles understood that Tom wasn't questioning his capability, just making sure, he knew all the facts. "I'm sure. I checked in using my ID and the only people who saw her were the two guys working the front desk."

"All right. Stand by for possible airport change, but be ready to make the New York flight."

"Roger that." He shifted on the edge of the tub, set into the wall across from the shower.

"What's the word on that Joseph guy? Are we bringing him in?"

"NSA's still verifying he's our man, but with all the agencies working on it now, I'd say our jurisdiction is well and truly fucked at this stage.

Whoever gets to arrest him, it won't be one of us."

Charles clenched his back teeth together in frustration. He may not like it, but there was nothing he or any of them could do to change it.

"Understood."

"Right. Charlie Mike."

Continue mission. "Yeah. Later." He went back into the bedroom and placed the phone on the nightstand.

Carmela had rolled onto her side, facing him. One hand was tucked beneath the long veil of curls that obscured her bare breast, exposed by the drape of the sheet, and the other lay next to his pillow, palm up.

She looked so peaceful like that; he didn't have the heart to wake her. No point in explaining the new development anyway because it would only cause her further stress.

Charles intended to ensure their last few hours together were as perfect as he could make them. He glanced at the digital clock on Carmela's nightstand. Only five thirty.

Plenty of time to climb back into bed and have her all to himself for a while longer. Easing onto the mattress, he stretched out beside her and eased an arm around her waist. She sighed and opened sleepy eyes to blink up at him. "What time, is it?" she mumbled, clearly still half asleep.

Charles set a hand on the back of her head and drew her down to his shoulder.

"Still early. Go back to sleep."

Something squeezed in his chest when Carmela sighed and snuggled into his body, dropping right off to sleep without a second thought. Her trust meant more to him than she'd ever know. She was a good person; she deserved a hell of a lot better than what life had dished out to her lately.

Though he knew he had to put her on a plane in a few hours, he wished like hell he could go back to Chicago with her and guard her there, to make sure she stayed safe. He didn't want anyone else entrusted with her safety, but that was just too damn bad for him, wasn't it?

Savoring the feel of her warm, naked curves nestled against him, Charles closed his eyes and allowed himself to slip back into a light doze. A slender hand roving down his chest woke him a little while later. He leaned his head back to see Carmela better and found her watching him. She held his gaze as her hand trailed lower, her fingers caressing his naked abdomen. His cock hardened instantly, his body punched with a sudden desire so sharp, it was as if he'd gone months without her touch instead of a few hours.

Her hand slid down to close around his aching length and Charles let out a soft groan. There was nothing hesitant in her grip this time. She worked him up and down, slowly, with a firm pressure that brought his lower back off the mattress in a wordless plea.

"Thought you needed some more sleep," he managed in a gravelly voice.

"Nope." She pressed an open mouth kiss to the frog bones tat on his shoulder and bent to replace her hand with her lips.

Charles relaxed against the pillow with a little smile and let her explore, reaching down to tangle one hand in her thick curls when her cheek grazed his cock.

Pulling back the sheets to get a better view, he watched, spellbound as she leaned down and took the flared head between her parted lips.

The feel of her hot mouth closing around him made him shudder. His hand contracted in her hair, tugging at the roots as a raw sound of need rumbled up from his chest.

She stared up at him, her pale eyes gleaming with a wicked, seductive light as she pleasured him with her mouth and tongue. Suddenly it was both too much and not enough. Charles squeezed his fist around her hair to bring her eyes to his.

"Do you want me to fuck you?" His voice was low, almost a growl.

He caught her swift intake of breath, saw the rise of excitement in her eyes.

She nodded, her velvety tongue teasing him.

Charles applied pressure on her hair again, gently forcing her mouth away from his aching cock. He wanted to be inside her, now. "Roll over," he commanded, and pushed her onto her side facing away from him.

She started to turn her head to look at him over her shoulder, but he caught her around the ribs with one arm and hauled her tight against his body.

After fumbling for a condom from the stash he'd left on the nightstand, he rolled it on and settled his cock against the curve of her ass. Pushing a hand between her thighs, he found her wet and ready. He groaned at the evidence of her desire for him.

Carmela arched toward his searching fingers, impatient. He smiled against her shoulder. "You sore, baby?"

"No. Do it." Her voice was hoarse with longing. He gripped her upper thigh and moved her leg forward, opening her to him. With one hand on her shoulder and the other between her thighs, he positioned himself and eased inside. Carmela let out a quiet whimper and grabbed his arm to anchor herself, pushing her hips back for more.

Charles stroked the pads of his fingers over her slick flesh and gave her a few slow thrusts, savoring every sensation. This wasn't enough. If this was their last time together, he wanted to stake his claim. He wanted her to feel him hours from now when she was sitting on that plane, for her to never forget what it felt like to have him buried inside her.

"I want in deeper," he rasped against her ear, and rolled her to her stomach beneath him. Trapping her thighs between his, he braced himself on one arm and slid his free hand around her hip to cup her mound.

When she rocked against his fingers and made a soft sound of need, Charles drove deep. Carmela moaned and tried to arch backward but he held her still. He needed her like this, desperate for the feel of him inside her, those soft, helpless sounds of pleasure spilling from her lips. He pressed his face against the sensitive spot where her neck joined her shoulder and scraped his teeth against her tender skin.

She pushed and threw her head back. "Ah! Charles…"

He soothed the little mark with his tongue. Her body quivered beneath him, her inner muscles squeezing and moving around his cock. With a primitive growl, Charles locked his free hand around the top of her shoulder and sunk deep, intent on imprinting himself in her memory forever.

Chapter 18

The Fire Alarm

Carmela was already drifting back toward consciousness when she felt Charles bump beside her. Her eyes sprang open in the darkness to find him pushing up into a sitting position. She immediately turned onto her side and propped herself up on one elbow. He'd thrown both legs over the side of the bed and his head was cocked slightly, his body eerily still.

"What is it?" she murmured, reaching out to stroke a hand down the length of his naked back. The muscles beneath her palm were rigid with tension.

Then she heard it. Faint popping noises, from either down the hall or maybe the floor beneath them.

Followed closely by what sounded like human screams. Carmela's heart stuttered as she realized what it was.

Gunfire. Bursts of it.

Shit! She shot upright, her eyes on Charles as she lunged for her bra and panties lying on the floor beside the bed. He was already up and reaching for his jeans, his phone to his ear. "We've got automatic fire in the hotel," he said to whoever he'd called. "Can you confirm?" He met her gaze and tossed the rest of her clothes at her. Carmela leaped out of bed and hurriedly dragged on her jeans and top, her heart hammering. "I'm getting her out right now. I'll contact you with a meeting point."

No sooner had he hung up than the fire alarm went off. The eerie, high-pitched wail skittered like fingernails over her taut nerves. A second after that the sprinkler system turned on overhead, drenching them with a spray of cold water.

She gasped and covered her head to block the worst of it. "Is there really a fire?" she asked. Charles strode to the window that overlooked the front of the hotel and pulled the curtain aside.

Weak rays of sunshine filled the room. "I can't tell. Get your stuff," he said curtly. "We're leaving."

She ran to the bathroom to grab her shoes and socks. Somewhere down the hallway, a heavy door crashed against the wall. Carmela froze. More screams, followed by a loud burst of automatic gunfire.

"Carmela," she cried, spinning around. He was right behind her, pistol in hand, his face a tight mask.

"They're on our floor," he told her, drawing her out of the bathroom and toward the window at the front of the room.

"What are we going to do?"

"I'm not taking you out there while there's still gunfire. We'll wait here."

He broke off and swiveled around as another door slammed against the wall out in the hall, this one sounding as though it came from the opposite end of the corridor.

"Shit. They're coming at us from both sides."

Carmela's insides shriveled. Those men were coming for her. She could barely breathe for the panic clawing at her, squeezing the air from her lungs.

"Charles …"

"Get in the tub," he ordered gruffly, having changed his mind and shoving her back toward the bathroom.

"Lie down flat and keep your head down." He grabbed her hand and pressed another pistol into it. "Know how to use this?"

Technically? Yes. Actually? No. "Wait, what do I ?"

"You need to be able to defend yourself if I'm taken down."

Oh, shit. At his shove she careened into the bathroom and climbed into the tub, pressing herself up against the side of it to leave room for him. Except he didn't join her. "What…"

"Just stay down and keep quiet." He flipped off the bathroom light and strode over to the window to steal another peek outside. When he turned back, she saw him still and lift his head, staring toward the hotel room's door.

As she watched him, frozen, she noticed the first telltale wisps of gray smoke curling through the air. Charles cursed under his breath and hurried toward her, pausing only to close and lock the bathroom door. This time he climbed over the lip of the tub and stretched out next to her.

"Keep your head down and stay still, understand?"

"Yes," she whispered, automatically curling her hands into his shirt and burying her face against his chest. His heart was racing, which scared her even more.

The shooters opened fire again, just outside in the hallway. More screaming.

Carmela's muscles tensed. She squeezed her eyes shut and held her breath.

Seconds later, shots exploded outside their room.

"Fuck." Charles instantly rolled her beneath him and pinned her to the bottom of the fiberglass tub. A heartbeat later, bullets slammed through the wall above them and buried themselves in the one across the room.

Glass and stone rained down around them as the full-length mirror and granite vanity shattered under the assault.

Carmela bit off a scream and hung on. The rounds peppered the room as the shooters sprayed fire back and forth before moving on to the next room. Then suddenly, inexplicably, the shooting stopped.

Men were shouting to each other in the hallway. She heard the pounding of their footsteps over the wail of the fire alarm as they ran away. She was shaking all over, gasping for air when Charles put his mouth to her ear.

"Are you all right?" he whispered. He ran his hands over her, probably checking for blood. All she could manage was a nod. "Stay right here. I'm just going to…"

She clutched at his shoulders. "No." The shooters might come back.

"Carmela. "Charles spoke right against her ear. "Don't move. I'll be right back."

She swallowed a cry of protest and shut her eyes as Charles eased off her and slid over the lip of the tub. Glass and other debris crunched under his boots as he opened the door and left the bathroom.

Less than a minute passed before he came back. She opened her eyes in the dim light coming from the bedroom to find him dragging down towels from the rack above the toilet. He closed the bathroom door, climbed back in the tub and handed her one.

"Are they gone?" Her voice sounded like she'd swallowed sandpaper, but her throat was so tight it was a miracle she could talk at all.

"Looks like for now, anyway."

"Did you get cut?"

"A few scratches, but I'm okay." He started to towel off his hair when suddenly the sprinklers stopped working and the lights went out, plunging them into near darkness, the only light now spilling in between the gap in the curtains at the front window.

She barely made out the way Charles's hand froze on the top of his head.

Carmela whispered to him. "What's going on?"

"Either they've cut the water supply, or the fire's already destroyed the system."

Her stomach took a collapse. Already the smoke was thickening. It floated in a shroud near the ceiling, strong enough that she could smell the acrid tang of it.

"How close do you think the fire is?"

"No idea, but I'm guessing fairly close."

They lapsed into silence, her mind racing frantically. He was motionless and tense beside her, and she desperately wanted to know what he was thinking. Out in the hall she could hear people beginning to move out of their rooms and into the corridor.

They were shouting, coughing, some of them crying. Carmela shuddered. The smoke was getting worse, the air hazy with it. She couldn't draw a breath without pulling it into her lungs.

Charles still hadn't moved, and she knew in her gut that he was keeping something from her.

"Shouldn't we go?" she asked.

A tight shake of his head. "They're waiting for us."

"Where?"

"They obviously knew which floor we were on, but not which room. The fire's a distraction, to force us out into the hallway because they know our only way out is through one of the stairwells at the ends. They'll be waiting when we do."

She hadn't thought it possible to get any colder, but at his words her blood iced up.

Charles exhaled and slid an arm around her waist. "Smoke's getting bad enough out there that they won't be coming back in for another sweep. Not without gas masks, anyway. I texted Gage and Tom to update them.

The police and fire department will be here soon." He stroked a hand over the back of her wet hair. "We'll wait until they clear the building before, we leave the room."

She nodded, unable to think of a single thing to say. The turn of events left her feeling like she had whiplash.

A few hours ago, she'd stood under the spray of the shower in this very same bathroom while Charles pleasured her with his mouth and his body, and now they were hunkered in the tub for protection from another militant attack. She bit her lip and concentrated on taking small breaths, wondering how long the air would stay breathable at their level.

Charles's phone rang a few minutes later and he checked the lit-up display.

"It's Gage. He and the others are on their way. They'll update us about the situation as soon as they can."

He typed something back and lowered his arm across her waist again. "Bet you can't wait to get out of New York, huh?"

A hysterical laugh bubbled up and she choked it back. "You have no idea. I'd say I wish I'd never come here, but I know I would have been ashamed of myself if I hadn't. And…I would never have met you."

He pressed a firm kiss to the middle of her forehead. "Some consolation I've turned out to be, huh?"

Carmela wet her lips. "If I must be shot at and trapped in a burning building with someone, I want it to be you."

His shoulders shook in a silent laugh, though nothing about this was even remotely funny. "Well, that's good then."

The wobbly smile on her lips vanished when he gathered her close and tucked her face into the broad expanse of his chest, the fabric of his T-shirt damp against her cheek.

Please let us out of here. Please let us live. Carmela squeezed her eyes shut and turned more fully into him.

Precious minutes ticked past while they waited for word from the others.

Charles held Carmela the whole time, using her as a distraction from the reminder that this was eerily like the night when Scottie died. The fire, the gunmen hunting them.

No matter how hard he tried to block them, the demons of his nightmares snapped their jaws at the edge of his consciousness. Carmela was silent and her initial trembling had stopped, but the way her hands were still bunched in the back of his shirt told him just how terrified she was. He wracked his brains for something to say to lighten the tension again and came up blank.

Giving her useless plainness right now would be beyond shitty. They had only two options at this point, and both sucked asses. Smoke continued to collect in the bathroom despite the closed door, seeping beneath the lower edge in a toxic veil. They were on the fifth floor.

It would take some time for any first responders to reach them. They wouldn't have much longer before the smoke became lethal, but staying put for the moment was a calculated risk they had to take.

Carmela stirred against him and let out a little cough. "Smoke's getting bad."

He could feel her heart racing, the panic building inside her.

"Hang on." He got up and snagged some wet towels, shoved them under the crack at the bottom of the door to buy them a bit more time.

Even close to the floor it was hard to get a good breath and he coughed at the irritation in his lungs. Carmela made room for him again when he came back to the tub.

"I'm really sorry you got caught up in all this," she whispered.

Charles shook his head. "My choice to take the job, sweetheart. It's not like you asked for any of this."

She ran a hand over the length of his back, taking a slight edge off his anxiety. "No. My life is usually much quieter. Downright boring. I miss boring."

Ha. "I'm looking forward to a little boring after this myself."

She tilted her head back. "I'd say you've earned it. Along with a giant raise."

He grunted. "Tell that to Tom later."

"Oh, I will."

Her voice was tight, her tenuous hold on her bravery slipping.

No sound now except the fire alarm blaring away, fed by some unknown power source. He was good under pressure, and his mental toughness was what had earned him a spot in the Teams in the first place, but at that moment he had to work hard to block out the incessant screech of that alarm.

He was relieved when his phone vibrated again. Gage, thank God. "What's the story?"

"What's your status?" Gage countered.

"We're in the bathtub with a wet towel stuffed under the door to keep the worst of the smoke out. It's getting bad in here though."

"Fire department and SWAT team are here, but that's one big fire.

It's on your floor, and it's already spread above and below you. I can see flames pouring out of the windows in some of the rooms."

Fuck. "What about the ends by the stairwells?"

"Can't tell, but if the fire's not there yet, it will be shortly."

Those stairs were their only way out, whether they took the ones up to a higher floor or down toward the lobby. "What about the shooters?"

"Still inside.

Parking lot's a nightmare right now. People are running around in hysterics. SWAT hasn't even entered the building yet because of the fire. Firemen are just hooking up the hoses now, but I doubt they'll let them start with the shooters there."

Charles's muscles were drawing tighter by the second. He could tell from how still Carmela was that she'd heard every word of what Gage said. "What about Tom?"

"He's working on getting the Italians to agree to a military takedown."

They'd never pull that off in time to save everyone trapped in the hotel.

"Where are you?"

"I'm on foot at the north side of the building. Police aren't letting anyone in, not even me. You're going to have to get out there right fucking now, Charles."

The words he'd been dreading. "Copy that." They had to somehow make it out of the room and down the hall to an exit through the suffocating smoke, then descend five flights of stairs with nothing but a single pistol for each of them, not knowing where the flames or militants were.

He wished he'd brought more weapons up when they'd checked in last night, but he'd never dreamed they'd have to fight their way out of the hotel like this.

"Get Tom here and station somebody at each entrance. I don't know which one'll be viable."

"Roger that. See you on the ground floor, brother."

They both knew he and Carmela had barely a chance in hell of making it out of the hotel alive. He hoped she didn't realize it too. "Yeah."

Charles hung up and shoved the phone into his back pocket before turning his attention to Carmela.

Inside the closed-up bathroom it was pitch black, and the smoke already stung his eyes and throat. "You got your shoes on, right?"

"Yes." She grasped his shoulder to pull herself up and he helped her to her knees. Probably for the best that he couldn't see her expression. This was going to be hard enough without seeing the pure terror in her eyes.

"Here." Reaching over the side of the tub, he shook out a soaked washcloth to make sure there were no bits of glass in it and handed it to her.

"Put this over your nose and mouth, it'll help filter the smoke out." In theory.

Grasping her shoulders, he squeezed to make sure she was paying attention to every single word he said.

"The smoke's going to be way thicker outside than it is in here. Once I open that door, we've got seconds, maximum, to get out of our room and down the hallway to an exit. The closest one's to the left, about thirty meters.

You get on the floor and crawl as fast as you can for it. Hold your breath if you can, and don't stop unless I tell you to. No matter what. Got it?"

"Yes." Her voice was a mere whisper, but she raised the cloth and held it to her face.

"It's going to be pitch dark out there and the smoke's going to make your eyes run so keep them closed and hug the wall. You're going to grab hold of me anyplace you can get a good grip and I'm going to lead us out, okay?"

This time she nodded, her curls brushing the backs of his hands. "What about the shooters?"

"The smoke's too thick for them to be up here. Just hold onto me and stay low once we hit the hallway. We've only got one shot at this."

Another fragile nod, and he could practically feel the terror pouring off her.

He squeezed her shoulders once more, fighting back the cold tendrils of fear snaking up his backbone.

Gut check time.

Charles pulled her to her feet, helped her over the edge of the tub and snagged a hand towel from the ruined vanity to press over his own face.

"Ready?"

She coughed, shot out a hand and snagged his arm. "Charles ..." A wealth of emotion laced that single word. Fear, hope, regret.

He couldn't let her panic. To calm her he took her face between his hands, pitched his voice low. "Listen to me."

Even though he couldn't see her, he could reach her with his words, the force of his will.

"You know we don't have a choice. I'm going to be right in front of you every moment, and you're not going to stop no matter what happens." He kept his voice harsh, authoritative.

"If something happens to me, you don't stop, you keep going. You keep going until you get down the stairs and out to where the guys will be waiting for you.

Now take a deep breath, and when I squeeze your hand, you hold all that air in because I'm going to open this door and get us the fuck out of here."

He released her, slid the hand holding the towel down to grip hers, tight, and grabbed his pistol with the other.

"On three. One." He heard her pull in a deep breath through the wet cloth. "Two." Her fingers dug into him like claws.

"Three." He sucked in a breath, ripped open the bathroom door and ran blindly for the only way out.

Chapter 19

The Hotel Room

O ut in the hotel parking lot, Gage shoved his way through the crowd of transfixed onlookers and headed straight for the armed officers maintaining the perimeter a good distance away from the hotel.

The SWAT team was doing dick all, standing around the command van. A continuous stream of guests flowed out of the hotel's ground floor exits, people in their sleepwear doubled over coughing, their clothes and skin tarnished with smoke and smoke.

No sign of Charles or Carmela. Neither of them had responded to the last two texts Gage had sent. Ignoring the gestures and shouts for him to stay back, Gage strode right up to the armed guards to find out what the hell was going on.

"I'm an American military contractor, and my team leader's inside," he told the angry corporal.

"No one goes in but law enforcement," the guy told him firmly. "Get back and give us some room."

He could have tried storming past them, but everyone was already on edge and the last thing he wanted to worry about was being shot by one of the good guys during chaos.

With a mental curse, he spun around and stalked back toward the road where he'd parked the SUV. Two steps from the door, his cell rang.

He snatched it out of his pocket and his heart gave a funny lurch when he saw Claire's number. "Hey," he answered, wondered if she had any worse news.

"Are you okay?" she blurted.

Any other time, the worry in her voice might have set off an issue of hope inside him.

"I'm fine. So, you heard?"

"I was just about to leave the office when the news broke. Everyone on my floor's glued to their monitors watching the live stream now. What's going on?"

Leaning against the vehicle, he looked back at the hotel. Considering he wasn't allowed within a hundred feet of the place, Claire probably knew more than he did at this point.

"There's smoke streaming from most of the fourth and fifth floor windows. I can see people waving towels and stuff through them, trying to get the emergency responders' attention. With the shooters still in there nobody's letting the fire crews near the building. SWAT team hasn't even gone inside yet and basically nobody knows shit, let alone how many shooters are in there."

"What about Charles? We heard that he might…"

"He's trapped inside somewhere on the fifth floor with Carmela." Her ragged gasp of dismay only amplified the helplessness inside him. "I talked to him a little while ago and they were okay, but I can't reach him now."

Staring at the burning building, the dread kept building. "Doesn't look good, Claire," he admitted quietly. With how intense the fire was and how fast it was spreading, it was likely many of those insides wouldn't get out in time.

She was silent for a moment as she absorbed that. "What about the others?"

"Tom's on his way, and the other two guys on the team should be here any minute." Fuck load of good any of them would do Charles and Carmela though.

"What can I do?" she asked, steel in her voice.

After the way she'd dropped him like a live grenade six months ago the offer shouldn't have meant much to him. Except it did, and more than he'd ever let her know.

"Alert me if you get any Intel that might be of use?"

"I'm on it."

Damned if those three little words didn't make him feel better even under these supremely shitty circumstances. When Claire sank her teeth into something she was like a bulldog, wouldn't let go until she'd got what she wanted. Knowing she was on this took an invisible weight off his shoulders.

"Thanks."

"Just promise me you won't do anything stupid."

A dry smile tugged at his mouth. "So, you do still care."

A huffing sound, and he had no trouble imagining the annoyed expression he knew was on her face.

"Gage, I mean it. No bullshit heroics or anything."

Ellis and Dunphy's SUV came into view down the street near where the police had blocked off traffic. He stuck out an arm to flag them down. "Got to do what I can."

"Gage"

"Have to go now. Talk to you later."

"Gage, wait, there's…!"

Ignoring the urgency in her voice he disconnected as the boys pulled up behind his vehicle.

Ellis stepped out of the passenger seat and pulled off his Oakley's, taking in the scene with a single glance. "Shit, it's like Mumbai all over again."

"No, it's worse," Gage corrected. "More shooters this time and so far, they're better organized." How had they found Carmela in so short a time?

He and Charles had been careful last night. Nobody had followed them, Gage was positive.

Tom's vehicle passed through the police barricade and sped toward them, stopping behind the second SUV with a screech of tires. The driver's side door popped open and Tom jumped out.

He ripped off his shades and stared at the burning spectacle before him. "Fuck me," he muttered. His hazel gaze shifted to Gage. "Nothing further?"

"Nope."

Tom set his hands on his hips and shook his head as he stared at the burning hotel. "I can't goddamn believe this. Shit, it's got to be hell on Charles. Especially this soon after Scottie…"

"Yeah." Tom had said what they were all thinking, but the back of Gage's neck prickled at the thought of being trapped in that burning building with active shooters hunting him yet again.

They were all quiet a moment as the gravity of the situation sunk in. This was fucked up, any way you looked at it. The ground floor exits were eerily inactive now.

"No one's come out of there for the past few minutes," Gage said finally, his gut sinking.

Tom flashed him a sharp look and narrowed his eyes. "Charles 'll get out."

Well, if anyone could get out of that deathtrap, it was Charles. Gage hoped like hell his friend and Carmela found a way.

With a nod he turned to Ellis and Dunphy. "Grab your weapons and med kits. We'll get in position, and each take an exit so we're ready for them when they come out."

Up on the fifth floor Charles burst through the hotel room's door into the hallway and crawled straight into hell.

Through the artificial darkness cast by the choking smoke he could just make out the orange glow of flames at the end of the hallway to the left. The sights, sounds and smells instantly transported him back to that burning ministry building.

For a moment, he was trapped in that memory as he and Scottie fought their way toward the staircase that led to the roof. Images flashed through his mind at high speed. The sound of the mob outside the building walls.

The desperate run to safety with no backup in sight. The rest of the team guided the diplomats up to the roof. Scottie slumped on the floor in a pool of blood. Him, hauling his buddy over his shoulder and pounding up the steps to the rooftop, praying the evac would be in time, that Scottie would make it if Charles could just get him out fast enough.

A hand on his lower leg snapped him back to the present, unfreezing him.

Carmela.

Move, asshole. With the wet cloth pressed over his mouth and nose, he laid flat on the debris-strewn carpet and took stock of their options. He was on his belly, braced on his forearms and she was right behind him.

He couldn't risk trying to run the metal glove of flames on the left, even though it meant the only remaining exit probably had shooters waiting for them. No telling how fast and where the flames were spreading to, and they had less than a minute to get out of here before the smoke suffocated them both.

Over the shriek of the fire alarm and the pounding of his heart he heard Carmela coughing, felt the convulsive grip of her hand around his right ankle, and made a snap decision.

He turned right and began to belly-crawl down the hallway. Nobody came towards them, and he didn't see or sense anyone else in the corridor. His eyes were streaming so much that he had to feel his way along, using the wall to orient himself.

Carmela stayed right with him. Steeling himself against the sounds of her gasping coughs he kept crawling forward, intent on getting to the exit. Only another thirty yards or so, though it seemed like a thousand.

Another ten yards and a few choked breaths later, the smoke got to him too. Deep, wracking coughs took hold as the toxic fumes clogged his lungs. Blind, gasping, he forced himself to crawl faster, prepared to bodily drag Carmela out of there if necessary.

He'd already lost Scottie despite his best efforts to save him. He wasn't losing Carmela too. His right hand fell along the wall as he moved closer to that unseen exit, hoping like hell it was clear.

Already he was lightheaded, his brain setting off its low oxygen alarm. His lungs burned, the exertion sapping his muscles of strength. He was running on full auto mode now, nothing but survival instinct propelling him forward.

Then Carmela failed. He felt her hand drop from his leg. Charles swept one arm back and managed to snag her forearm. She gripped him like a lifeline, quickly transferring her grip to his ankle as he kept going.

He couldn't see shit. The exit had to be close now. He stretched his arm out to feel for the door, hit empty air.

Pushing his trembling muscles onward, he made another sweep. Nothing. Hell, where was that goddamn door?

Fragments on the carpet dug into his elbows and belly. Carmela's hand remained firm around his ankle, a constant reminder that she was counting on him to find a way out. He flung his right arm out again and this time his fingertips met the plaster of the end wall.

Forcing his eyes open to slits in the dense smoke, he reached up and found the metal latch on the door. God only knew what was waiting for them on the other side, but he couldn't afford to hesitate. He was almost out of air.

Dropping the damp cloth that was doing jack all at this point, he yanked his pistol from the waistband at the small of his back as he turned the handle and shoved the door open with a grunt.

It swung open easily. A wash of cool, comparatively clean air hit him. When no one shot at them he reached back for Carmela, grabbed her by the upper arm and hauled her through the opening.

The moment she cleared the jambs he dragged her sideways to lie behind him and slammed the heavy door shut with one foot. They collapsed together there in the stairwell, heaving and coughing like a couple of drowning victims.

Charles forced his head up, wiped at his watering eyes to see what the hell they were facing. No flames below in the stairwell as far as he could tell from this angle, and the smoke was much thinner here, curling in a thick layer that hugged the ceiling and left the bottom foot or so near the floor relatively clear.

He rolled onto his side to get a look at Carmela. "Okay?" he wheezed.

She dropped the soot-stained washcloth she was holding and kept coughing, managed a nod. Her face was streaked with grime and blood oozed from little cuts in her forearms, but otherwise she didn't seem hurt besides the smoke inhalation.

"Keep low," he told her, stopped to hack a few times to clear his lungs.

"Smoke's still bad enough to do damage here." Flipping back onto his hands and knees, he gripped his weapon and started for the edge of the stairs.

Other than the fire alarm, he didn't hear anything. No shouts, no pounding of feet. Didn't promise well. There should've been plenty of other people scrambling to get out of the building.

He'd just started down the first set of stairs when he heard running footsteps.

An instant later a spray of bullets gave him his answer. He jerked back a split second before they slammed into the concrete wall less than a foot from his head.

With a mental curse he reared back to shove Carmela into the corner between the wall and emergency exit door. She grabbed hold of his sides and froze with a blurted, "Oh, shit."

A chilling stillness followed the shots. He could feel her tensed up against his back but she reached behind her and withdrew the semi-auto Hunter had given her, aimed it with both hands over his shoulder.

Ready to fight her way out and kill if necessary. A rise of pride swept through him because he knew just how foreign a concept it was to her.

"Don't move," he whispered, still sprawled out on the cold concrete. They couldn't stay here in the stairwell with the smoke thickening and the fire encroaching on their position.

Carmela didn't have the training to help him eliminate the shooters and they certainly couldn't go back through the emergency door into that deathtrap of a hallway.

That left him the only option of clearing this goddamn stairwell to give him and Carmela a fighting chance at escape.

"Stay put. I'll yell once it's safe. When you move, hug the ground, and keep your head down."

"Ok-kay," she stammered. "Please be careful."

Since there was nothing, he could say to reassure her, he didn't answer.

Squeezing her leg once in a gesture meant to give her encouragement, he hugged the wall and inched forward. He was willing to bet the shooters weren't trained in taking a stairwell the way, he was, but that didn't make them any less dangerous.

Unfortunately, fuckwads like them seemed to have a knack for getting lucky in close quarters. Creeping low and slow, he peered over the lip of the staircase to check the place where the lower landing made a ninety degree turn and disappeared from view. No one was there.

He eased forward with his weapon up and ready, wishing he had a rifle instead. Thankfully Carmela stayed where he'd left her, giving him one less thing to worry about.

At last, he reached the bottom of the first staircase. The air here was clearer than at the top. He drew in a full breath, stifled a cough as his lungs attempted to expel more smoke. The minimal sound that emerged triggered an immediate response.

A burst of bullets smacked into the wall below him and pinged off the metal railing. Charles swore and readied himself, bracing for the attack he knew was coming. He heard the shuffle of feet, caught sight of the muzzle end of the rifle as it appeared around the corner.

The second the man's head came into view, Charles opened fire. His shot hit the guy in the side of the head and dropped him like a sack of sand. The rifle clattered to the ground.

The frantic shout rose from below. Charles shifted his attention to the AK, lying there to take into its dead owner's hands. Only twelve stairs separated him from increased firepower and his best shot at evening the odds. If he was quick enough, he might be able to get it. He leaned forward to make a lunge for it and heard the heavy footfalls racing up the steps below him.

At least two men, maybe more. He snapped up into a better firing position and took a slow, deep breath. This time the shooters didn't wait for visual contact to start shooting. Their weapons barked; a hail of bullets sprayed the lower stairwell. Bits of concrete and plaster exploded in a hail of white around him. He bit the inside of his cheek and covered a grunt when he felt a hot sting in the back of his left calf.

A cold, deadly resolve came over him. He was not going down like this. Not with Carmela waiting helplessly behind him. Blood pumping fast, he stayed in position and rode out the initial barrage, forcing himself not to move and maintain the pitiful cover the bend in the stairs and metal railing provided him. Time screeched to a halt.

The men were still coming; he could feel the subtle vibrations of their boots on the steps. They were still firing, rushing at him headlong when the first one appeared below. Charles took aim and hit him twice in the chest. The guy fell back but didn't stay down, and Charles realized the assholes were wearing ballistic vests.

He eased forward a couple of inches to get a better line of sight and fired again, with a head shot. This time the round plowed into the first shooter's forehead.

The guy's upper body dropped back where he lay, unmoving. A split second later an enraged cry split the relative quiet and another explosion of gunfire ripped into the stairs where Charles waited.

Wickedly sharp bits of concrete peppered his arms and legs, then he felt a heavy thud and couldn't hold back the curse as one of the rounds buried itself in the back of his upper arm.

Angry beyond belief, fighting through the pain, Charles kept his sidearm raised with his good arm and started firing as soon as he detected motion below him.

One round hit the second attacker in the shoulder. He spun back out of sight and the muzzle of his weapon dropped. Charles charged forward, exploding down the stairs. As swipe number two was picking himself off the floor, blood pouring from the wound in his shoulder. His head snapped around when he saw Charles coming. In slow motion he started to raise the barrel of the AK, his eyes fixed on Charles.

Charles let fly with a double tap, grazing the man's temple. He hit the floor and Charles didn't hesitate. He sent a final round through the fucker's brain and snatched up both fallen AKs, tossing his near empty pistol aside.

In the wake of the initial rush, the tide of adrenaline flooding his body died down a little, enough for him to become aware of the burn of the shrapnel and bullet wounds. Blood flowed down the back of his left arm and calf, warm and sticky. They burned like hell. He was still mobile, still in the fight.

For the moment nobody else was coming at them and they had to keep moving.

Without taking his eyes off the next portion of the stairwell, he called up to Carmela. "We're clear for now. Come quick but stay a few yards behind me, and keep down." They had a lot of stairs left to take before they reached the ground floor and he had a gut feeling they weren't in the clear yet.

Chapter 20

Gun Fires

At the sound of Charles voice, Carmela closed her eyes for a second and sent up a silent prayer of thanks. She had no idea how he'd survived all that gunfire, or how she'd remained safe with all those bullets flying around.

Pushing to her feet, she threw out a hand to steady herself when her legs wobbled. The inside of her chest burned from the smoke and her coughing had done little to clear her lungs. Her left hand gripped the railing, her right holding fast to the pistol. It felt strange against her palm, but she wouldn't hesitate to pull the trigger if she had to, lack of training or not.

A few unsteady steps down, she stretches out her head around to see Charles and the two men lying crumpled on the floor. Bile rose in her throat. Her gaze swung from the bodies to Charles, taking in the rifles and Charles was bleeding.

"You were shot!" She rushed down the remaining steps, ignoring his muttered dismissal, her attention on the blood spilling down his upper arm and the back of his leg in scarlet streams.

"Don't worry about it now, I'm fine," he said sternly, blocking her hand as she reached out to halt the bleeding in his upper arm.

"We've got to move fast. Same drill, stay back and stay low. Come on." He turned away from her and staggered down the stairs, trailing blood behind him.

A door slammed open somewhere below them. Charles dropped to one knee on the stairs and Carmela did the same. Heart in her throat, she waited there for a few tense seconds before she heard it.

People coughing, a woman crying. Then shouting. More screams. The primitive fear in them caused a gut reaction deep inside her. An automatic and an   uncontrollable curling in her guts.

Chills broke out across her cold skin, the hair on her arms and the back of her neck standing on end. The clatter of panicked feet further down the stairwell had barely registered when the door banged open again and another gun opened fire.

Charles remained frozen in place ahead of her, his full attention riveted to the lower stairwell. Then he shifted slightly, the muscles across his back and shoulders tensing, and Carmela knew the assault was coming. She gripped the pistol in both hands and started to bring it upward when Charles suddenly fired the rifle.

Precise, controlled bursts of a few rounds each. A cold trickle of sweat rolled down her spine. She had to remind herself to breathe. Charles rose slightly from his crouch and went down a few steps to the landing, pausing.

Without looking back or giving any sort of signal, he turned the corner and disappeared. Carmela forced herself to follow at a distance, the weight of the gun still a foreign sensation in her hands.

She dove onto the landing before the last syllable was out. Raising her eyes, she stared in horror at the carnage revealed before her. Blood everywhere.

Splattered on the walls and the stairs and the floor. Bodies lay crumpled in the narrow stairwell.

An elderly couple was curled around each other, the man on top of the woman as though he'd attempted to shield her in their final moments. Their eyes were still open, staring at each other in terror even in death.

The roar of gunfire jerked Carmela's attention to Charles. It drowned out the shouts and screams of the victims as the gunmen mowed down anyone left moving. Charles returned fire.

Her eyes were glued to him during that massacre when he ran out of ammo. He flung the now useless rifle away and reached over his shoulder for a second, then suddenly tugged and Carmela knew he'd been hit again.

A cry of denial built in her throat, but it was blocked by the tightness there. She rose to her hands and knees and began crawling toward him without realizing it, intent only on getting to him.

All she knew was that he was down, and the shooters were still coming.

She was only a few yards from him when he reared up with the second rifle and let loose with another stream of bullets.

She stopped and risked a glance past him, caught sight of three men bursting into view down the spiral of the staircase. Charles had held his own so far, but he couldn't hold off that much firepower alone.

At that moment a rush of cold, hard determination flooded her system. She brought her pistol up, finger on the trigger, prepared to shoot at anything coming up those stairs, but Charles suddenly swept an arm out and knocked her flat.

The air rushed out of her as her chest hit the hard concrete and something hot and sharp tore into her back, just below her right shoulder blade. A split second later, Charles's weight crashed down on top of her. She went dead still beneath him, the repeated boom of gunfire echoing in her ears.

She felt Charles shift and heard the answering bark of his rifle, then he twitched and grunted, rolling away slightly. Carmela snapped her head up in time to see two of the three gunmen appear at the bottom of the stairs.

Charles must have taken out the third. The remaining two were so close now she could see the whites of their eyes. She didn't think, only reacted. If she was going to die, she was going to die fighting, not cowering in the corner begging for her life.

Rage and adrenaline crashed through her in a toxic, dizzying tide. Everything slowed. Charles was still struggling to turn over when she brought both arms up to grasp the pistol grip and pulled the trigger over and over. The gun kicked in her grip. Her first two rounds slammed harmlessly into the concrete wall behind the men.

The one in the lead brought the muzzle of his rifle up, pointed it straight at her. In the space of a heartbeat, her senses crystallized. She was aware of her choppy breathing, the feel of the gun bucking in her hands as she adjusted her aim and squeezed the trigger.

A bullet hit him high in the shoulder, causing him to cry out and drop the barrel of the rifle. She fired again, managed to hit him on the chest. He didn't go down, but he stumbled back, crashing into the man behind him.

In that split second lapse, Charles appeared in her secondary vision. The bark of his weapon filled the air. A spray of blood went up on the wall behind the lead man, a dark red hole appearing in the middle of his forehead. Carmela was already focused on the second one.

She was on her knees, arms trembling as she fired and fired again along with Charles. All her focus remained on the last shooter as she pulled the trigger repeatedly. Another red bloom on the wall, a hole in his bearded face. Even as he toppled back, Carmela kept firing.

She dimly realized she was screaming, venting her terror and rage, her finger continuously squeezing the trigger. It took her a moment to realize the gun was clicking on empty.

A hard hand seized her wrist, wrenching the weapon away. Shaking, chest throwing, she blinked up at Charles. He had a hand on the side of her face, his urgent voice finally breaking through the haze.

"Baby, stop. It's over. They're dead." His eyes were earnest, diving into hers with concern, as though he was afraid, she'd cracked and lost her fragile grip on sanity.

Dead. She gave a jerky nod in response. Her throat was locked too tight for her to get a word out. A ragged sound came out instead. The tension in her stomach and muscles suddenly evaporated, leaving her nauseated and her bones like jelly. She was shaking apart, didn't know how to stop it.

Charles's gaze softened. "Hey," he whispered, curving that steadying hand behind her neck as he leaned his forehead to hers. "Stay with me. You got to stay with me."

Yes. Stay with him. Her muscles refused to cooperate when he began to drag her upright. She let out a choked breath and shot a handout for the railing to give her time to lock her knees. Jesus, she was ice cold, trembling so hard her teeth were chattering. The wail of the fire alarm suddenly turned piercing, made her want to clap her hands over her ears.

Charles's hand slid to her wrist. "Come on, we are almost there."

Carmela ran her gaze over him. He was bleeding in a few more places now but somehow still on his feet, and she prayed that meant he was going to be okay.

"How f-far?" she managed, lips and tongue so numb the words came out slurred.

"One more flight, then we're on the ground floor."

So close. She could make it.

Charles started down with a pronounced limp, his fingers curled around her wrist, but she shook him loose. If there were more threats, he'd need both hands and she could walk down these last stairs on her own.

The scent of gunpowder and blood mixed with the acrid tang of smoke, the reek of it all burning her nostrils. Charles swept past the dead gunmen. Bodies of their innocent victims lay sprawled in a tangle of limbs on the stairs, so heartbreakingly close to the exit and escape.

Another wave of nausea twisted her stomach. She swallowed a gag and kept her eyes on Charles's wide shoulders to block out the hideous sights. Putting one unsteady foot in front of the other, she curled both hands around the cold metal railing for support, her focus on that heavy steel door below them.

Stepping between the bodies, Charles stopped at the side of the door and glanced back at her. "I'm going out first. Stay here until I tell you to come out.

There are going to be first responders everywhere out there, and we don't want any of them shooting at us by mistake."

No, she really didn't want that. "How do y-you know it's s-safe to…"

"I'm going to make it safe." His voice rang with certainty, his eyes burning with resolve. Even wounded and covered with blood, he was prepared to risk his life for hers. The knowledge made her tear up. "Stand back, flat against the side wall," he told her.

When she'd picked her way through the bodies to get in position, he turned his back to her, waited beside that door, then reached out and slammed it open with one hand. He ducked back behind the cover of the concrete wall as brilliant sunshine flooded the room. Carmela flinched and closed her eyes, bracing for more shooting.

Nothing happened. No bullets, nobody running at them. A gust of fresh air rushed through the tight space. When she opened her eyes, the rifle he'd been holding lay on the floor by the open door and Charles was gone.

She dragged in a shuddering breath and got ready to run. The brilliant rectangle of light in the open doorway seemed like a portal into another world, leading from this satanic blood-sprayed place of murder and terror into safety and freedom.

A shadow appeared between the sides. She tensed, but then Charles materialized in the opening. "It's safe. Come on out." He stretched out a hand to her, palm up.

Her gaze locked onto that strong, capable hand. Carmela shoved away from the wall and lunged for it. The moment their palms touched he curled his fingers around hers and pulled her outside.

Blinking in the glare, she instinctively shielded her eyes with one hand as she followed Charles on an unsteady jog. A wall of men appeared in front of them.

Black uniforms, blue ones, military fatigues. They descended upon her and Charles, surrounding them, everyone shouting at once.

Someone grabbed her around the waist and ripped her from Charles's hold.

He wore a police uniform but that meant shit to her right now. She twisted and kicked out, felt a sharp twinge in her back where she'd been hit earlier. A scuffle broke out in front of her and she could hear Charles yelling her name, swearing.

She whirled and struggled, casting a frantic glance around for him, but he'd already been swallowed up by the sea of humanity engulfing them.

"I'm trying to get you to safety!" the officer shouted at her, clearly exasperated by her resistance. "Come this way, to where the medics can look at you." "I want to find my friend," she insisted, pulling away from him.

"You're bleeding and need to do as I say." He snagged her arm again, his grip tighter this time and started walking despite her protests. The scuffle in the crowd was still going on as the policeman towed her away from the hotel, firing questions at her as he went. Were there any more shooters still inside, was anyone else shot, was she hurt, how much smoke had she breathed in.

"I'm f-fine," she shouted at him, yanking against his hold. The wound in her back couldn't be too serious, or she wouldn't be able to walk.

Finally, he stopped and let her go long enough for her to turn around and look for Charles. Her gaze snagged on the front of the hotel, the windows of the middle floors streaming smoke and flame. Black clouds of it boiled into the clear blue sky.

More smoke gulped from the doorway she'd just fled through. She still couldn't believe they'd come out of there alive. So many others hadn't been as fortunate.

The sudden, violent stumble in her gut gave her just enough warning to bend over.

She heaved up bile until she had to lean her hands on her thighs to stay upright. Someone laid a hand on her back and a water bottle appeared in front of her watering eyes. She coughed and sputtered, struggled to get her breath back, but her knees finally gave out and she sank to the hot pavement.

The Paramedics arrived. A team of what looked like SWAT guys rushed past her toward the open exit door.

"Bodies," she gasped.

"What?" one of the medics asked.

"Bodies in there," she said, pointing. "All over the floor." Oh shit, she was going to throw up again.

The officer pushed her head down. "Take some deep breaths," he said, his accented voice adding to the unreality of the situation. She should have been at the airport right now, getting ready to board her flight home. "Are you hurt anywhere?"

She shook her head, not caring about the stinging on her back. Cuts and scrapes were nothing. "Charles was shot. Is he...."

"Let's get you over to one of the ambulances." He dragged her to her feet.

She allowed him to lead her through the swarm of people, but after seeing what had happened to the ambulances after the bombings downtown, she didn't want to get near them. Carmela dug in her heels. "I told you, I'm fine," she snapped. "Now let me go find my friend."

"You have cuts that need bandaging and oxygen will help with the smoke inhalation."

Even if her lungs felt roasted on the inside, she wasn't going over there.

"Dammit, I said no..."

"Carmela"

At the shout she whipped her head around to search the crowd for a friendly face and saw Gage shoving his way through toward her. The policeman backed up a step when Gage burst through and pulled her into a tight hug. She flinched at the pain in her back, flooded with relief.

"Jesus, you guys scared the shit out of us," Gage said. "Are you okay?"

"Just scraped up, but they hit Charles a few times. Have you seen him?"

Gage frowned and looked around them. "There he is. Tom's got him at an ambulance."

Though she was still afraid that someone had planted a bomb somewhere, Carmela didn't protest as Gage bent and swung her up in his arms, careful of the wound on her back.

She closed her eyes and rested her head on his shoulder. When she opened them again, she saw Charles searching the scene, and the moment his gaze landed on her he visibly relaxed. Gage carried her straight over and settled her in the back of the next ambulance, then the medics took over.

Tom appeared at the back door a few moments later. "Thank God you're okay. I thought I was going to have to pin Charles and choke him out to keep him from going to find you."

Carmela pulled the oxygen mask away to speak, fired a glare at the paramedic when he quickly shoved it back into place. She looked back at Tom. "Is he okay?"

"Got some holes in him they're trying to patch up, but their job will be way easier now that he knows you're safe."

"Sir, we need to start treatment on her now," another paramedic said from beside her. "Please step back and let us get to work."

"Are you taking her to the hospital?" Gage asked.

She shook her head, adamant. "I don't need to go to the hospital." What she wanted was to see Charles and make sure he was okay.

Then she wanted to hide in his arms and wake up to find this was only a nightmare.

"They're transporting Charles now," Tom said, then glanced at Gage. "Meet you there?"

"Yeah." Gage climbed inside and parked it beside Carmela despite the exasperated sighs of the paramedics.

With one lift of an eyebrow, Gage silently dared them to kick him out. They didn't and a moment later the driver slammed the rear doors shut.

Needing human contact to reassure her that she was finally safe, Carmela reached over for his hand. Without a word Gage closed his fingers around hers and held on tight the entire ride to the hospital.

Chapter 21

The Emergency Room

Over an hour after being wheeled into the emergency room on a fucking rolling bed, Charles was done with people poking and digging at him. The wounds in his upper arm and calf hurt the worst, but the doctor had already confirmed there were no bullets in him, just bits of concrete and splinters of metal.

Two nurses were currently pulling some of them out of his back with tweezers while the doctor sewed up the hole in his arm in preparation for a precautionary round of x-rays.

Biting back a roar when one of the nurses dug deep into the middle of his back to extract a splinter of shrapnel, he gritted his teeth and fought for patience.

Carmela was safe; she was being looked over somewhere in this same ER, he just couldn't go to her, and he needed to. He wanted to see for himself that she was truly okay.

The doctor, a young Italian woman, tied off the last stitch and set down her needle driver on the metal tray beside his bed. "I stopped all the bleeding so that should do for now.

Once we verify via x-ray that all the large fragments are out and the bone is intact, we'll have a better idea of what we're dealing with, and whether you'll require surgery."

Hell, "How long's that going to take?" He didn't have time for a surgery and the recovery that would follow. Considering all he'd been through the past few days, wasn't it time the universe cut him?

The doctor raised her eyebrows at his curt tone, aimed at crushing look at him.

"Could be a long wait, considering how many patients we're treating from the hotel. It will depend." Meaning, she could make it take all day if he insisted on being an asshole to her and the rest of the staff.

Charles forced out a slow, calming breath and tried for a reasonable tone. "My arm's not broken. As soon as I'm bandaged up, I'll be good to go, and I'm sure someone else needs the bed worse than me anyway."

Ambulances were still arriving with new victims from the hotel every few minutes.

"Well, let's just wait and see what the x-rays tell us, so we know for sure.

You said your tetanus vaccinations were up to date?" She bent to make some notes in his chart.

"Yeah." He barely kept from growling it. The wounds scattered across his body stung and throbbed, adding to his agitation. He wanted to find this Joseph asshole, hunt him down along with the rest of his militant buddies and expedite their journey to the afterlife.

The second nurse, a male, finished up with cleaning and bandaging the last of the lacerations in his back and stepped away to look at him. "Do you want anything for the pain?"

Of course, he'd ask that after all the poking and stitching. "No, I'm good." He started to sit up, using his good arm for leverage. The nurse grabbed him and helped him upright, ignoring the dark look Charles shot him. He wanted to see Carmela and get the hell out of here. "How long until those x-rays?" he demanded.

The local police, ISI and US State Department must have launched their own intensive investigations by now. Charles wanted his team to be the ones who brought Joseph and the rest of the cell down.

The nurse looked over just as another orderly appeared at the end of the room. "I was going to say at least another half hour, but I think you just got lucky." The orderly headed straight for them, nodded once.

Luck? Charles snorted. More like Gage or Tom had taken charge and moved Charles to the front of the line. He stood despite the doctor's and nurse's protests and insisted on walking to the x-ray room without assistance.

While the tech fussed with his positioning on the table Charles was a good boy and did what he was told. He would do anything to hurry this process.

By the time he finished and wandered back into the ER to await the results so they could discharge him, Gage was there waiting for him.

"How's Carmela ?"Charles asked as he neared the bed Gage stood beside.

"She's good. Good sized piece of metal was buried in her back, but they got it out and stitched up, so it's all good now."

Fuck, he hated thinking about anything penetrating her silky soft skin. He looked around the ER, a hive of activity with more and more patients being brought in. "Where is she?"

"With Tom. He didn't want to wait and take any more chances with getting her and Ray to a different city, so Tom's working on getting them both on the next flight out of New York."

Good. Much as he hated to lose her, he wanted to see her safe more. He just hoped he'd get some time alone with her, at least a few minutes in private, so he could tell her everything he needed to before she left. "Any word on the investigation?"

"Ongoing, but nothing concrete or specific yet. You know how it is, everything's chaos right now."

"That sucks ass." He loosened his hand and moved his wounded arm, testing the muscles. The surge of pain and tightness there assured him everything was still attached and in working order. He pretty much hurt everywhere. All he needed now was the doctor's official okay.

"Hey."

He swiveled around at the sound of Carmela's voice, found her walking toward him across the ER. Immediately he scanned her for injury, noted the bandages on her forearms and the streaks of dust on the sides of her face. He moved without even being aware of it, rushing over as fast as his limp would allow.

Careful of the bandage beneath the back of her T-shirt where they'd stitched her up, he slid both arms around her. Returning the embrace, she leaned into him with a hard sigh and buried her face on his chest.

The sheer relief at having her pressed up close against his body made him a little dizzy, but maybe it was partially due to blood loss as well. "How are you doing, sweetheart?" he murmured against her hair, grateful she was safe and in his arms.

"Doing the best, I can," she answered in a rough voice.

"I hear you." But damn, she completely melted him. Even after everything they'd been through together these past few days, she'd flat out amazed him in that smoky stairwell.

She was keeping it together while under fire with nowhere to go, crawling over to help him when he was hit and then emptying a clip into the shooters when firing a pistol was as foreign to her.

The bravest thing he'd ever seen. He felt so much for her, he didn't know what to do with it all, let alone how to put it into words. "Gage said you got hit in the back. Do you need anything?"

"No, they gave me a shot of something already. Stitches just kind of burn and pull, you know?"

"I do," he answered sardonically. "And whatever they didn't get out will eventually work its way out of your skin on its own."

"Ew. Seriously?" She shuddered.

"Yeah, it's fun times." God knew he'd be pulling splinters of metal and concrete out of his hide for months to come.

"What about you?" She pulled her head back slightly to study his bandaged arm, then looked up into his face. "Gage is hassling the doctors right now to get them to fast track your x-ray results.

He told me he saw the films and there's no break or bullet in there, but I'm not sure how good his x-ray reading is."

"I'd say he's right on this one. I'm all stitched up and ready to roll."

Carmela was frowning in concern, clearly not approving of his answer. She unwound her arms from his ribs and placed her palms flat against his chest, gazing up at him with pale green eyes shadowed by fear and worry. "Come back with me. Get on the plane with Ray and me and leave here this morning."

He was such a selfish prick for thinking it, but man he loved that she was so worried about him.

"Wish I could, sweetheart, but I've got a job to finish first."

She closed her eyes for a second, exhaustion and strain written in every line of her face. Then she peered back up at him, tried once more. "Please."

Something ached inside him at the plea in her voice. Other than his mother, he couldn't remember having anyone worry about him.

Carmela had already seen firsthand the sort of danger his job could entail. Though there wasn't much he would deny this woman, this was one thing he couldn't give her. "I can't, I'm team leader. I wouldn't be good enough for you if I left the rest of the guys to take care of this without me." Didn't matter that he wasn't in the Teams anymore; he'd always be a SEAL at heart.

"Yes, you would." She reached up and took his face between her hands, her expression earnest. "Because you know what? I love you. And you coming back home with me now isn't going to change my opinion of you one bit. I just want you safe."

He barely heard the last sentence, still stuck back on the three-word bomb she'd just dropped on him. Except instead of freaking him out, her declaration made him feel like the luckiest bastard on the planet.

He couldn't wipe the grin off his face. "You love me? You sure it's not just because of everything that's gone down since you got here?" As soon as the words were out, he wanted to take them back, in case her answer might be yes.

"Yes, I'm sure," she retorted, eyes flashing with indignation, that stubborn chin lifting. "You think that's something I'd say without meaning it?"

He smothered a chuckle and opened his mouth to reassure her by telling her exactly how hard he'd fallen for her when a clipped female voice called out.

"Charles."

He looked over his shoulder, annoyed at the interruption. Really, universe?

Really? The female doctor was striding toward him, her irritation clear on her face. "Yes?"

She stopped a few feet from him, casting an aggravated glance at Carmela as she tugged on the hem of her scrubs top and pinned him with an outraged glare.

"It seems you and your American friends have no interest in following protocol and allowing us to do our jobs properly, so considering the bleeding is taken care of and that I see no visible fractures in your humorous or other large fragments in your arm, you are free to go."

The words were spat at him like bullets, her opinion of him and his "friends" made plain. Her speech had just ended when Gage appeared around the corner and spotted them all. The doctor glanced over at him, humped, and stormed off.

Charles grinned at him. "I love you, man."

Gage smiled back and nodded toward the exit. "Shall we?"

Charles reached down to take Carmela's hand, aware of the color in her cheeks and that he'd just said the L word to Gage instead of her. Hell. There was plenty he wanted to say to her, just not in front of anyone.

He held her hand as they walked out of the hospital and into the hot afternoon sunshine. The moment they exited the building, Charles spotted Ellis and Dunphy leaning against their parked SUV at the entrance. They headed straight over, their posture and expressions telling him something else was going on.

"What's up?" he asked them, bracing for more bad news. He felt Carmela's hand tense in his, squeezed gently in reassurance.

Ellis shot a look at Dunphy before turning his attention back to Charles.

"Think we've got something."

Oh, hell yes. Not wanting her to overhear in case it made her more upset, he released Carmela's hand and limped over to them, Gage right beside him. "What?"

"Had someone in Joseph 's office keeps tabs on him for us before we headed to the hotel. Word is he's nervous and just left the office," Ellis said.

"Ah, hell…"

"No, it's good." A huge grin spread across Dunphy's face as he held up his phone. "Because we're tracing his every move via the tracking device, we had his co-worker plant on him."

Charles smiled back, the adrenaline already pumping as he watched the tiny red dots move on the screen. "Awesome. So where is he now?"

"Just leaving downtown. Dot's moving fast, so he must be in a vehicle of some sort. Co-worker told me Joseph rides the bus a lot.

My guess is he's headed back to the city, to hook up with someone from the cell to take him into hiding."

Excitement ignited in his blood. "Let's nail the bastard." He glanced back at Carmela, who stood watching them, just as Tom pulled his vehicle up behind Ellis and Dunphy. Charles watched her eyes shift from him to Tom and back, and knew the instant she realized what was happening. Her face crumpled. The devastation in her eyes hit him like a roundhouse to the gut.

Christ, she thought he was deserting her. It was all over her face. Baby, no. He closed the distance between them with four limping strides and pulled her into a hug, careful of her bandage. She was stiff in his arms, but thankfully didn't pull away.

"Hey," he whispered. "I'm sorry, but we have to act on this right now."

She gave a jerky nod, refused to look up at him.

Charles sighed. This timing was shit. She needed him and he wanted to be there for her, but this lead passed everything else because it was consumable and every second mattered. "You know I must do this.

It's my job, and I want this guy. I'm going to get him and bring down this whole cell for everything it did to you, me, your father, and Scottie. I'm going to get him, Carmela.

One of her hands crept up to grasp the front of his shirt and he felt her shoulders shake. A lump settled in the center of his chest, and he gathered her closer. "Hey. This isn't goodbye, it's just see you later.

You think I'd let you go after everything we've been through together?" He set her back a little, just enough to look down into her face. The tears glimmering in her eyes sliced him.

"You won't lose me," he promised, then let out a breath and laid it all on the line. "You couldn't because I've fallen for you. Hard."

She stared up at him with surprised, tear-bright eyes. "Really?"

"Yeah, really." He was done for, he knew it, and was glad he'd admitted it.

Charles leaned down and kissed her, swallowed a groan of relief when she wound her arms around his neck and kissed him back. Someone honked the SUV's horn.

Charles pulled away and forced a smile, the pain of his wounds all but forgotten for the moment. "Go with Tom. Right now, I need you safe so I can finish this.

Tomorrow night when I go to sleep, I want to know you're home safe and sound with your family. I'll be in touch as soon as I can."

She didn't fully believe him; he could tell by the dread waiting in her eyes.

He shook his head, tried once more to reassure her. "You got to trust me again this one last time, baby.

Please just trust me. I won't let you down, I swear."

Before she could answer the SUV's horn blared again; and Charles bit back a curse as he turned away and looked at Tom, waiting by his rental. "You take care of her."

He nodded; face solemn. "You know it, brother."

With that Charles headed straight for the SUV, too chicken shit to look back and see the tears in Carmela's eyes.

Near the back of the city bus, Joseph fumbled in his pocket and dug out the last of the Pepto Bismol tablets he'd snagged from the office medicine cabinet.

The chalky-sweet things made him gag but at least if he threw up again, he'd have something in his stomach this time. His throat felt like it had second degree burns in it from all the bile he'd retched up throughout the morning at work.

Rubbing his sweaty palms on his thighs, he stared out the grimy window and went over his plan once more. Flying was too great a risk now, and he couldn't buy anything that requires ID, credit, or debit card. The small amount of cash he had on him wasn't going to last long and he knew better than to show up at his parents' home for help.

They didn't deserve to be dragged into this mess any farther, and Joseph knew they were already being watched by the man who'd threatened him, and probably other agencies as well.

The cell leader in New York was pleased with Joseph's work in this operation, and he was hopeful the man would help him get over the border into New Jersey.

If he could make it to New York and find some TTP members, from there he could slip over the border into New Jersey and wait in a safe house until he came up with a long-term plan.

Because as of this morning, life as he'd known it was over for good. If he stayed, the man from the warehouse would kill him. His only option was to run.

He heard the sirens approach behind them and felt a sickening lurch in his stomach. His face, palms and back were slick with the cold sweat of fear, his heart racing so fast he felt dizzy.

A glance out the window showed two police vehicles racing up behind the bus. Every muscle in his body drew wired, and natural response to the futility of his situation.

The vehicles didn't pull up beside the bus. They passed it and sped onward, the blast of their sirens eventually fading into nothing. Joseph sagged against the seat and closed his eyes with a silent prayer of thanks.

A few moments later, the bus slammed on its brakes. Joseph barely threw a handout in time to stop his face from crashing into the back of the seat in front of him. The vehicle skidded and staggered, came to a violent stop there in the middle of the road.

All around him people were chattering, stretching out their necks toward the driver and then outside to see what the matter was. A second after that, someone pounded on the front door.

A bone-chilling flash of fear ripped through him. The door opened and a group of men boarded the bus. The first one was a big man with a reddish skull trim. Two full sleeves of tattoos showed below the cuffs of his T-shirt, which was stretched taut across the defined muscles in his arms and chest. He was right in the driver's face, and though Joseph couldn't hear what was being said, the driver had his hands up and was leaning away as though to show he was no threat and wasn't about to put up a fight.

The passengers were beginning to move to the rear, watching everything unfold with uneasy expressions.

Trapped at the back, Joseph had nowhere to go. Two more men came aboard, ne with darker skin and a slightly shorter one with black hair. All were armed with pistols. They did a visual sweep of the bus.

Unable to look away, Joseph slowly sank down in his seat to try and avoid detection. The first man's gaze traveled over the passengers at the back of the bus and landed on him. Stopped. Held.

He murmured something to the darker skinned man behind him, who immediately pinned him with startling hazel eyes. Joseph didn't dare move, didn't dare breathe, convinced this was a nightmare and wasn't really happening at all. It was too bizarre.

There was no way they could have found him. Not this soon. The thought had barely formed when a fourth man stepped aboard the bus. Taller than the last, with short dark hair, and made of solid muscle. He strode down the aisle with a pronounced limp and a bandaged upper arm that did nothing to detract from his menacing appearance. This man had done hard time in the military, and he meant business.

His gaze locked onto Joseph, and he saw the fire burning in the other man's light brown eyes. Victory and revenge.

Instinct drove Joseph to leap up and dive for the lock on the emergency window. His right knee landed on the lap of the lady cowering beside him. He barely heard her cry of pain, didn't even feel the blows as she struck out at him.

His hands clawed at the release latch, managed to slide it open. He shoved it free and had his head stuck out of it when he heard the shout behind him.

Powerful hands grabbed his waist. He cried out and lashed back with both feet, the soles of his shoes hitting an unforgiving wall of muscle.

In the blink of an eye, he was yanked backward through the window and slammed to his back on the aisle floor. The air rushed out of his lungs and spots of light danced when his head smacked into the floor. A hard weight landed on him, flipped him over then seized his wrists and wrenched them up and back, the brute force of it nearly snapping the bones.

With a scream of terror and pain, Joseph arched up against his assailant, but it was like trying to move a bulldozer. His lungs seized once more when he found himself staring up into that hard, livid face.

"Who are you?" the man growled, the muscles in his jaw so tight they stood out in sharp relief.

Don't answer. Don't answer.

A vicious jerk on his arms, sending a sharp stab of pain into his shoulder sockets. "Who are you?"

"No one!" he cried; certain his arms were going to be ripped free. "I'm no one!"

The man sat back slightly, but didn't ease up on his grip as he spoke to the man behind him, the redhead with the skull trim. "Search him."

The big American wasted no time in frisking him, coming up with the empty packet of tablets and his wallet. Joseph closed his eyes but couldn't bear being both blind and helpless.

He looked up in time to see the man reading his driver's license and show it to he brutish dark-haired man who pinned him. Then he held up something small and flat, like a watch battery, and Joseph recognized what it was designating. That bitch had somehow planted a tracking device in his wallet for these men when he hadn't been looking. Probably while he was in the men's room, throwing up. Fear and helplessness washed through him.

His kidnapper glanced at the license, his expression becoming even more frightening in its triumph as he turned that angry glare back on him.

"Joseph," he murmured in a silky tone that made Joseph's skin crawl and gave a tsking sound. "You've been a very bad boy."

Had he really feared dying this morning in that warehouse? As they unceremoniously hauled him to his feet and shoved him toward the bus's door, Joseph had a feeling he would soon wish he was already dead.

References

Q. L. Pearce. Native American Mythology. Greenhaven Publishing LLC, 2012. ISBN 978-1-4205-0951-9; and "Native American Literature", Britannica online. The article on "American literature" links to this article. Archived September 28, 2020, at the Wayback Machine

Lease, Benjamin (1972). That Wild Fellow John Neal and the American Literary Revolution. Chicago, Illinois: University of Chicago Press. p. 80. ISBN 0-226-46969-7.

Kellman, Steven G. (2020), "Ch. 22: American Literature in Languages Other Than English", in Belasco, Susan (ed.), A Companion to American Literature, Wiley, pp. 349–364, doi:10.1002/9781119056157.ch84, S2CID 216443099, archived from the original on May 31, 2022, retrieved May 31, 2022

Gunther, Erna. "Native American Literature". Britannica. Britannica. com. Archived from the original on September 28, 2020. Retrieved December 4, 2021.

MacKay, K.L. "Native American Literature". faculty.weber.edu. Weber State University. Archived from the original on December 4, 2021. Retrieved December 3, 2021.

Baym, Nina, ed. The Norton Anthology of American Literature. New York: W.W. Norton & Company, 2007. Print.

Henry L. Schoolcraft, "The Capture of New Amsterdam", English Historical Review (1907) 22#88 674–693 in JSTOR Archived August 7, 2020, at the Wayback Machine

Skipp, Francis E. American Literature, Barron's Educational, 1992.

A Short History of Boston by Robert J. Allison, p.14 the Bay Psalm Book exhibition at the Library of Congress 2015

"Sarah Kemble Knight | American diarist | Britannica". www.britannica. com. Retrieved March 27, 2023.

Gray, Richard. A History of American Literature. Blackwell, 2004.

Colden, Cadwallader, and John G. Shea. The History of the Five Indian Nations Depending on the Province of New-York. New York: T.H. Morrell, 1866.

Gitin, Louis L. Cadwallader Colden: As Scientist and Philosopher. Burlington, Vt, 1935.

Hoermann, Alfred R. Cadwallader Colden: A Figure of the American Enlightenment. Westport, Conn: Greenwood Press, 2002.

Julian P. Boyd, "The Declaration of Independence: The Mystery of the Lost Original" Archived February 12, 2015, at the Wayback Machine. Pennsylvania Magazine of History and Biography 100, number 4 (October 1976), p. 456.

Parker, Patricia L. "Charlotte Temple by Susanna Rowson". The English Journal. 65.1: (1976) 59-60. JSTOR. Web. 1 March 2010.

Schweitzer, Ivy. "Review". Early American Literature. 23.2: (1988) 221-225. JSTOR. Web. 1 March 2010.

Hamilton, Kristie. "An Assault on the Will: Republican Virtue and the City in Hannah Webster Foster's 'The Coquette'". Early American Literature. 24.2: (1989) 135-151. JSTOR. Web. 1 March 2010

Joudrey, Thomas J. (2013). "Maintaining Stability: Fancy and Passion in the Coquette". The New England Quarterly. 86: 60–88. doi:10.1162/TNEQ_a_00257. S2CID 57567236. Archived from the original on February 5, 2023. Retrieved September 21, 2017.

Campbell, Donna M. (July 14, 2008). "The Early American Novel: Introductory Notes". Literary Movements. Archived from the original on September 29, 2005. Retrieved March 1, 2010.

Rutherford, Mildred. American Authors. Atlanta: The Franklin Printing and Publishing Co., 1902.

Reynolds, Guy. "The Winning of the West: Washington Irving's 'A Tour on the Prairies'". The Yearbook of English Studies. 34: (2004) 88-99. JSTOR. Web. 1 March 2010.

Sears, Donald A. (1978). John Neal. Twayne Publishers. p. 82. ISBN 080-5-7723-08.

Marfo, Florence (2009). "African Muslims in African American Literature". Callaloo. 32 (4): 1213–1222. doi:10.1353/cal.0.0567. ISSN 0161-2492. JSTOR 27743138. S2CID 161625199. Archived from the original on February 6, 2021. Retrieved August 8, 2020.

Said, Omar Ibn. (2014). Muslim American Slave : the Life of Omar Ibn Said. University of Wisconsin Press. ISBN 978-0-299-24953-3. OCLC 1043364329. Archived from the original on February 5, 2023. Retrieved August 8, 2020.

"Summary of Autobiography of Omar ibn Said, Slave in North Carolina, 1831. Ed. John Franklin Jameson. From The American Historical Review, 30, No. 4. (July 1925), 787-795". docsouth.unc.edu. Archived from the original on July 12, 2020. Retrieved August 8, 2020.

Lease 1972, pp. 42, 69

Sears 1978, p. 80

Sears 1978, p. 57

Pattee, Fred Lewis (1937). "Introduction". In Pattee, Fred Lewis (ed.). American Writers: A Series of Papers Contributed to Blackwood's Magazine (1824-1825). Durham, North Carolina: Duke University Press. p. 22. Archived from the original on January 17, 2021. Retrieved August 10, 2020.

Lease 1972, p. 70, quoting Harold C. Martin

Gura, Philip F. American Transcendentalism: A History. New York: Hill and Wang, 2007: 7–8. ISBN 978-0-8090-3477-2

"Garland, Hamlin 1860 - 1940". Dictionary of Wisconsin History. Wisconsin Historical Society. Archived from the original on November 10, 2012. Retrieved October 17, 2009.

"Hamlin Garland and Henry George". Archived from the original on February 3, 2014. Retrieved January 29, 2014.

Hazel Hutchison, The War That Used Up Words: American Writers and the First World War (Yale University Press, 2015)

Jeffrey Meyers, Scott Fitzgerald: A Biography (HarperCollins, 1994).

Dos Passos, John (1932). Three Soldiers. United States of America: The Modern Library.

Maxwell Geismar, American moderns, from rebellion to conformity (1958)

Keith Ferrell, Ernest Hemingway: The Search for Courage (Rowman & Littlefield, 2014)

John T. Matthews, William Faulkner: seeing through the South (Wiley, 2011).

Kimball, Roger "Existentialism, Semiotics and Iced Tea, Review of Conversations with Walker Percy" Archived December 13, 2007, at the Wayback Machine. New York Times, August 4, 1985, Accessed September 24, 2006

Kakutani, Michiko (January 12, 1996). "Seeking Salvation On the Silver Screen". The New York Times Books. Archived from the original on May 20, 2013. Retrieved December 3, 2009.

Bloom, Harold: How to Read and Why, page 269. Touchstone Press, 2000.

Allén, Sture. "Nobel Prize Award Ceremony Speech". NobelPrize.org. Archived from the original on May 31, 2022. Retrieved May 31, 2022.

"What Is the Best Work of American Fiction of the Last 25 Years?". The New York Times. May 21, 2006. Archived from the original on August 8, 2020. Retrieved December 4, 2009.

Bloom, Harold (June 15, 2009). "Harold Bloom on Blood Meridian". A.V. Club. Archived from the original on November 5, 2013. Retrieved March 3, 2010.

Bloom, Harold (September 24, 2003). "Dumbing down American readers". The Boston Globe. Archived from the original on June 17, 2006. Retrieved December 4, 2009.

"All-Time 100 Novels: The Complete List". Time. October 16, 2005. Archived from the original on October 19, 2005. Retrieved December 4, 2009.

Grossman, Lev (August 12, 2010). "Jonathan Franzen: Great American Novelist". Time. Archived from the original on August 15, 2010. Retrieved August 16, 2010.

Kakutani, Michiko (August 15, 2010). "A Family Full of Unhappiness, Hoping for Transcendence". The New York Times. Archived from the original on May 12, 2011. Retrieved August 16, 2010.

Tanenhaus, Sam (August 19, 2010). "Peace and War". The New York Times. Archived from the original on September 3, 2011. Retrieved August 19, 2010.

Kakutani, Michiko (August 31, 2007). "In Vietnam: Stars and Stripes, and Innocence Undone". The New York Times. Archived from the original on June 23, 2011. Retrieved April 17, 2010.

"2012 National Book Awards". National Book Foundation. November 14, 2012. Archived from the original on October 26, 2018. Retrieved December 2, 2012.

Lubbers, Klaus (1994). Born for the Shade: Stereotypes of the Native American in United States Literature and the Visual Arts, 1776–1894. Rodopi. ISBN 978-90-5183-628-8.

"Our Land, Our Literature: Literature - Rebecca Lard". digitalresearch. bsu.edu. Archived from the original on December 1, 2022. Retrieved May 31, 2022.

"A Brief Guide to the Fireside Poets" Archived January 16, 2014, at the Wayback Machine at Poets.org Archived December 18, 2015, at the Wayback Machine. Accessed 10-07-2015

"Emily Dickinson Archive". January 24, 2018. Archived from the original on January 24, 2018. Retrieved January 24, 2018.

Noel Stock, The Life of Ezra Pound (1970)

Hugh Kenner, The invisible poet: TS Eliot (1965).

"The Nobel Prize in Literature 2020". NobelPrize.org. Archived from the original on October 8, 2020. Retrieved March 21, 2021.

Groundbreaking Book: Life Studies by Robert Lowell (1959) Archived May 29, 2010, at the Wayback Machine Accessed May 5, 2010

Lopate, Phillip (April 6, 2021). The Golden Age of the American Essay: 1945-1970. Knopf Doubleday Publishing Group. ISBN 978-0-525-56733-2.

Madsen 2000, p. 107

"Giannina Braschi". National Book Festival. Library of Congress. 2012. Archived from the original on August 28, 2017. Retrieved February 17, 2015. 'Braschi: one of the most revolutionary voices in Latin America today'

Ilan Stavans (2011). Norton Anthology of Latino Literature. Norton. OCLC 607322888.

"Luis A. Miranda, Jr. Doesn't 'Need To Be Liked' but This New Documentary Will Make You Like Him Anyway". Remezcla. October 5, 2020. Archived from the original on January 26, 2021. Retrieved October 12, 2020.

Bibliography

For references on specific authors or topics, please see the relevant article.

Bercovitch, Sacvan (1994–2005). The Cambridge History of American Literature. Cambridge: Cambridge University Press.

Delbanco, Andrew (Spring 2006). "American Literature: A Vanishing subject?". Daedalus. 135 (2): 22–37. doi:10.1162/daed.2006.135.2.22. S2CID 57567897..

Gray, Richard (2011). A History of American Literature. Malden: Wiley-Blackwell.

Madsen, Deborah L. (2000). Understanding Contemporary Chicana Literature. Columbia, SC: University of South Carolina Press. ISBN 978-1-57003-379-7.

Moore, Michelle E. (2019). Chicago and the Making of American Modernism: Cather, Hemingway, Faulkner, and Fitzgerald in Conflict. New York and London: Bloomsbury Academic.

Müller, Timo (2017). Handbook of the American Novel of the Twentieth and Twenty-First Centuries. Boston: de Gruyter.

Shell, Marc; Sollors, Werner, eds. (2000). The Multilingual Anthology of American Literature: A Reader of Original Texts with English Translations. New York: NYU Press. ISBN 978-0814797525.

Woodberry, George Edward (1911). "American Literature". In Chisholm, Hugh (ed.). Encyclopædia Britannica. Vol. 1 (11th ed.). Cambridge University Press. pp. 831–842.

About the Author

Norma Iris Pagan Morales was born in Ponce, Puerto Rico. Her parents, Juan Jose Pagan Rodriguez, and Digna Morales Figueroa, now deceased, always helped her with her projects as a writer and teaching career.

Norma had three siblings, Adelin Milagros Pagan Morales, Juan Jose Pagan Morales, and Julio Manuel Pagan Morales. Adelin Milagros Pagan Morales died on February 17, 2023 and Julio Manuel Pagan Morales died on September 19, 1998. He was also known for his writing / composer skills.

Norma did all her academic studies in New York City, Puerto Rico, and Canada. She worked in the City of New York Police Department where she oversaw the full investigation of every new civilian and uniform member of the department.

As an Educator, she worked in New York City Bd. of Education, in Puerto Rico Bd. of Education as an English teacher. She also worked for the Puerto Rico Army National as an English Teacher.

She has teaching certifications for English as a Second Language and Teaching English as a Foreign Language. She also has teaching licenses to teach the following:

1. English Literature
2. Spanish Literature
3. Communication Skills in both English and Spanish
4. Office Procedures= These classes consisted of basic filing to writing memorandums and full company or organization reports.
5. Computers - Certified to teach Long Distance Learning

She has published Thirteen books: Proud of My Puerto Rican Bequest, Porque Soy Boricua? Poemas del Alma, Art in Written Form, A Baffling Short Stories Collection, On Job in the Big Apple, Nature's Rage in the Caribbean, Puerto Rican Soldiers Serving with Pride, Poemas de Ternura and Violence in the City.